Losing the Peace

Losing the Peace

Georgia Republicans and Reconstruction, 1865-1871

ELIZABETH STUDLEY NATHANS

Louisiana State University Press
Baton Rouge

To my parents

PREFACE

Congressional Reconstruction, we now know, was a dismal failure.[1] In the North, racism and lack of commitment to sweeping reforms, whether social or economic, brought about a retreat from the moral fervor of the early 1860's and an abandonment of attempts to rebuild the South. And with retreat in the North came the collapse of Reconstruction in the former Confederate states—for reform of the South seemed impossible without sustained Congressional intervention. One need only look at the record. Abandonment of Southern Republicans by Northern party leaders led to the

[1] See, for example, Harold M. Hyman (ed.), *New Frontiers of the American Reconstruction* (Urbana: University of Illinois Press, 1966), especially the essays by John Hope Franklin and C. Vann Woodward. The theme of uncertain northern commitment is also central to Kenneth M. Stampp's *The Era of Reconstruction 1865–1877* (New York: Alfred A. Knopf, 1965). It received perhaps its most eloquent formulation in C. Vann Woodward's "Reconstruction and Revision," an address before a General Session of the Southern Historical Association at Atlanta, November 8, 1967.

downfall of that party in the South and to subsequent Democratic "redemption" of the region. And the Democrats rejected all that Reconstruction had implied. Having acquiesced in freedom for the Negro, they relegated him to virtual economic bondage. Having courted his vote during the Reconstruction years, they disfranchised him when it suited their partisan purposes. Having accepted the results of the Civil War in good faith and having sworn evermore to uphold the Union, they resurrected Confederate generals and Rebel politicians as United States Senators and state governors. So complete was the wreckage of social and economic reconstruction under the restored Democratic governments that the task remained to be begun anew in the twentieth century.

Because the ultimate result of Reconstruction was failure, we have come to assume that failure was inevitable. And surely it seems that in Georgia, if anywhere in the conquered South, failure could scarcely have been avoided. The most recalcitrant of the Southern states, the only one to undergo two military reconstructions, and the last to be readmitted to the Union, Georgia had more than her share of unrepentent rebels. Only constant vigilance by Congress, so the implication is, could have kept this state squarely on the road toward reform and reconstruction.

Yet in Georgia, I think, failure was not inevitable. For there was in Georgia during Reconstruction a very real prospect of a Republican party which would have united a natural majority of the state's voters, which would have sustained itself whatever the vacillations of the national Congress, and which would have embarked on a program of economic and social development for the state similar to that advanced by Henry Grady in the 1880's and urged by Atlanta businessmen in the twentieth century. That such a party did not materialize in Georgia during the early months of Congressional Reconstruction may be blamed on Georgia Republicans' misplaced reliance on Congressional support. That efforts to develop such a coalition failed in 1870 may be laid to the stigma of corruption and Negro rule which by then had become attached to all Southern Republicans.

Georgia Republicans, I suggest, were confronted with clear alternatives of strategy and tactics as they began the process of party-building shortly after the passage of the first Military Reconstruction Act in March, 1867. The choices the party leaders made, and the effect those choices had on the development of a Republican organization in Georgia, are the subjects of this book. Georgia Republicans doomed themselves to destruction, and the end result in Georgia, as elsewhere in the South, was failure. But, because it might have been otherwise, it was a failure whose importance for Georgia went far beyond the mere unseating of a single, short-lived, unpopular, state administration.

ACKNOWLEDGMENTS

Members of the staffs of the Georgia Department of Archives and History, the Atlanta Historical Society, the Georgia State Library, Emory University, the University of Georgia, Duke University, the University of North Carolina at Chapel Hill, the University of Virginia, the Library of Congress, the National Archives, the Historical Society of Pennsylvania, the Massachusetts Historical Society, and Widener Library of Harvard University have been unfailingly kind and efficient in the face of what must often have seemed excessive demands on their time and skills. At the Johns Hopkins University Library, Miss Margaret Lough, Miss Ethel De-Muth, Miss Adelaide Eisenhart, and Mrs. Ione B. Hoover were especially generous with their help.

To Professors Horace Mann Bond, Clarence A. Bacote, Adrian E. Cook, E. Merton Coulter, Carl N. Degler, Fletcher M. Green, Larry G. Kincaid, James Z. Rabun, Willie Lee

Rose, Joel R. Williamson, and Charles Wynes, who guided me to materials I had overlooked or who offered ideas or suggestions, I am deeply grateful. I am particularly indebted to Professor C. Vann Woodward for his careful reading of an earlier version of this manuscript and for his consistent encouragement and support. The members of my dissertation committee at the Johns Hopkins University, Professors Stephen E. Ambrose and Harold M. Hyman, and my dissertation director, Professor David Donald, all gave the original manuscript a close reading and made dozens of suggestions for improvements in style and content.

Permission to examine a group of Joseph E. Brown Papers still in private possession was granted me during the summer of 1964. Only the wish of those who hold the papers to remain anonymous prevents a fuller acknowledgment of their contributions to my work. But I am deeply indebted to them for their faith in my project and for the freedom to use and quote fully from papers which had not previously been opened.

Fellowship grants from Vassar College, the Johns Hopkins University, and the Social Science Research Council helped finance the preliminary work upon which this volume is based. A grant from the Faculty Research Council of the University of North Carolina at Chapel Hill eased the burdens of preparing the manuscript for publication.

For their patience with a neophyte author, I am very grateful to Richard L. Wentworth and Charles East of the Louisiana State University Press.

My husband, Professor Sydney Nathans of Duke University, has shared the crises of research and writing, from beginning to end.

ELIZABETH STUDLEY NATHANS

Chapel Hill, North Carolina
March 16, 1968

CONTENTS

Counties and Major Cities of Georgia in 1868

Defiant Acquiescence

The spring of 1865 brought little joy to the white citizens of Georgia. Dazed by the destruction wrought by William Tecumseh Sherman's Yankee "bummers" during the march from Atlanta to the sea the previous fall and winter, grieved by the loss of loved ones, and impoverished by four years of war, they now faced the formidable task of rebuilding their state.

As spring turned into summer and Georgians took stock of the work ahead, the labor of reconstruction seemed difficult, indeed.[1] In the rural counties, failure to plant cotton in the early spring augured badly for the year's crop. A plant-

[1] C. Mildred Thompson, *Reconstruction in Georgia: Economic, Social, Political, 1865-1872* (New York: Columbia University Press, 1915), Chap. 2-5, contains an extensive summary of economic and social difficulties in Georgia at the end of the Civil War. See also Alan Conway, *The Reconstruction of Georgia* (Minneapolis: University of Minnesota Press, 1966), Chap. 2, 4, 5.

ing class already impoverished by the loss of $300 million in slave property found itself plagued by labor shortages as freedmen wandered off to test their liberty.[2] Many who had lived comfortably in antebellum years on the income from their plantations now in desperation moved to the towns, seeking to use long-rusty professional skills to support struggling families.[3] Soldiers returning home faced run-down farms and pressing debts; few found ready jobs. On the outskirts of once proud cities, the squalor of refugee camps, both Negro and white, bespoke the personal tragedy of war.

Scars of battle were everywhere apparent. Railroads and telegraph lines, severed during Sherman's march, had not yet been repaired. The port city of Savannah remained cut off from the interior of the state, her mail service disrupted and her railroads halted by miles of twisted and broken track.[4] In cities like Augusta, bypassed by Sherman's plundering troops, only the presence of an "idle crowd" of Negroes in the streets testified to the changes war had brought. But along Sherman's track, blank walls and skeleton houses stood as mute and somber reminders of the events of barely a half year before.[5]

Political disorganization in Georgia at the war's end matched the economic and social dislocation. The last decade before the war had seen the breakup of the national Whig party and had brought important changes to Georgia

[2] *Annual Report of the Comptroller General of the State of Georgia . . . October 16, 1866* (Macon: J. W. Burke & Co., Stationers and State Printers, 1866), 30; John W. Kennaway, *On Sherman's Track: or, the South After the War* (London: Seeley, Jackson, and Halliday, 1867), 122; Whitelaw Reid, *After the War: A Southern Tour. May 1, 1865, to May 1, 1866* (New York: Moore, Wilstach & Baldwin, 1866), 146.

[3] W. W. Paine to Alexander H. Stephens, October 6, 1865, and J. Henly Smith to Stephens, December 30, 1865, in Alexander H. Stephens Papers, Library of Congress.

[4] Reid, *After the War,* 149–50.

[5] Kennaway, *On Sherman's Track,* 107, 122.

state politics. As their own party splintered, state Whig leaders—including Robert Toombs and Alexander H. Stephens—reluctantly joined other nationally prominent Georgians like Howell Cobb and Herschel V. Johnson in the Democracy. Their change of affiliation precipitated a struggle for leadership within the Democratic party itself, a struggle for supremacy between older, established politicians and a rising generation of leaders. In the popular mind, the contest quickly became one between the planters and merchants of the wealthy "Black Belt" and seacoast counties and the white farmers of the barren North Georgia mountains and south-central wiregrass region, whose leader was a shrewd North Georgia lawyer, Joseph E. Brown. In 1857 Brown won a crucial gubernatorial contest over a young, diehard Whig, Benjamin H. Hill. His victory pointed the direction in which Georgia's Democratic party would move throughout the Civil War years, for Brown built a personal following which ensured his reelection in 1859, 1861, and 1863. By 1865—despite the enmity of most Georgia editors and of former Whigs like Stephens and Toombs—Brown almost singlehandedly controlled the state. The end of the war, the imprisonment of prominent Confederate leaders, and, above all, the arrest of Brown by Federal troops in May, 1865, left a political vacuum in Georgia.

Had the banishment of old leaders been the only problem which plagued Georgia politicians in the spring of 1865, political reorganization would doubtless have been swift and relatively painless. But the removal of Brown and the exile of other leaders forcibly recalled to Georgians a fundamental, gnawing concern. Abraham Lincoln was dead; Andrew Johnson was President. Johnson's policies were unformulated, and his probable course toward the South was unknown. Until the new President made some public announce-

ment of his plans, Georgians—like all Southerners—could do
little except watch and wait.[6]

They waited in apprehension, for all knew the power of
the Congressional Radicals who were pressing their advice
on Johnson. Reconstruction of the South, these men believed,
devolved by right to the legislative branch of the government. The Confederates, defeated by force of arms, must be
broken in spirit. To this end, the most militant of the Radicals urged full civil rights for Negroes, confiscation of Southern lands, and punishment of all who had led in the rebellion
against the government of the United States. Their demands
were not new; Lincoln had faced them and had responded
with his own moderate "10 percent plan" of restoration and
with the pocket veto of the Radical Wade-Davis bill in the
summer of 1864. What the Congressional Radicals had
failed to secure from Lincoln, Southerners feared, they might
now secure from his successor.

Andrew Johnson, however, proved more temperate in his
course than Georgians had dared to hope. Restoration of the
Southern states, he suggested, was an executive, not a legislative, function. Proclamations throughout the spring and
summer of 1865 made it clear that the new President would
not easily relinquish leadership to the Radicals.

Military rule had supplanted civilian government in Georgia as in the rest of the South, and Johnson believed his first
task to be the establishment of some form of supervised
civilian authority. On May 29 he issued the first of several
proclamations designating provisional governors for the
Southern states, and Georgians hastened to Washington to
press the claims of candidates for the office in their state.
Most thought Joshua Hill, a staunch Unionist and longtime

[6] On the problems and uncertainties facing both South and North at
the end of the war, see Eric L. McKitrick, *Andrew Johnson and Reconstruction* (Chicago: University of Chicago Press, 1960), Chap. 2.

opponent of Joseph Brown, the logical choice for Georgia, but Johnson apparently feared Hill's Radical leanings.[7] Instead, he turned to one of his own acquaintances, an obscure Columbus lawyer, a "plain and unassuming man" with a "pleasantly inexpressive face" and timid manner who was, nonetheless, reputed among Georgians to act with cool deliberation and good sense.[8] A presidential proclamation of June 17, 1865, named James Johnson provisional governor of Georgia. It would be his task to cooperate with the President and the army in directing civil affairs in Georgia, to supervise elections for a new constitutional convention, and to lead that convention in repealing the secession ordinance, abolishing slavery, and repudiating the Confederate debt.

The President kept in close touch with his provisional governor during the summer, but not even presidential prestige would have sufficed had Georgians been determined to resist federal authority. The mood in Georgia, however, was for the moment one not of resistance but of acquiescence. Federal officials in the state could not cope with the numbers of Georgians who flocked to take the oath of allegiance to the Union prescribed by the President for those wishing to vote in the fall elections or sit in the constitutional convention.[9] Prominent antebellum and wartime politicians en-

[7] Joshua Hill to Andrew Johnson, May 10, 1865, in Andrew Johnson Papers, Library of Congress; Thompson, *Reconstruction in Georgia*, 146–47; Augusta *Chronicle and Sentinel*, June, 20, 1865; Olive Hall Shadgett, "James Johnson, Provisional Governor of Georgia," *Georgia Historical Quarterly*, XXXVI (March, 1952), 3; Macon *Telegraph*, June 7, 1865.

[8] Quotations from Sidney Andrews, *The South Since the War: As Shown by Fourteen Weeks of Travel and Observation in Georgia and the Carolinas* (Boston: Ticknor and Fields, 1866), 241. See also *ibid.*, 243. Alexander H. Stephens characterized James Johnson as timid; see Myrta Lockett Avary (ed.), *Recollections of Alexander H. Stephens* (New York: Doubleday, Page & Company, 1910), 231.

[9] Joseph E. Brown to Andrew Johnson, July 21, 1865, July 25, 1865, both in Andrew Johnson Papers; Albany *Patriot*, July 22, 1865; Augusta *Constitutionalist*, August 6, 1865.

dorsed the President, the provisional governor, and their programs. Even Joseph E. Brown applied for and secured a presidential pardon on his promise to return to Georgia and stump the state in support of Andrew Johnson's plan for Southern restoration.[10]

As Georgians prepared to elect their delegates to the new constitutional convention, it indeed seemed that all were prepared to cooperate in restoring their state speedily to the Union.[11] Old party ties had been broken, and no new ones had developed to take their place. Surrender to Federal armies had meant the eclipse of the fire-eating secessionist Democrats. Old-line Whigs, long thought to be unhappy in their alliance with the Democracy, made no attempt to revive their party. Party committees gave way to Union clubs, where old-line Whigs, antebellum Democrats of the Stephen A. Douglas persuasion, and even former secessionists like Brown united in bowing before the fact of defeat and urging cooperation with federal authorities.

Preparations for the election of delegates to the new constitutional convention proceeded smoothly. Most counties apparently made only a single nomination for each convention place, and there were no real contests. Eager to procure

[10] Brown to Edwin M. Stanton, May 21, 1865, in Joseph E. Brown Papers in private possession; New York *Tribune,* June 2, 1865; Andrew Johnson to Edwin M. Stanton, copies of two letters dated June 3, 1865, in Edwin M. Stanton Papers, Library of Congress; Joseph E. Brown's "Address to the People of Georgia," June 30, 1865, in Executive Minutes of the State of Georgia, Georgia Department of Archives and History; and frequent letters from Brown to the President during the summer of 1865, in Andrew Johnson Papers.

[11] Executive Minutes of the State of Georgia, Georgia Department of Archives and History; Allen D. Chandler (Comp.), *The Confederate Records of the State of Georgia* (Atlanta: By authority of the Legislature, 1909), IV, 14ff; Macon *Telegraph,* July 16, 1865; Benjamin H. Hill to James Johnson, July 14, 1865, in Benjamin H. Hill Papers, Georgia Department of Archives and History; Augusta *Chronicle and Sentinel,* July 25, 1865; Rome *Courier,* September 28, 1865. For somewhat different reasoning on the need for Georgians to cooperate with the federal government, see the Albany *Patriot,* July 22, 1865.

pardons and gain the right to vote, few Georgians cared as much, apparently, about casting their ballots when the elections were held on October 4. So slight was the attention paid to the elections that no voting returns were published.

But Northerners lulled into dreams of an easy and painless reconstruction by Georgians' acceptance of federal authority in the summer of 1865 awoke with a start when the convention met on October 25. Though the nearly three hundred delegates failed to include the established leaders of Georgia politics, the antebellum and wartime chieftans who were themselves ineligible to serve under the terms of presidential proclamations had maneuvered to secure nominations for their own favorites.[12] Those who would lead the convention might never have served in Congress or the cabinet, but most had held state or local office. Though these leaders were not ardent secessionists, most had been co-operationists in 1861 and had willingly followed their state into rebellion.[13] Little consoled that the convention president, Herschel V. Johnson, had been vice-presidential candidate on the Stephen A. Douglas ticket in 1860, Northern observers grumbled that members of the convention failed to represent the truly loyal men of Georgia.[14]

James Johnson's message to the convention charged its delegates with four tasks. They must abolish slavery, repeal the secession ordinance of 1861, repudiate the Confederate

[12] W. W. Paine to Alexander H. Stephens, October 6, 1865, and G. F. Bristow to Stephens, September 14, 1865, in Alexander Stephens Papers, Library of Congress.

[13] These conclusions about the social, economic, and political backgrounds of convention members are drawn from career line analysis of members of the Committee on Business, which prepared the agenda and controlled debate, and from generalizations in Thompson, *Reconstruction in Georgia*, 148–49, and Lucian Lamar Knight, *A Standard History of Georgia and Georgians* (Chicago: Lewis Publishing Company, 1917), II, 803–804.

[14] Andrews, *The South Since the War*, 281–83. On Herschel V. Johnson, see Percy Scott Flippen, *Herschel V. Johnson of Georgia: States Rights Unionist* (Richmond: Press of the Dietz Printing Co., Publishers, 1931).

war debt, and frame a new constitution which would provide
for the election of civil officers to replace the military authorities and the provisional government. Action on the
secession ordinance and on slavery, urged by President Johnson, the provisional governor, and Brown, came swiftly.[15] But
repudiation of the Confederate debt came more slowly and
only after repeated proddings from the worried provisional
governor and repeated threats from Andrew Johnson to delay the readmission of Georgia to the Union.[16]

Despite this minor difficulty, however, most observers
conceded that the convention acted with restraint during its
three-week session. Though it passed ordinances permitting
the provisional governor to borrow to meet the state's pressing expenses, and though it adopted a stay ordinance, designed to aid Georgians burdened by heavy debts and failing
crops or business until the General Assembly could enact a
permanent relief law, it stayed generally within the bounds
prescribed by the President and the provisional governor.[17]
Major problems of rebuilding—legislation defining the rights
of the freedmen, permanent provisions for debtor relief, and
measures for the financial rehabilitation of Georgia—remained unsolved as the delegates prepared to adjourn. But
permanent legislation had not been their job. Under their
guidance, under the leadership of this curious coalition of
old-line Whigs and lifelong Democrats, Georgia had taken
what appeared to be the first steps toward recovery. The
delegates who in their final act before adjournment had

[15] Candler (comp.), *Confederate Records of Georgia*, IV, 38–45, 145–
46, 171–72; Georgia *Constitution of 1865*, Art. I, Sec. 20.
[16] James Johnson to Andrew Johnson, October 27, 1865; Andrew Johnson
to James Johnson, copy, October 28, 1865; James Johnson to Andrew
Johnson, telegram, November 7, 1865, all in Andrew Johnson Papers. See
also Candler (comp.), *Confederate Records of Georgia*, IV, 167–68, 305,
345–46, 403–404.
[17] Candler (comp.), *Confederate Records of Georgia*, IV, 40, 76–77,
104–105, 167, 183, 224–25, 324, 395.

petitioned Andrew Johnson for Georgia's readmission to the Union could well expect a swift and agreeable response to their plea.[18]

But those who so confidently petitioned the President did not, and perhaps could not, realize that even as the convention adjourned and preparations began for new elections and the installation of a new state government, the unquestioning submission to federal authority which had marked Georgia politics in the summer of 1865 was breaking down. To be sure, the breakdown was not evident in the elections. The convention ordinance providing for balloting for governor, Congressmen, and state legislators on November 15 seemed innocuous enough, and Georgians appeared no more interested in these contests than they had been in the convention elections a few weeks before. Voters knew of but one candidate for the governorship—Charles Jones Jenkins, an antebellum Whig turned Democrat, who had chaired the powerful Committee of Sixteen which had determined the agenda of the constitutional convention.[19] Many candidates for the General Assembly and for Congress also ran unopposed. All had little time to mobilize popular opinion, and all confined their campaign efforts to public letters urging support for James Johnson and the work of the constitutional convention. Most editors followed the lead of the Macon *Telegraph* in avoiding discussion of specific issues and in merely urging the election of the "best" men for each office.[20]

Those admitted to the innermost councils of Georgia politics, however, should have noted the warning signs. The loose, bipartisan coalition which had dominated state politics in 1865 had seriously considered nominating both Joseph E. Brown and Confederate Vice-President Alexander H.

[18] *Ibid.*, IV, 325–26.
[19] Albany *Patriot*, November 11, 1865.
[20] Macon *Telegraph*, October 28, 1865.

Stephens for the governorship before deciding to ensure the continued support of former Whigs by selecting Jenkins.[21] Of the seven Congressmen-elect, one had been an ardent secessionist, and all had served the Confederacy. Georgians, it seemed, would submit to federal authority—but they would not repudiate their old leaders. And repudiation of antebellum and wartime leaders was precisely what an increasingly restive Congress demanded.

Matters came to a head in Georgia soon after Jenkins replaced Provisional Governor Johnson and the new General Assembly convened. At first, there seemed little reason to expect difficulty. The legislature speedily ratified the Thirteenth Amendment to the federal Constitution, and Governor Jenkins' inaugural message painted a cheerful picture of Georgia's progress toward economic and political recovery.[22] Though the new governor dwelt on the inferiority of the Negro and demanded stringent measures for his control, he called for the admission of Negro testimony in the courts.

[21] Alexander H. Stephens to Joseph E. Brown, November 11, 1865; Stephens to Brown, November 15, 1865; Stephens to Brown, November 30, 1865, all in Joseph E. Brown Papers, Felix Hargrett Collection, University of Georgia. See also Robert Toombs to Stephens, Havana, Cuba, December 15, 1865, in Ulrich Bonnell Phillips (ed.), *The Correspondence of Robert Toombs, Alexander H. Stephens, and Howell Cobb* (Washington: Government Printing Office, 1913), 673–76; M. C. Fulton to Stephens, November 29, 1865, in Alexander Stephens Papers, Library of Congress; and Brown to Stephens, November 14, 1865, in Alexander H. Stephens Papers, Emory University. On the negotiations leading to Jenkins' nomination, see also Howell Cobb to his wife, November 5, 1865, in Howell Cobb Papers, University of Georgia; A. R. Watson to Stephens, November 6, 1865, P. Thweatt to Stephens, November 10, 1865, O. A. Lochrane to Stephens, November 22, 1865, all in Alexander Stephens Papers, Library of Congress; J. B. Dumble to Stephens, Macon, November 17, 1865, in Alexander Stephens Papers, Emory University; Linton Stephens to Alexander H. Stephens, November 20, 1865, in Alexander Stephens Papers, Manhattanville College of the Sacred Heart; and Stephens to Jenkins, November 12, 1865, in Telamon Cuyler Collection, University of Georgia.

[22] *Journal of the Senate of the State of Georgia, 1865–6*, 17–18; *Journal of the House of Representatives of the State of Georgia, 1865–6*, 16–17.

A correspondent for the New York *Times* reported that Jenkins' remarks had included a "handsome tribute" to the conduct of the freedmen, and the *Times* seemed impressed by the new governor's "liberal, kindly . . . [and] temperate" speech.[23] Even Georgia's Black Code, moderate by comparison with those in other states, occasioned no unfavorable comment.[24] Rather, it was the election of the United States Senators which helped dash hopes that Georgia would gain prompt readmission to the Union and which furnished fresh ammunition to Northern Radical Republicans already angered by the President's policies and eager to place Reconstruction more directly under Congressional control.

Although President Johnson on November 24, 1865, had made clear his wish that Alexander Stephens not be chosen,[25] the General Assembly in January, 1866, rejected the candidacy of Georgia's foremost Unionist, Joshua Hill, and elected Stephens and Herschel V. Johnson to the state's two United States Senate seats.[26] Stephens and Johnson, doubtless pleased by their selection, nonetheless understood better than most Georgians the probable effect of the balloting. While Johnson mourned to Stephens that the legislature had acted unwisely, and while Stephens dispatched pained assurances of his loyalty and regard to the President in Washington,[27] white Georgians rejoiced in the assembly's choice.[28]

Georgians' reaction contrasted sharply with that of North-

[23] New York *Times*, December 17, 18, 1865.
[24] Thompson, *Reconstruction in Georgia*, 159.
[25] Johnson to Gen. J. B. Steedman, telegram, November 24, 1865, in Andrew Johnson Papers.
[26] *Journal of the House of Representatives of the State of Georgia, 1865–6*, 190–201.
[27] Herschel V. Johnson to Alexander H. Stephens, Augusta, February 1, 1866, in Herschel V. Johnson Papers, Duke University; Stephens to Andrew Johnson, telegram, January 31, 1866, in Andrew Johnson Papers.
[28] Augusta *Chronicle and Sentinel*, February 8, 1866; Augusta *Constitutionalist*, February 11, 1866; Macon *Telegraph*, February 7, 1866.

ern editors and most Republican Congressmen, who saw in the election of such prominent Confederates as Stephens irrefutable proof of continuing Southern recalcitrance. Georgia's seven Congressmen-elect had never been seated, and the Senate's refusal to accept the credentials of either Stephens or Johnson was hardly surprising.

Understanding that the presidential program of Reconstruction was rapidly falling before the onslaughts of Congressional Radicals and that they themselves had contributed to the process came only slowly to Georgians in the summer of 1866. A few of the most prominent antebellum leaders were the first to sense the situation, and these men responded to pleas from Andrew Johnson's backers for all moderate Republicans and Democrats to unite in a National Union convention at Philadelphia in September.[29] Correspondence between Georgia leaders and the President's supporters led quickly to a flock of public meetings in July and August, summoned to ratify the convention call and nominate delegates to district, state, and finally the national gatherings.[30]

In the local and state rallies, Democratic stalwarts temporarily silenced at the end of the war formally reentered politics. At no level did the lists of those prominent in the convention proceedings contain many surprises, for these men were scarcely newcomers to Georgia politics. Local leaders

[29] Alexander H. Stephens to Montgomery Blair, July 13, 1866, in Blair-Gist Family Papers, Library of Congress; Herschel V. Johnson to Stephens, Augusta, July 5 and 16, 1866, in Herschel V. Johnson Papers, Duke University. See also Stephens to Johnson, July 18, 1866, Johnson to Stephens, July 20, 1866, and Johnson to "My Dear Sir," July 2, 1866, all in Herschel V. Johnson Papers, Duke University.

[30] Rome *Courier,* July 12, 1866; Dawson *Journal,* July 13 and 27, August 3, 1866; Sandersville *Central Georgian,* August 15, 1866; Albany *Patriot,* August 4, 1866; Augusta *Chronicle and Sentinel,* July 3, 5, 6, 10, 12, and 15, 1866. A complete list of delegates and alternates to the Philadelphia convention appears in the Augusta *Constitutionalist,* August 8, 1866.

—David Irwin, E. G. Cabaniss, Augustus Reese, E. A. Nisbet, James Jackson, and A. H. Colquitt—had rendered active service in earlier Democratic campaigns. Behind them and behind several of the delegates to the Philadelphia convention, including Linton Stephens, Judge Hiram Warner, and General John Brown Gordon, Democrats united in the summer of 1866 to begin rebuilding their party at the local, county, and state levels. In 1867 these supporters of the National Union movement would combine with other opponents of Congressional Reconstruction to form the new statewide Democratic Executive Committee.

In the autumn of 1866, however, there seemed even to leaders like Herschel Johnson and Alexander Stephens little need for such permanent, formal party organizations. As enthusiasm for the abortive National Union movement waned, apparent political stagnation returned. Candidates for Congress in the fall of 1866 met only apathy; even their denunciations of the Radical program for Reconstruction and of the proposed Fourteenth Amendment failed to evoke popular response.[31] Preoccupied with crop failures and plagued by economic distress more severe than they had experienced even in 1865, most Georgians seemed unconcerned with political events and failed to grasp the import of Radical victories in the nationwide Congressional elections.

Equally uncomprehending were Governor Jenkins and the members of the General Assembly. Presented by Congress with the Fourteenth Amendment, the Georgia legislature—like its counterparts in other Southern states—rejected ratification on November 9 by a nearly unanimous vote.[32]

A humiliated and discredited Andrew Johnson, no longer

[31] Rome *Courier*, November 20, 1866; James P. Hambleton, "To the Voters of the Seventh Congressional District," Atlanta, October 26, 1866, in Broadsides Collection, Henry P. Farrow Collection, University of Georgia.

[32] *Journal of the Senate of the State of Georgia, 1866*, 65–72; *Journal of the House of Representatives of the State of Georgia, 1866*, 68–69.

in close touch with the progress of Georgia Reconstruction, could do nothing to control the enraged Radical Republicans. That Congress would itself seize control over Reconstruction seemed likely; that the Southern refusal to accept the Fourteenth Amendment would speed the process seemed inevitable. The form Congressional control would take depended only on the outcome of a fierce struggle between radical and moderate members of the House and Senate in the closing hours of the Thirty-ninth Congress.

CHAPTER I

Toward a Political Party

The Republican organization which took shape in Georgia late in 1865 and in 1866 developed without the blessings of President Andrew Johnson. Indeed, there is no indication that the President ever sought to create a Republican party in the state. As long as Johnson remained in firm control of Southern Reconstruction, few Georgians openly discussed the formation of a Republican organization. By the summer of 1866, however, the breach between the President and the Congressional Radicals was clear, and Johnson in fact, if not yet in law, had lost control of events in the South. In the early fall, leaders who had earlier disavowed party labels talked openly of the rise of Republicanism in Georgia. Though Democrats and Republicans remained curiously unconscious of each other's activities, the revival of the Democratic party and the formation of a Republican organization proceeded almost in step. In both cases, the foundations were laid in 1865, and frankly partisan activity began only in 1866.

Never during their party's tortured history in post-Civil War Georgia would Republicans agree on the groups which should make up their coalition. From the outset, however, all recognized that reliance solely upon the freedmen was not a viable plan. Northern race prejudice would make the national Republican party wary of encouraging such a course, and in Georgia whites outnumbered Negroes by nearly twenty thousand. The freedmen would probably be enfranchised and nearly all would doubtless become loyal Republican partisans, but Georgia Republicans would also have to woo reliable white support. Beyond recognizing this fact, it seems doubtful that most Republicans before 1867 developed any blueprint for constructing a party in the state. The party's development in 1865 and 1866 was at best a chaotic process. Such order as it had was imposed by party workers in Georgia, for Congressional leaders took little interest in the new organization until they had openly avowed their own partisan motives and had seized control of Reconstruction at the national level.

The story of the Republican party in Georgia properly begins in 1865, with the arrival of United States occupation troops, Freedmen's Bureau agents, missionaries of the Methodist Church, and federal appointees who entered the state after Appomattox. The army troops, the bureau agents, and the missionaries were the official emissaries of no political party, and Andrew Johnson's appointments were not designed to aid the Republican cause. Most of those who came South at first engaged in no political activity whatever. But it is likely that the majority of bureau officers and missionaries supported the humanitarian policy toward the Negro which had become identified with the national Republican party. Most were probably loyal Union men in a decade which identified Republicanism with patriotism and the Democratic party with treason. That some would eventually combine their social, economic, or religious missions with political proselytizing was inevitable. Too little can be ascertained about the formation of the Republican party in Georgia, but one fact seems clear. The party did not grow out of a diabolical plot by Congressional Radicals to enslave the South. It was instead a predictable by-product of the social and economic rehabilitation of the section.

The power given Freedmen's Bureau agents to call meetings, issue circulars, and serve as general counselors to the Negroes made bureau posts ideal starting points for those who aspired to political careers in the postwar South. By the end of 1865, the bureau had over two hundred agents in Georgia. Political activity was officially forbidden them, but many agents did not hesitate to tell the Negroes which national party represented their true friends. Because they served as the closest link between the federal government and the freedmen, they eventually became an excellent means of communication between Republican organizers and the Union Republican Congressional Committee in Washington.[1]

Bureau agents were not always mere intermediaries between the developing Georgia party and the national organization. In 1865 and 1866, before the national party showed sustained interest in its Georgia counterpart, bureau officers often served as party organizers—holding meetings, making speeches, coordinating activities throughout the state, and encouraging the development of a party press. At least twenty such agents later held office under Georgia's Republican government, and at least three became prominent in party councils. James L. Dunning, a resident of Georgia for nineteen years before his appointment as bureau agent in

[1] Leslie Paul Rowan, "The Rise and Development of the Republican Party in Georgia" (M.A. thesis, Emory University, 1948), 7–8.

1865, served as a delegate to the Radical constitutional convention in 1867.[2] J. Clarke Swayze, named agent for Spalding County in January, 1866, moved on to become editor of the Republican *American Union* in Griffin and Macon.[3] John E. Bryant, a native of Maine and a former captain in the Union army, was the most prominent Georgia carpetbagger and probably the most politically active of the state's bureau officers. It is no accident that the lines of communication in Georgia's developing Republican organization during 1865 and 1866 radiated from Augusta, where Bryant was bureau agent. The founder of a Negro political association and of a weekly Republican paper in Augusta, he served in the constitutional convention of 1867, on the state Republican Executive Committee, and later led a revolt within the Republican party against the administration of the Radical Republican governor.

Intimately connected with bureau activities in matters both of philanthropy and of politics were the efforts of clergymen and missionaries of the Northern Methodist Church. Though most churchmen avoided political activity, a few Northern missionaries journeyed South "with a Bible in one hand and the equivalent of the *Republican Fact Book* in the other."[4] For such men, activity under the auspices of the Freedmen's Bureau seemed to offer the best field for political proselytizing. Only three Methodist missionaries became prominent in Republican activities; of these, one, J. H. Caldwell, had no demonstrable connection with the bu-

[2] Candler (comp.), *Confederate Records of Georgia,* VI, 1021; Bureau of Refugees, Freedmen and Abandoned Lands, Georgia, Roster of Civil Agents, in R. G. 105, National Archives, hereafter cited as Freedmen's Bureau Records, Georgia.

[3] Freedmen's Bureau Records, Georgia, Special Orders No. 19, January 23, 1866, in R. G. 105, National Archives. Swayze's appointment, made at the request of the Georgia General Assembly, was revoked on January 30; see Special Orders No. 24, *ibid.*

[4] Rowan, "Rise and Development of the Republican Party," 8.

reau.[5] Two of Caldwell's Negro colleagues, however, served as federal agents; Henry M. Turner was an army chaplain assigned to the bureau,[6] and Tunis G. Campbell, Sr., served under General Rufus B. Saxton as military governor of one of the Sea Islands at the close of the war.[7] Caldwell, Turner, and Campbell all participated in the 1867 convention. Though none of the three found a secure place in the highest echelons of the party, all became prominent Republican spokesmen and popular campaign orators.

Executive patronage, a traditional means of party-building, was never an important factor in the early development of Georgia's Republican party, for Andrew Johnson seems to have paid little heed to party considerations in making appointments within the state. Appointments in 1865 and 1866 went to men whom the President believed to be sincere supporters of his program. Probably most of the appointees did support the President in 1865 and 1866, and many became Democrats after the Congressional Radicals seized control of events in the South in 1867. Those who used the minor offices bestowed on them by the President as a ladder to higher political posts were those with the greatest talent for staying a half-step ahead of political changes. When Johnson lost control of Reconstruction to the Congress, these men espoused the Congressional program of restoration as fervently as they had once espoused the President's plan.

A few of the state appointees were carpetbaggers, such as

[5] *Ibid.*, and Freedmen's Bureau Records, Georgia, Roster of Civil Officers, in R. G. 105, National Archives. On Caldwell's later activities, see Ralph E. Morrow, *Northern Methodism and Reconstruction* (East Lansing: Michigan State University Press, 1956), 225.

[6] E. Merton Coulter, "Henry M. Turner: Georgia Negro Preacher–Politician During the Reconstruction Era," *Georgia Historical Quarterly,* XLVIII (December, 1964), 374.

[7] Frances Butler Leigh, *Ten Years on a Georgia Plantation since the War* (London: Richard Bentley & Son, 1883), 113*ff*; Thompson, *Reconstruction in Georgia*, 190.

A. L. "Fatty" Harris, a rotund Ohio editor who traveled
South after the war. Appointed special agent of the Post
Office Department at Augusta in 1865, Harris had moved to
Savannah by January, 1866.[8] Most of the new officials, however, were native Southerners like Foster Blodgett. Blodgett,
born in South Carolina, moved to Georgia as a youth and
won immediate success as a lawyer and Whig politician. By
1860, at the age of thirty-two, he was mayor of Augusta.
In 1865 he received the Augusta postmastership. When the
feud between Andrew Johnson and the national Republican
party flared, Blodgett espoused the Radical cause and was
removed from the office by order of the President. His
rewards, however, seemed greater than his losses. He became one of the leaders in the developing Republican organization at Augusta and, later, a prominent officeholder under
the Republican state regime. To the Congressional Radicals,
he was a martyr to his convictions, to be paraded before the
Senate during Johnson's impeachment trial in 1868.[9]

The bureau agents, missionaries, and minor officeholders
who used their official positions for partisan purposes were
usually stationed in Georgia's major cities and towns. In the
countryside, where communications were poor and farms
were scattered, the difficulties incident to arranging mass
meetings of freedmen, organizing political clubs for native
whites, or founding newspapers to advocate the Republican
cause were forbidding. Agents in the cities and towns, how-

[8] Thompson, *Reconstruction in Georgia*, 191; Harris to John Sherman,
June 29, 1866, in John Sherman Papers, Library of Congress; Augusta
Chronicle and Sentinel, July 7, 1865; Savannah *Morning Herald*, January
13, 1866.

[9] Eighth Census of the United States (1860), Schedule I, Population,
Richmond County, Georgia, Manuscript Returns, in National Archives;
*Trial of Andrew Johnson . . . Before the Senate of the United States, on
Impeachment . . . for High Crimes and Misdemeanors* (Washington:
Government Printing Office, 1868), I, 375–76, 708–25.

ever, had a ready audience, and they could more easily supervise the day-to-day activities of their followers. The first organized Republican activity, then, occurred in Augusta, Atlanta, Macon, Savannah, and Columbus, and in such smaller towns as Albany and Griffin. From these centers, the party organization eventually spread over the entire state.

That Georgia Republicans made early if only moderately successful efforts to develop a party press in the state suggests their determination to appeal to native whites as well as to the freedmen. Most freedmen were illiterate and presumably could not be reached directly through a party press, though in the cities and towns whites might be employed or might volunteer to read the papers to the Negroes. On the other hand, whites who would never be seen at meetings dominated by freedmen might be willing to subscribe to a Republican paper.

Georgia Democrats refused to believe that any respectable citizen could sympathize with the Radical cause, and they expressed their surprise that any Republican papers could flourish in the state.[10] One of the earliest Republican papers in Georgia, however, was also one of the oldest and most respected dailies in Savannah. Even before the end of the war, the *Daily Republican* had advocated acceptance of whatever measures the federal government might take toward reconstructing the state. After the surrender, John E. Hayes, editor of the *Republican* and a former reporter for the New York *Tribune*, became increasingly radical. By the winter of 1865 he was publishing vituperative attacks on

[10] Augusta *Chronicle and Sentinel*, October 2, 1866. The *Chronicle and Sentinel* noted with surprise that the Savannah *Daily Republican* had appeared on a list of Radical papers in Georgia. They could scarcely believe the report, the editors announced, for the *Republican* was "liberally patronized by the old merchants and citizens of Savannah."

Solomon Cohen, a former secessionist elected by his district
to represent Georgia in the Thirty-ninth Congress.[11]

Not often, however, were the editors of old, well-estab-
lished papers Republican partisans. More often, Republicans
founded their own papers, and they complained bitterly of
the financial reverses suffered when circulation proved to be
less than they had anticipated. In Augusta, John E. Bryant
joined with a mulatto, Simeon Beaird, to purchase a mori-
bund Negro paper, the *Colored American*. Using funds
contributed by loyal whites, Bryant and Beaird founded
the Georgia Printing Company and began publication of the
Loyal Georgian, a weekly journal devoted to encouraging
the political aspirations of the freedmen. Not surprisingly,
the paper reached only a small audience, and other Republican papers founded in Georgia in 1865 and 1866 fared little
better.[12] Though there were only a few Republican journals
in the state by the end of 1866—the Augusta *Daily Press*, Bryant's *Loyal Georgian*, Hayes's Savannah *Daily Republican*,
and the Griffin *American Union*—all were apparently in financial straits. Early in 1867, when passage of the Military Reconstruction Act by a Republican Congress made a redistri-

[11] John E. Hayes to N. P. Banks, February 5, 1867, in Nathaniel P.
Banks Papers, Library of Congress. Hayes was tried for and convicted of
libel against Cohen. He reported to Banks that he had always "struggled
to maintain" the *Daily Republican* "as a loyal newspaper without soliciting
any aid from the North," but that he had fallen "the first victim of rebel
spleen in Georgia."

[12] *Proceedings of the Council of the Georgia Equal Rights Association.
Assembled at Augusta, Ga., April 4, 1866.* (Augusta: Office of the *Loyal
Georgian*, 1866); *Proceedings of the Convention of the Equal Rights &
Educational Association of Georgia, Assembled at Macon, October 29, 1866*
(Augusta: Office of the *Loyal Georgian*, 1866), 6. Bryant's activities as
a Republican editor incurred the wrath of the military authorities, who
stationed a guard in the press room of the *Loyal Georgian* after editorials
critical of the local military commanders had appeared. See Bvt. Brig.
Gen. Samuel Thomas to Bvt. Maj. Gen. C. R. Wood, June 11, 1866, in
Freedmen's Bureau Records, Georgia, Letters Sent, R. G. 105, National
Archives.

bution of government newspaper patronage seem imminent, Georgia's Republican editors pleaded with their Congressional friends for aid. If money from government contracts were not forthcoming, many hinted, they would be forced to suspend publication.[13]

Because so few freedmen could read and because Republican papers were of such small number and had such limited circulation, the activities of Republican editors were never as important in the organization of the party in Georgia as were the meetings held and associations formed by bureau agents, minor officeholders, and clergymen. In 1865, the problems of economic and social readjustment were paramount in the minds of most Georgians, and meetings called by bureau officers or other officials generally confined their deliberations to these subjects.[14] By the winter of 1865–66, however, the first steps toward economic recovery and social adjustment had been taken, and agents who were so inclined began to turn their attention to politics.

The most active of these agents was Bryant. In January, 1866, he led in calling a convention of freedmen to meet at Augusta. The gathering had the reluctant blessing of the bureau commander in Georgia, General Davis Tillson, a moderate whose protection of planters as well as freedmen had won marked approval from Georgia conservatives. Tillson could, he reported to Alexander Stephens, "give no sufficient reason" for withholding his consent; he doubted "very much" that the freedmen had "any definite [political] intention or purpose." Somewhat naively, Tillson hoped that

[13] Undated flyer from editors of loyal southern papers, in N. P. Banks Papers, filed under February, 1867; Bryant to Edward McPherson, March 4, 1867, James L. Dunning to Edwin M. Stanton, March 5, 1867, Charles Whittlesey to McPherson, March 4, 1867, George W. Ashburn to McPherson, March 14, 1867, and A. G. Murray to [McPherson?], March 2, 1867, all in Edward McPherson Papers, Library of Congress.

[14] See, for example, Augusta *Chronicle and Sentinel*, June 3, 1865.

"if the more intelligent members of the freed people should thus assemble together," he could "make use of the opportunity to disseminate correct views among them throughout the State."[15] The "correct views" he had in mind doubtless did not include the formation of a Negro political association. Yet it was to this end that Bryant's movement was dedicated.

The Augusta convention itself took no extreme action. It met on January 10 with representatives of only 18 of Georgia's 132 counties present and with a Negro, James Porter, in the chair.[16] Its delegates opposed universal suffrage, demanded property and education qualifications for the franchise, and asked appointment of a board to oversee the establishment of schools for Negroes. Though they resolved that lands along the Georgia coast and on the Sea Islands, temporarily given to the Negroes by Union General Rufus B. Saxton during the war, should not be taken from the freedmen, the delegates also voted to oppose sweeping Congressional confiscation of Southern lands.

Out of the January meetings came a new organization, the Georgia Equal Rights Association. Nominally, the association was a nonpolitical group, headed by Bryant and dedicated to the program approved by the Negro convention. But its political purposes were quickly apparent to all observers, and it immediately became the scapegoat wherever Georgia whites had complaints about the conduct of the

[15] Davis Tillson to Alexander H. Stephens, Augusta, January 6, 1866, in Alexander Stephens Papers, Library of Congress.

[16] A good secondary account of the convention appears in Ethel Maude Christler, "Participation of Negroes in the Government of Georgia 1867–1870" (M.A. thesis, Atlanta University, 1932), 4–6. See also the Milledgeville *Southern Recorder*, January 30, 1866, and, for the convention proceedings, *Proceedings of the Freedmen's Convention of Georgia, Assembled at Augusta, January 10, 1866* (Augusta: Office of the *Loyal Georgian*, 1866), which includes the constitution and resolutions adopted by the convention.

freedmen.[17] Apparently because he ignored Tillson's wish that bureau agents remain aloof from Republican politics, Bryant lost his Freedmen's Bureau post.[18] His was universally recognized as the guiding hand behind the new Negro organization. "The negroes," reported the Macon *Telegraph,* "are in the foreground and make all the moves, but certain wicked Northern Men, representatives of the Radical faction, are behind the scenes, fix up the documents and pull the wires."[19]

In fact, white leadership of the Negro was precisely what Bryant encouraged. It was vital to the political success of the Negro race, he told the freedmen, that they cultivate friendly relations with the whites and associate with them in their political endeavors. He believed, therefore, that the Negro convention acted wisely in January, 1866, when it chose him president of the Equal Rights Association in preference to a Negro who sought the office.[20] Though he encouraged the hopes of educated Negroes for the ballot and urged that the freedmen send a delegate to Washington to "advocate the cause of equal rights with the President and members of Congress," Bryant concentrated his major efforts on organizing the freedmen in Georgia within his Equal Rights Association.[21] Using as bases of operation the major cities and towns where United States troops were stationed

[17] Dawson *Journal,* April 20, 1866.

[18] Charles Stearns, *The Black Man of the South, and The Rebels* (New York: American News Co., 1872), 106; George R. Bentley, *A History of the Freedmen's Bureau* (Philadelphia: University of Pennsylvania Press, 1955), 69–70, 129.

[19] Quoted in Dawson *Journal,* March 30, 1866.

[20] *Proceedings of the Freedmen's Convention. . . . At Augusta, January 10, 1866,* 23, 27.

[21] *Proceedings of the Council of the Georgia Equal Rights Association . . . April 4, 1866,* 3. For the reaction of the Georgia press to Bryant's plans, see Augusta *Chronicle and Sentinel,* March 25, 1866; Dawson *Journal,* March 30, 1866; Rome *Courier,* March 17, 1866.

and where whites already had their own Republican-oriented
political clubs, Bryant and the Equal Rights Executive Council in April, 1866, established ten membership districts for
the state.[22] Six months later, Bryant claimed organizations
in fifty counties, but he reported considerable difficulty in
mobilizing the freedmen outside the cities and towns.[23]

It was through Bryant's association that such Negroes as
Aaron Alpeoria Bradley and Henry M. Turner first entered
Georgia politics. Bradley, a native of Brooklyn who came to
Georgia by way of the New York state prison system (he had
been incarcerated for seduction), was as unpopular among
his Radical colleagues as he was among Democratic white
Georgians. His forte was persuading the freedmen of the
coastal counties that they should refuse to cooperate with
any federal Reconstruction agencies; he was, strictly speaking, a rabble-rouser rather than a serious party organizer.
Turner was at once more influential than Bradley among the
freedmen and more respected by the whites. Though Turner
attended meetings and conventions of the Equal Rights
Association, he apparently avoided formal membership, and
he shrewdly presented a cooperative and moderate front to
observant whites.[24] But he was an active participant in the
crusade to awaken Georgia Negroes to political self-con-
sciousness. Carleton B. Cole, a conservative judge, later
claimed to have attended two meetings called and conducted
by Turner "in the fall of 1866, or early in 1867." At a morning
session attended by whites, Cole testified before a Congressional committee, Turner made a "conservative and satisfactory" speech. In the evening, however, he addressed a

[22] *Proceedings of the Council of the Georgia Equal Rights Association
. . . April 4, 1866,* 10.

[23] *Proceedings of the Convention of the Equal Rights & Educational
Association of Georgia . . . at Macon, October 29, 1866,* 5.

[24] *Proceedings of the Freedmen's Convention . . . At Augusta, January
10, 1866;* Coulter, "Henry M. Turner," 375–77.

second meeting, from which whites were excluded. To the evening meeting, he made "entirely a political speech for the purpose of organizing a political party and cautioning the negroes against being influenced in any manner, shape or form by the white people, and [advising them] to band together for their own protection."[25]

Like Bryant, Turner never advocated the formation of an independent Negro political party. The Equal Rights Association was a necessary step in Georgia; only through it or some similar organization could the freedmen be mobilized for political action. But almost as soon as the association was founded, its leaders began to look beyond to its eventual alliance with the Union League in a true Republican party organization throughout the state.[26]

The activities of the Union League in Georgia before 1867 remain shrouded in obscurity. This secret society, organized in the North during the war, spread South after Appomattox. In the former Confederate states, it was first popular among the Unionist whites—in Georgia, especially among those in the northern counties.[27] Though the leagues became prominent in Georgia only late in 1866 or early in 1867, their political activities long antedated that time. By the early months of 1866, league councils were reported active in Georgia's

[25] *Report of the Joint Select Committee to Inquire into the Condition of Affairs in the Late Insurrectionary States* (Washington: Government Printing Office, 1872), VII, 1188, hereafter cited by the binder's title, *Ku Klux Conspiracy*. Cole's testimony, solicited by a Democratic member of the committee, may be unreliable.

[26] *Proceedings of the Equal Rights & Educational Association of Georgia . . . at Macon, October 29, 1866; Proceedings of the Council of the Georgia Equal Rights Association . . . April 4, 1866*, 6.

[27] Olive Hall Shadgett, *The Republican Party in Georgia from Reconstruction through 1900* (Athens: University of Georgia Press, 1964), 3. See also Maj. Gen. George H. Thomas to Asa Seward and others, May 3, 1865, in George H. Thomas Papers, Duke University, and Roberta F. Cason, "The Loyal League in Georgia," *Georgia Historical Quarterly*, XX (June, 1936), 131.

major cities and towns—Rome, Macon, Savannah, Atlanta, and Griffin—and it was league funds which early in 1866 enabled Bryant and Beaird to purchase the presses of the Augusta *Colored American* and establish the *Loyal Georgian*.[28] Not until 1866 were statistics of league membership published, however, and since these figures reflect membership in the fall of 1867, after the Republican party had formally organized in Georgia, they are doubtless unreliable for 1866. The league president's exultation in the fact that by the fall of 1867 there were councils in 117 Georgia counties does suggest that in 1866 the organization had been much more limited.[29] Probably the league, like the Equal Rights Association, continued throughout 1866 to be most active and most successful in the cities and towns.

The traditional story of the Union League in Georgia is that the membership rolls in 1866 were increasingly dominated by freedmen. Historians have made much of the attractions which league rituals held for the Negro and of the elaborate catechisms devised by league councils to convince the ignorant freedmen that the Republican party and not the Democratic was their true friend.[30] The implication, of course, is that the Union Leagues spared nothing in their efforts to attract Negro members. In fact, however, the Union League in Georgia did little to attract the freedmen. Negroes were excluded from membership in 1865, and, even after they were admitted in 1866, they were segregated in

[28] *Proceedings of the Council of the Georgia Equal Rights Association . . . April 4, 1866*, 9; *Proceedings of the Convention of the Equal Rights & Education Association of Georgia . . . at Macon, October 29, 1866*, 6; testimony of B. F. Sawyer, *Ku Klux Conspiracy*, VII, 901; Davis Tillson to W. A. Rozar, January 18, 1867, in Freedmen's Bureau Records, Georgia, Letters Sent, R. G. 105, National Archives.

[29] Henry P. Farrow, President of the Union League of America in Georgia, *To the Subordinate Councils, U. L. A., in Georgia, February 5, 1866*, pamphlet in Henry P. Farrow Collection, University of Georgia.

[30] See, for example, Cason, "The Loyal League in Georgia," 134.

their own councils. It was the Negro Equal Rights Association, not the white Union League, which took the initiative in calling for the coordination of Negro and white political activities.[31]

John E. Bryant accurately foresaw the process by which the Republicans would finally establish a viable political organization in Georgia. There were, he noted, three groups in Georgia by the summer of 1866 which espoused Republican principles. One was his own Equal Rights Association. The second was the Union League. The third was a disorganized mass of whites and potential Negro voters who favored the Republican party but who had as yet made no political commitments. To reach this third group, Bryant argued, the Equal Rights Association and the Union League must join hands. They must work together to hold meetings and to preach the Republican gospel through the party press.[32]

By the end of 1866, however, the fusion which Bryant sought had yet to take place.[33] Not until the Congressional Republicans provided the impetus in the passage of the Military Reconstruction Bill would the scattered Republican forces in Georgia join to form a true political party.

[31] *Proceedings of the Convention of the Equal Rights & Educational Association of Georgia . . . at Macon, October 29, 1866,* 6.

[32] *Ibid., passim.*

[33] Miss Cason suggests, however, that the Equal Rights Association merged with the Union League in 1867. Cason, "The Loyal League in Georgia," 134.

CHAPTER II

Victory by Default

Passage of the Military Reconstruction Bill over Andrew Johnson's veto on March 2, 1867, served as a catalyst both to speed the fusion of the Union League, the Equal Rights Association, and many hitherto uncommitted Georgians into the new Republican party and to hasten the formal reentry into Georgia politics of the old Democratic coalition. In their first formal campaigns, in the spring and summer of 1867, both Republicans and Democrats made their first pronouncements on the issues which would distinguish their parties and divide their state for the next three years.

The Military Reconstruction Act formally removed much of the control over Reconstruction from Andrew Johnson's hands and placed the restoration of the South under Congressional direction. It divided the South into military districts, each under the command of a major general. Civilian authority again became merely provisional. The prospect of new constitutional conventions, Negro suffrage, and disfranchisement of former Rebels cheered Republicans and haunted Democrats. The organization of military rule proceeded in Georgia under the direction of Major General John Pope. In April, 1867, Atlanta became the headquarters of the Third Military District, and Pope almost immediately began preparations for elections to be held in October under the provisions of the Supplementary Reconstruction Act which became law on March 23.[1]

The military commander dictated preparations for the election in a series of registration orders. Two questions would confront the voters in October—they would have to decide whether to call a constitutional convention and would have to select the delegates should a convention be summoned. Ratification of the convention call would require the assent of a majority of all voters registered. Pope divided Georgia into registration districts; for each district, he ordered the appointment of one Negro and two white registrars. Ed. Hulbert, a Republican, became superintendent of registration. The freedmen were guaranteed the ballot by terms of the Military Reconstruction Act and Pope's registration orders. Registrars were specifically instructed to explain to the freedmen their privileges and obligations as voters and to impress upon them their duty to exercise the franchise at every opportunity.[2] Whites eligible to vote included all except those who had held civil office under the Confederacy or who had taken an oath to uphold the federal Constitution

[1] Ulysses S. Grant to John Pope, April 8 and 13, 1867, in Headquarters Records, Ulysses S. Grant Papers, Library of Congress.

[2] General Orders No. 20, *Report of the Secretary of War, 1867* (Washington: Government Printing Office, 1867), Pt. 1, pp. 336–37; Pope to Grant, October 28, 1867, in Andrew Johnson Papers. White registrars were usually appointed on the recommendation of local Freedmen's Bureau agents. The whites then selected the Negro member of the board. Bentley, *History of the Freedmen's Bureau*, 185. Pope issued two registration orders, the first on April 8 and the second on May 21.

and had later supported the rebellion. Those whites who were disfranchised could petition Congress for removal of their political disabilities.

Whether the registration figures for Georgia in 1867 accurately reflected the number of qualified voters is impossible to determine. When registration ended on September 1, 95,214 whites and 93,457 Negroes had registered.[3] During the summer, however, the supplemental Reconstruction Act had provided for revisions of the voter registration lists, and, on September 19, Pope reopened registration. Before the lists were again closed, the registrars had added more whites than Negroes to the rolls; the final registration figures showed 102,411 whites and 98,507 Negroes eligible to participate in the elections which were scheduled to begin on October 29.[4]

Reaction to the registration procedures was mixed and partisan. Some Democratic editors might concede that the registrars had discharged their duties impartially, but most were less satisfied. In Sumter, Democrats charged that a white Republican had threatened Negroes who failed to register with a $200 fine.[5] In Augusta, a stronghold of the developing Republican organization, the Democratic *Constitutionalist* complained bitterly of "a deep-laid plot to engineer the whites out of their registration." Only two days' notice of the registration was posted, complained the editors, and, though registration books remained open for nearly two weeks, the mails were so slow than many whites living in the outlying sections of Richmond County failed to learn of the dates until too late. The Negroes, on the other hand, were thoroughly organized—presumably by the Union

[3] Thompson, *Reconstruction in Georgia*, 186.
[4] *Ibid.*, 186. *n2.*
[5] Augusta *Constitutionalist*, July 24, 1867.

League or by Bryant's Equal Rights Association.[6] Others noted irregularities in the Richmond County figures. The county had a white majority, but Negro registrants exceeded whites by over a thousand. In other counties, too, registration figures appeared distorted. In Baldwin County, in Bibb, in Brooks, in Pulaski, in Spalding, and in Washington, the whites comprised a majority of the population but a decided minority of the registered voters.[7]

Irregularities in the registration procedures and disfranchisement of native whites cut down or wiped out entirely white majorities in many Georgia counties, but they do not alone explain the large number of Negroes and the relatively small number of whites on Georgia's voting rolls.[8] There is little evidence that Georgia registrars were reluctant to enroll eligible whites. Instead, Negro voter majorities in most counties resulted from the refusal of many white Democrats to recognize the constitutionality of the Reconstruction Acts by registering under their provisions.

When passage of the Military Reconstruction Act seemed imminent in February, 1867, the various groups in Georgia whose sympathies lay with the Republican cause at last joined together to form a true political party. The guarantee that the freedmen could vote for delegates to the new constitutional convention for the first time gave Republicans a clear chance for political success in Georgia. No longer were Georgia Republicans waging a hopeless battle; now they could count on the support of the Congressional Radicals and, so long as Pope was in command, of the military.

Republican political organization in Georgia in the spring

[6] Quoted in Atlanta *Daily Intelligencer*, June 20, 1867.
[7] Thompson, *Reconstruction in Georgia*, 186, 187n.
[8] William A. Russ, Jr., "Registration and Disfranchisement under Radical Reconstruction," *Mississippi Valley Historical Review*, XXI (September, 1934), 177–78. See also Russ's "Radical Disfranchisement in Georgia, 1867–1871," *Georgia Historical Quarterly*, XIX (September, 1935), 175–209.

and summer of 1867 coincided with vigorous efforts to obtain support from the national party. Particularly importunate were pleas for government patronage of Republican newspapers. The award of government printing contracts to Republican papers in Georgia would mean increased circulation and greater prosperity for the hard-pressed editors. Virtually every Republican editor in the state wrote during February and March of 1867 to Edward McPherson, who as clerk of the House of Representatives had power to dispense such government favors. In cities like Atlanta and Augusta, which after the passage of the Military Reconstruction Act briefly boasted two Republican papers, the editors vied with each other for government patronage.[9]

More confident after the passage of the military bill that the national party would sustain them, Georgians made other demands on national leaders. Rufus Bullock in March of 1867 asked the War Department to exercise closer control over voter registration in Georgia. Bullock was a New Yorker who had arrived in Georgia in the 1850's and established himself in Augusta as an agent of the Southern Express Company; Republicans early saw in him, as they did in Henry P. Farrow and Foster Blodgett, a promising convert to their party. By 1867 a prominent member of the Augusta group of Republicans headed by Blodgett and Bryant, Bullock telegraphed Stanton on behalf of the local party, demanding that military force be used in Georgia to guarantee full Negro registration.[10]

[9] The extensive correspondence between Republican editors and national party leaders is filed with Edward McPherson's correspondence for March and April, 1867, in the McPherson Papers. Especially revealing of squabbles over government patronage are William L. Scruggs to Horace Maynard, March 22, 1867, Scruggs to McPherson, April 3, 1867, William Dunn to McPherson, May 25, 1867; E. H. Pughe to McPherson, March 20, April 6, 1867, Citizens of Augusta to McPherson, April 6, 1867, and Rufus B. Bullock to Freeman Clarke, March 19, 1867.

[10] Thomas T. Eckert to Charles A. Tinker, March 27, 1867, in Records

Some Republicans hoped to ensure their party's ascendancy in Georgia by securing the removal of political disabilities imposed on former Confederate officeholders who now promised to support the Republican program. In March, 1867, Georgians learned that Senator John Sherman had agreed to sponsor a bill to remove the disabilities of Alabama's Governor R. M. Patton and Georgia's Joseph E. Brown.[11] Others who professed conversion to the Republican faith at once sought to have their names added to the measure;[12] still others demanded a more sweeping Congressional policy. Athens party worker R. S. Taylor suggested to Sherman that Congress should remove all disabilities and entrust the Georgia party with offices to be filled by loyal Republicans. Only if Georgians had patronage to bestow and freedom to bestow it on all potential supporters could they hope to build a lasting organization among white voters in the state.[13] Others seemed concerned that the Georgia organization would be labeled a Negro-dominated party, unwilling to accept the support of any but a selected few whites. L. P. Gudger, the nearly illiterate president of the Union League Council at Dalton and a voting registrar for the Forty-third District, urged that disabilities be removed to demonstrate that "we are not a proscriptive Party but [are] able and willing to be both generous and forgiving to those who bring forth fruit meet for repentence."[14] Only Republican sym-

of the Secretary of War, Telegrams Received, War Department Records, R. G. 107, National Archives.

[11] Jonathan Truman Dorris, *Pardon and Amnesty under Lincoln and Johnson* (Chapel Hill: The University of North Carolina Press, 1953), 363. Brown professed surprise over Sherman's bill, but the former governor had visited Washington in February, and it seems likely that Brown and Sherman reached at least an informal understanding. See Brown to John Sherman, Atlanta, March 21, 1867, in John Sherman Papers.

[12] Dorris, *Pardon and Amnesty*, 363.

[13] R. S. Taylor to John Sherman, April 1, 1867, in John Sherman Papers.

[14] L. P. Gudger to Benjamin F. Wade, July 8, 1867, in Benjamin F. Wade Papers, Library of Congress.

pathizers should benefit from Congressional action, however; the sweeping pardons granted by President Johnson had hurt, not helped, the cause in the South. "If all those who obtained Parden from the President is to be regestered ... as voters as Seems to be the prevailing Ide[a], now there is no use for Regestration," Gudger assured Radical Republican Benjamin F. Wade. "The Law itself dose not fulle protect Union Soldiers Union citizens nor, coloreded citizens," Gudger added. "If congress dose not do some thing to more fulle protect Union citizens than we have no use for the South nor use to live here. We will have no interest in these States. Good bye to Republican Government If Rebels is to Rule."[15] Congress failed, however, to do anything to remove political disabilities until 1868—too late to please Gudger and his colleagues, and too late to affect the outcome of the convention elections in Georgia.[16]

Despite the help which Congress did give, help in the form of the Military Reconstruction Acts themselves and in the award of government printing contracts, the major tasks of extending the Republican organization throughout Georgia in 1867 fell to the state's small coterie of established party leaders. The Republican campaign for convention delegates proceeded with remarkable precision during the spring and summer.

Not the least of the party's advantages was the apparent conversion of Joseph Brown to Republicanism, for the former governor still commanded the largest single following in the state. He visited Washington in February, 1867, while the Military Reconstruction Bill was pending before Congress, and he came away convinced that passage of the measure was inevitable and that Georgians must accept what they could not hope to change. Republican organizers, quick to

---

[15] Gudger to Benjamin Wade, July 5, 1867, in Wade Papers.
[16] Dorris, *Pardon and Amnesty*, 367–68.

sense Brown's attitude, begged him to make his views known, and Brown obliged with a letter which appeared in Georgia's Republican papers on February 26.[17] Southerners, he argued, must cooperate with Congress; his advice was "agree with thine adversary quickly." Georgians should call a convention and alter their state constitution to provide for Negro suffrage. "If we reject the terms proposed [by Congress]," he warned, "I confess I see no hope for the future."[18]

Georgia Democrats, aghast at Brown's letter, could only regard it as a temporary aberration. All were certain that the former governor had capitulated to Radicalism, and they noted darkly that Brown and General Pope seemed "on very good terms."[19] However, the Democrats worried needlessly —even as the Republicans rejoiced prematurely. Brown had not joined the Republican party, nor had he espoused the Radical faith.[20] He simply believed the political allegiances and prejudices of the antebellum and war years to be irrelevant in 1867. The only course open was to look at things as they then were, "to start out anew."[21] Congress could control the South whatever Southerners wanted or said, and Southerners, as the conquered, could no longer expect any better terms than those contained in the military bill.[22] No one yet knew precisely what military Reconstruction would in-

[17] Brown's letter, dated February 23, 1867, appeared in the Atlanta *New Era*, February 26. It was widely reprinted. An undated letter, identified by Henry P. Farrow as the original letter sent to Brown by the Georgia Republican organizers, is filed in the Henry Farrow Collection.

[18] Atlanta *New Era*, February 26, 1867.

[19] P. Thweatt to Alexander H. Stephens, April 27, 1867, in Alexander Stephens Papers, Library of Congress.

[20] Joseph E. Brown to Henry M. Turner, June 17, 1867, unsigned copy, and Brown to "Dear Sir," June 19, 1867, in Joseph E. Brown Papers, Felix Hargrett Collection.

[21] Augusta *Daily Press*, April 28, 1867.

[22] Quoted in New York *Times*, April 2, 1867. See also Cincinnati *Commerical*, May 7, 1867, a clipping in Joseph E. Brown Scrapbooks, Joseph E. Brown and Elizabeth G. Brown Collection, University of Georgia.

volve, or whether the first military bill represented the final
Congressional terms. No one yet knew how many unrepentent ex-Confederates would be disfranchised, or for how
long political disabilities would continue. Better, then, to
work to shape the conquering, dominant party than by
clinging mindlessly to past loyalties to be stripped of all
political responsibility.

The shadings of Brown's thought little concerned the Republican organizers who gleefully added his name to their
rolls in 1867. Not until later would they realize that Brown's
conversion was not so complete as they had imagined. For
the moment, they rejoiced in his support for the military bill
and in the prospect that Brown's name would win to their
party the Georgia farmers who had long been the former
governor's staunchest supporters.

Fortunately for the Republicans, however, success in 1867
depended less on the strength of a single man than on the
smooth operation of the party organization which now
evolved out of the separate, scattered Republican efforts of
1865 and 1866. By mid-March, 1867, the Republicans had
formed a state-wide organization, with a State Executive
Committee and a party chairman.[23] By May 20 they had laid
plans for a state convention, and they invited Republican
Senator John Sherman to attend and address the meeting.[24]

In the formal organization of the Republican party during
the early months of 1867, the Union League played a dominant role. The league even before the passage of the Military
Reconstruction Act had a state-wide organization in Georgia
and, through its ties with the national Union League, probably had closer connections with the national Republican

[23] George W. Ashburn to Edward McPherson, Washington, March 14,
1867, in McPherson Papers. See also Rowan, "Rise and Development of the
Republican Party," 10.
[24] Atlanta *Opinion*, May 20, 1867; William Bassford to John Sherman,
Atlanta, May 30, 1867, in John Sherman Papers.

party than the Georgia-based Equal Rights Association could hope to develop. White members of the league, furthermore, had the financial resources for party-building which the Negro association had never been able to command, and they had the political experience which the former slaves sorely lacked. The call for the Republican state convention bore the signatures of William Markham, an Atlanta railroad promoter and former slave trader who served as president of the state Union League, and Henry Farrow, the league's executive secretary.[25]

When the Republicans gathered at Atlanta on July 4 to perfect their party organization and adopt a platform for the coming campaign, however, the league officers shared convention leadership with other prominent Republicans. Augusta Postmaster Foster Blodgett was named permanent chairman and chairman of the revamped State Executive Committee. John E. Bryant, editor of the *Loyal Georgian,* was chosen secretary. Farrow headed the committee which drew up a platform and resolutions. After his report, the convention unanimously adopted planks approving the Congressional program of Reconstruction, promising what were vaguely termed "equal rights" for all citizens, and pledging Republican support for relief measures, homestead laws, and free schools.[26]

The platform planks adopted at Atlanta made it clear that the new party had already taken a decision of crucial importance, one which virtually dictated its tactics in the fall campaign. The Republican party in Georgia, its first platform made clear, would direct its strongest appeals to the Negroes and to the whites in North Georgia and in the Wiregrass Country of South Georgia. Most of the latter had been stalwart Democrats before 1865, but many had been Union-

[25] Shadgett, *Republican Party in Georgia,* 5–6.
[26] Atlanta *Opinion,* July 5, 1867.

ists or cooperationists in the secession crisis. Now, plagued
by debts and poor harvests, they could be won away from a
Democratic party tainted by secession and increasingly ori-
ented to the needs and aspirations of wealthy planters and
merchants in the Black Belt. Republicans would need only
to invoke Joseph Brown's name to show his former supporters
among the yeoman farmers where their interests now lay.

In appeals to their potential supporters, however, Republican leaders discovered that their newspapers were of little
use. Only a few Republican papers existed in the state,
and they were still, in the summer of 1867, based in Georgia's
major cities and towns. Furthermore, most Negroes and
many yeoman whites were illiterate. Even had the Republican press been well developed in Georgia, party leaders
could not have reached these groups without relying on the
services of paid or volunteer "readers." Only through a series
of mass meetings could Republican leaders rapidly and efficiently educate the Negroes and yeoman whites in the cor-
rectness of Republican views.

Though a few such meetings took place before the July
state convention, organized campaigning began only after
the adoption of the platform and the election of permanent
party officers.[27] Most rallies were called to ratify the Republican state platform, but they obviously were occasions
for campaign speeches and served to arouse enthusiasm for
the Republican cause. Savannah, which boasted a large com-
munity of Negro voters, was the scene of a particularly impressive gathering in September. The speakers included
Republicans prominent at the local level, as well as state
leaders like Markham, the Negro agitator Bradley, and
Walter L. Clift, soon to be elected a convention delegate and

[27] See, for example, reports of meetings in the Augusta *Constitutionalist*,
April, 14, 1867; Rome *Courier*, March 28, 1867; Macon *Georgia Journal
and Messenger*, March 6, 1867; New York *Times*, April 2, 1867.

later to be nominated as a candidate for Congress.[28] Hand-bills summoned "all the white and colored people" of the seacoast counties, those who desired suffrage for "colored voters and poor white persons without property." In their demands for homestead exemptions "to stop pauperism and dignify labor," for the eight-hour working day and for reduced city taxes, the broadsides merely echoed the planks and principles of the platform adopted at Atlanta in July.[29]

Republican campaign appeals, like the party organization itself, developed as the campaign progressed. To the freed-men, whom party leaders believed safe in the Republican fold, Republican campaigners preached the evils of the Democracy. Democrats had fought to keep Georgia's Negroes enslaved, and the Democracy now had no interest in the freedmen's welfare. Instead, the party represented the aristocracy of the state. Republicans urged all Negroes eligi-ble to register to do so and exhorted them to organize in Union Leagues and vote in the fall elections.[30]

Appeals to potential white supporters were well formu-lated by mid-September. To the yeoman farmers, the party's principal targets, the Republican rallying cry became "Con-vention and Relief."[31] Though they added promises of

[28] Macon *Georgia Journal and Messenger,* September 25, 1867. The scrapbooks in the Henry Farrow Collection contain several clippings de-scribing meetings at which Farrow spoke.

[29] Atlanta *Daily Intelligencer,* September 21, 1867. For reports of other Republican meetings see Quinea O'Neal to Alexander H. Stephens, October 1, 1867, in Alexander Stephens Papers, Library of Congress; and Linton Stephens to Alexander H. Stephens, September 6, 1867, in Alexander Ste-phens Papers, Manhattanville College of the Sacred Heart. Linton Ste-phens was frightened by signs of political activity among the freedmen in Sparta. He planned to send his wife and children away until after the elections.

[30] Augusta *Loyal Georgian,* August 10, 24, 1867.

[31] New York *Herald,* September 27, 1867; Atlanta *Daily Intelligencer,* September 21, 1867. The slogan "Convention and Relief" was apparently suggested by Republican registration superintendent Ed. Hulbert.

shorter working hours for the cities' laboring men, of homestead exemptions, and of free schools to appeal to voters
throughout the state, Republican workers concentrated their
attention on the relief issue. The stay law passed by the
General Assembly in 1866, they reminded white farmers,
was now "practically dead," emasculated by a state supreme
court whose Democratic chief justice, Hiram Warner, believed relief laws inconsistent with the contract clause of the
federal Constitution. The only hope for Georgia's struggling
debtors lay with a Republican constitutional convention.[32]

Republicans who counted on Joseph E. Brown's name and
presence on the campaign trail to win the yeoman whites
must have found Brown's own attitude during the campaign
puzzling. Throughout the spring, he had avoided specific
endorsement of Radicalism or its programs, and he now
shunned Republican rallies whenever possible. Instead, he
joined with Samuel Bard, editor of Atlanta's largest Republican paper, the *New Era,* to urge a broader coalition than that
envisaged by the State Executive Committee. Taking their
cue from the name of Bard's paper, the two men argued that
a "new era" had arrived in the South. Those who would
prosper most would be those who most sincerely renounced
slavery and an economy based solely upon agriculture and
accepted the changes war had wrought. Negroes and yeoman whites should be welcomed into the Republican party,
but Republicans must not build their platform around the
needs of a single economic class or racial group. Instead,
they must welcome all supporters, of whatever past political
persuasion, and must labor diligently to attract all the capital
they could to Georgia.[33] Only then would both their party
and their state prosper.

The split between Republicans of Brown's ilk and those

[32] Atlanta *Daily Intelligencer,* September 21, 1867.
[33] Augusta *Daily Press,* April 28, 1867.

who sought to build the party around a nucleus of Negroes and yeoman whites was the only one which intruded noticeably into the party's 1867 campaign. And Brown's failure to advance his own views with his customary vigor lulled party leaders into a false sense of security. Had they been alerted to the danger, they could scarcely have failed to see that the activities of the campaign, the efficiency of the new party committee, and the apparent unity of the mass meetings concealed only for the moment other deep dissensions within Republican ranks. Some Republicans, like L. P. Gudger, demanded stringent measures against unreconstructed Rebels; others, including Brown, favored a more moderate course. There were Republicans committed to universal suffrage and to full civil equality for the Negro, but there were also others who confessed themselves "at times stopped by the great ignorance of a large class of the colored people, being allowed the elective franchise when the greater portion of the intelligent whites are disfranchised."[34] The party's platform promised debtor relief, but to many prominent Republicans, such as convention candidate Amos T. Akerman, statesponsored relief measures had long seemed undesirable.[35] These dissensions lay smoldering beneath the apparently smooth surface of the Republican organization as the fall elections approached.

II

Unlike the Republicans, to whom the Military Reconstruction Act was an immediate call to unity and action, Georgia's Democrats seemed stunned by the events of March, 1867. At first incredulous, they sought to escape the provisions of the measure. Belated acceptance of the Fourteenth Amend-

[34] J. C. Morrill to William Pitt Fessenden, October 14, 1867, in William Pitt Fessenden Papers, Library of Congress.
[35] Augusta *Chronicle and Sentinel,* September 17, 1867.

ment, they concluded, would satisfy Republican demands. While the major spokesmen of the Georgia Democracy remained silent, local leaders organized meetings. In Thomas County, in Atlanta, in Cartersville, and in Hancock County, Democrats gathered to urge acquiescence in the amendment Georgians had so defiantly repudiated only weeks before.[36] The press clung to the hope that the Reconstruction Acts, so patently unconstitutional and "actuated . . . by malignant hate towards the South," would fall before the United States Supreme Court.[37] Two weeks after the military bill became law, New York *Times* correspondent "Quondam" described to his readers the downcast mien of Democratic Georgians. Most, he concluded, had yet to settle on a course of action.[38] Not until April would Georgia Democrats rally for political battle.

Democrats who at first urged that Georgians take no action under the Military Reconstruction Act found a ready champion in Governor Charles Jones Jenkins.[39] At the beginning of April, the governor journeyed to Washington and engaged Jeremiah S. Black, Edgar Cowan, and Charles O'Connor as counsel in an effort to obtain an injunction preventing the administration and the new military commander from enforcing the Reconstruction Acts in Georgia.[40] Then, on April 10, Jenkins issued an address to the people of his state. Condemning the military bills as unconstitutional, he advised his constituents to refuse to register for the fall elections.[41]

[36] New York *Times*, March 10, 1867.

[37] Milledgeville *Southern Recorder*, March 26, 1867.

[38] New York *Times*, March 16, 1867.

[39] *Ibid.*, March 11, 1867; Milledgeville *Southern Recorder*, March 26, 1867.

[40] The suit instituted by Jenkins became *Georgia* v. *Stanton*; eventually, it was dismissed by the Court.

[41] Thompson, *Reconstruction in Georgia*, 175. Jenkins' persistent refusal to recognize General Pope's authority in Georgia kept him in constant trouble with the military commander. See Ulysses S. Grant to Pope, April

The confusion of Georgia Democrats was understandable, for that party faced different kinds of problems in 1867 than did the Republican organization. Confronted by a measure they were convinced was unconstitutional, opposed by Congress and the military authorities, the Democrats who had seemed near to achieving a formal reorganization of their party in the summer of 1866 fell victim in the spring and summer of 1867 to divisions within their own ranks. Though the party was older and more firmly established than was the Republican coalition, the Democratic campaign lacked the confidence and style of the Republican effort.

By the time General Pope issued his first order for the registration of voters on April 8, the Democratic response to military Reconstruction had taken two divergent forms. A minority of party leaders, including Jenkins, continued to advocate a policy of non-action. Georgians would "infinitely prefer" rule by General Pope, the non-actionists insisted, to registration and voting under the Military Reconstruction Act.[42] A convention called under military rule would "be certain to do *some,* and in all probability much mischief"; it would likely "result in putting the control of the State Government in the hands of Negroes and Southern white men of the . . . [Republican] stripe; and this would be a Thousandfold worse than Military rule."[43] "We trust," said the Augusta *Constitutionalist* on the eve of the election, "the numbers of white participants will be magnificently few and conspicuously despicable."[44] By refusing to register and vote

21, 1867, in Headquarters Records, Grant Papers; Pope to Jenkins, April 22, 1867, in *Report of the Secretary of War, 1867*, Pt. 1, pp. 323–24; and Jenkins to Pope, April 26, 1867, in Governor's Letterbooks, Georgia Department of Archives and History.

[42] Augusta *Constitutionalist,* May 18, 1867.

[43] James D. Russ to Alexander Stephens, June 8, 1867, in Alexander Stephens Papers, Library of Congress.

[44] Augusta *Constitutionalist,* October 29, 1867. See also "Bill Arp on

for a convention, the non-actionists hoped to "wait for a reaction North"—a retreat from the Radical Republican position in Congress which would mean easier terms for the
South.[45]

Most Democrats, however, took a different stance. Though
they agreed with Jenkins that Georgia should test the constitutionality of the Reconstruction Acts, they counseled
cooperation by qualified whites in the voter registration procedures and full participation in the elections for the constitutional convention.[46] Georgians, they believed, should
recognize the fact of Congressional Reconstruction and "elect
[to the convention] good men, men of sterling integrity and
worth," who could "save the State and protect the rights of
the people."[47] The New York *Times* reported on April 2 that
most Democratic Georgians would register and vote.[48] Only
by doing so could the Democrats defeat the new Republican
organization.[49] Democratic leaders continued to divide, however, over whether Georgians should vote to elect Democratic delegates to the convention, vote to hold no convention
at all, or cast token, complimentary ballots for Democratic
candidates but bend all efforts to defeating the convention
call.

Reconstruction!" March 9, 1867, in Georgia Broadsides Collection, Duke
University.

[45] James D. Russ to Alexander H. Stephens, Butler, June 8, 1867, in
Alexander Stephens Papers, Library of Congress.

[46] Herschel V. Johnson to Charles Jones Jenkins, Augusta, April 25, 1867,
in Herschel V. Johnson Papers, Duke University.

[47] Atlanta *Daily Intelligencer*, June 1, 1867. See also the *Intelligencer*
for October 4 and 17, 1867; Herschel V. Johnson to Maj. John G. West-
moreland and others, Augusta, June 29, 1867, in Herschel V. Johnson
Papers, Duke University; Address of the Chatham County Committee,
printed in Atlanta *Daily Intelligencer*, July 3, 1867.

[48] New York *Times*, April 2, 1867.

[49] See, for example, Dawson *Journal*, April 19, 1867; Rome *Courier*, May
14, 1867; Sandersville *Central Georgian*, June 26, 1867; James D. Russ to
Alexander H. Stephens, June 8, 1867, in Alexander Stephens Papers, Library
of Congress.

The keynote of the Democratic campaign was sounded by Benjamin H. Hill, who offered Democrats a new choice—a plan of opposition to military rule which fell midway between Jenkins' call for non-action and the programs of those who urged full participation in registration and the fall elections. Hill's "Notes on the Situation," which appeared in the Augusta *Chronicle and Sentinel* and several other Georgia papers between June 19 and August 1, were an extended argument against the constitutionality of the military bills and a plea to Georgia Democrats to unite for political action. Probably few Georgians read all of Hill's "Notes," however, and the real impetus for the Democratic campaign came not from these articles, but from a mass meeting held at Davis Hall in Atlanta on July 16. In a fiery speech, Hill excoriated the Congressional Radicals, denounced the Military Reconstruction Act, and pleaded with Democrats to unite in combatting the Republican menace. He joined with other Democrats in appealing to the freedmen. The former masters, Hill argued, were the freedmen's best friends; Republican promises of votes, offices, and homestead exemptions were only designed to deceive the Negro. The freedmen needed only patient education by Democratic spokesmen to help them recognize their true interests.[50] Whites, Hill announced, should register, but they should not vote for a convention.[51] If Democrats voted against the convention or remained at home, the convention call would not receive the required approval of a majority of all registered voters.

[50] Letter from John Brown Gordon, printed in the New York *Times*, April 30, 1867; R. J. Moses to Alexander H. Stephens, April 2, 1867, in Alexander Stephens Papers, Library of Congress; Sandersville *Central Georgian*, October 9, July 3, 1867.

[51] There was no stenographic transcript of Hill's speech. Probably the most accurate report is that by J. Henly Smith, Atlanta *Daily Intelligencer*, July 18, 1867.

Hill's activities spurred other Democrats to action. A party committee for Fulton and DeKalb counties in June issued an address to antebellum Congressman and Governor Howell Cobb, and Robert Toombs promised the Cincinnati *Enquirer* that a Democratic anti-Reconstruction party would soon emerge in Georgia.[52] A series of ratification meetings followed the Davis Hall rally.[53] Most echoed Hill's plea for unity, but their calls for a more vigorous Democratic campaign met only an apathetic response as the first enthusiasm over Hill's Davis Hall speech waned. Except in opposition to Congressional Reconstruction, there could be no unity in the Democratic ranks in 1867. The party had no positive program, and it appeared seriously divided. Most Democrats seemed determined either to vote against the convention or to remain away from the polls. As a recent student has shrewdly remarked, the Democratic party line itself encouraged the disorganization which in the fall of 1867 claimed the Democratic cause as its first victim.[54] Hoping to defeat the convention call, most Democrats did not bestir themselves to nominate a full slate of candidates or to support the few who were nominated. What was remarkable about the results of the fall elections in Georgia was not the fact of Republican victory, but that the Democratic defeat was not more shattering than it was.

[52] Address to Hon. Howell Cobb, Atlanta, June 26, 1867, in Howell Cobb Papers, University of Georgia. I am indebted to Mr. Howell Cobb Erwin for permission to use and quote from this collection. Toombs's remarks to the *Enquirer* appear in an undated clipping from that paper in Joseph E. Brown Scrapbooks, Joseph E. Brown and Elizabeth G. Brown Collection, University of Georgia.

[53] Augusta *Contitutionalist*, August 17, 1867; Atlanta *Daily Intelligencer*, October 4, 1867.

[54] Charles G. Bloom, "The Georgia Election of April, 1868: A Re-examination of the Politics of Georgia Reconstruction" (M.A. thesis, University of Chicago, 1963), 16–17.

III

The policies pursued by Major General Pope during the summer of 1867 encouraged and sustained the Republicans and contributed to the discouragement and disorganization so evident among Georgia's Democrats. Though Pope in June had complained of the difficulties caused him by confusion among Republicans in Washington—by the passage of the new Reconstruction acts to supplement the original military bill and by conflicting military directives—by July he reported that "the Acts of Congress settle things pretty effectively in this region."[55] The military commander had enjoyed a certain uneasy popularity at the outset of his regime, but his strict enforcement of the military bills had by midsummer led Democratic Georgians to both fear and hate him.

Pope had power to fill vacancies in the civil administration and to remove officers who obstructed enforcement of the Congressional Reconstruction Acts. It was his avowed policy to place only loyal men in office, "loyal" citizens being those who favored Congressional Reconstruction.[56] Even incompetence proved no barrier to appointment; surely, Pope wrote, an incompetent but loyal man in office was better than a competent but disloyal one.[57] Yet Pope's practices were never as partisan as his letters to his superiors in the War Department suggest. Official records mention only a few men removed for openly opposing Reconstruction, and Pope refused to entertain a petition from Savannah Republicans who demanded the removal of Democratic Mayor Edward C.

[55] Pope to William Tecumseh Sherman, June 29, 1867, in William Tecumseh Sherman Papers, Library of Congress; Pope to Col. J. T. Sprague, July 16, 1867, in Otis Norcross Papers, Massachusetts Historical Society.

[56] Lt. O. C. Knapp, Pope's aide, to the Judge of the County Court, Heard County, May 27, in Department of the South, Headquarters Post Atlanta, War Department Records, R. G. 98, National Archives.

[57] Pope to Ulysses S. Grant, Atlanta, July 24, 1867, in *Report of the Secretary of War, 1867*, Pt. 1, pp. 325–26.

Anderson and the appointment of a Republican in his place.[58]

If they were aware of these facts, Democrats ignored them. To the Democrats, a single act—the removal of the mayor and city council of Augusta and their replacement by leading Republicans including Blodgett, Benjamin F. Conley, Ephraim Tweedy, and Bullock—represented Pope's entire policy.[59] The military commander, they were sure, was the lackey of the Republican party.

Pope's other actions during the summer only confirmed the suspicions of Democrats who believed that a fair election could not be had in Georgia while Pope remained in command. Though Pope only once ordered a Georgia civilian tried in a military court, he removed from office about a dozen judges, justices of the peace, and sheriffs whose decisions were allegedly biased against the freedmen, and he prohibited state courts from entertaining suits against any person for acts done under military authority.[60]

Two of the military commander's general orders, however, rankled more than all the rest. On August 12, Pope issued General Order No. 49, the "public printing" order. Official pronouncements could no longer appear in papers which opposed Congressional Reconstruction.[61] As Governor Jenkins quickly pointed out, the order was unrealistic. State law required the governor to publish official notices throughout the state; yet scarcely a half dozen papers in Georgia met Pope's requirements. The commander's inability fully to

[58] *Report of the Secretary of War, 1867*, Pt. 1, pp. 370–74. For the rejection of the Savannah petition, see Rome *Courier*, September 3, 1867.

[59] After Pope relinquished command and left Georgia at the end of December, 1867, Augusta Democrats pleaded with his successor, Maj. Gen. George G. Meade, to restore the original members of the city council to office. See Citizens of Augusta to Meade, January 1, 1868, in Andrew Johnson Papers.

[60] Edwin C. Woolley, *The Reconstruction of Georgia* (New York: Columbia University Press, 1901), 42–43.

[61] Pope to Edward McPherson, August 17, 1867, in McPherson Papers.

implement his new policy failed to stop the abuse which Democrats showered on him.

Even more obnoxious to Democrats was the "jury order" of August 19. A statute passed in 1866 had excluded Negroes from service on juries, but henceforth, Pope decreed, jurors must be drawn from the lists of registered voters without discrimination against the freedmen. The order led to a confrontation between Pope and Augustus Reese, the respected Democratic judge of the Ocmulgee circuit. Reese announced his intention of disobeying the order. Pope, at first not wishing to remove so popular an official but finally driven to uphold his own order, demanded Reese's resignation.[62]

Rumors that Pope would lose his command spread among hopeful Democrats as early as September. In Washington, controversy had erupted between Andrew Johnson and the War Department over Reconstruction policies. The President, still bitter over the passage of the military bills, apparently hoped by retaining control over the military commanders in the South to prevent full implementation of the Congressional policy. The War Department, on the other hand, had ranged itself on the side of the Congressional Radicals. In Washington, Secretary of War Edwin Stanton became the target of Johnson's wrath; in the South, the President directed his anger at such commanders as Pope and Philip Sheridan, who had warmly supported Congressional Reconstruction.[63]

Pope himself feared that he would be removed. Early in

[62] Jenkins to Pope, August 20, 1867, in Governor's Letterbooks, Georgia Department of Archives and History. The entire correspondence between Reese and Pope appears in the Augusta *Constitutionalist* for September 25, 1867.

[63] On the War Department controversy, see Harold M. Hyman, "Johnson, Stanton, and Grant: A Reconsideration of the Army's Role in the Events Leading to Impeachment," *American Historical Review*, LXVI (October, 1960), 85–100.

September he wrote to Ulysses S. Grant, reporting the rumors of his imminent dismissal and inquiring whether he should trouble to rent a house in Atlanta for the winter. Indeed, Grant replied, he too had heard the rumors, but he would argue for Pope's retention himself. Were he in Pope's place, however, he would make no long-term commitments.[64] Grant's counsel proved sound. Pope retained his post long enough to oversee the fall elections and the gathering of the constitutional convention. Then, in the last week of December, he relinquished command to Major General George G. Meade, who arrived in Atlanta prepared to assume his new duties on January 6.[65]

Pope's original election orders had provided for balloting on three consecutive days, October 29 through October 31. By October 30, however, Republicans began to doubt that they could poll the majority of registered voters that was necessary to carry the call for a convention. At Pope's direction, therefore, Superintendent of Registration Hulbert ordered the election extended until November 2.[66]

As their campaign apathy had suggested would be the case, Democrats seemed inclined to let the election go by default.[67] From Albany, Democratic partisan William E. Smith observed that "the whites" were "not voting at all"; only two had voted in Albany, none in Macon, and none in Columbus by October 30. Though over 100,000 whites had registered, only 36,500 cast ballots in the election. Votes for

[64] Pope to Grant, September 7, 1867; and Grant to Pope, September 9, 1867, in Headquarters Records, Grant Papers.

[65] Foster Blodgett to John Sherman, Augusta, December 30, 1867, in John Sherman Papers; General Orders No. 104, December 28, 1867, in Sandersville *Central Georgian*, January 1, 1868.

[66] Ed. Hulbert to Andrew Johnson, transmitting Pope's General Order No. 83, telegram, October 30, 1867, in Andrew Johnson Papers.

[67] Howell Cobb to his wife, November 2, 1867, in Howell Cobb Papers, University of Georgia; R. L. McWhorter to Alexander H. Stephens, November 4, 1867, in Alexander Stephens Papers, Library of Congress.

the convention totalled 102,282; those against, only 4,127.[68] The Democratic refusal to participate in the elections makes meaningful analysis of the votes for and against the convention impossible, and no results of the balloting for delegates are available. Republicans won substantial majorities in the Black Belt and seacoast counties, and they made significant inroads into Democratic strength in the areas of North Georgia and the Wiregrass Country to which they had directed their campaign appeals.

Republicans had elected a decided majority of the convention delegates, but what appeared at first a sweeping Republican triumph was in fact a portentously close contest. Ballots cast for the convention exceeded the required majority of registered voters by only 1,823. Divided and disorganized as it was, the Democratic party had nearly succeeded in thwarting the entire program of Congressional Reconstruction. Perhaps the Republican party in Georgia was, after all, not as strong as its leaders believed it to be.

[68] William E. Smith to his sisters, October 30, 1867, in William E. Smith Papers, University of Georgia; LaWanda and John H. Cox, *Politics, Principle, and Prejudice, 1865–1866: Dilemma of Reconstruction America* (New York: The Free Press of Glencoe, 1963), 509. Votes for and against the convention appear in the *Tribune Almanac* for 1869 (New York: Tribune Publishing Company, 1869), 77–79.

CHAPTER III

A Divided Party

The Republicans' success in carrying the call for a constitutional convention in 1867 and in securing the election of Republican delegates obscured for many Georgians the narrow margin of the party's triumph. More important, it had obscured the dissensions within the Republican ranks which the party had successfully concealed during the 1867 campaign. When the convention met, however, and Republican delegates were forced to take definite positions on controversial issues, these dissensions inevitably came to the fore. During the sessions of the constitutional convention at Atlanta, the Georgia Republican party split into opposing Radical and Moderate factions.

The Democratic strategy of abstaining from the elections had virtually dictated the party composition of the convention. Of 165 delegates who took their seats and voted in the convention, only 46 were staunch Democrats.[1] Twenty more

[1] My conclusions about party affiliation of convention delegates are

were probably elected as Democrats, but they bolted their party on important issues and allied with the Radical wing of the Republican coalition. The other 99 delegates, including 35 Negroes from the Black Belt and seacoast counties, were Republicans of various persuasions.[2] The convention, reported a Democratic paper on December 18, was "full of factions," and the delegates would have a "stormy time of it."[3] The Negroes were an obvious minority among the delegates, and within the Republican party itself the Northern carpetbaggers—who represented Republicanism to so many Southern Democrats—comprised only a small group. Only 16 delegates who voted consistently with the Republican party during the convention had arrived in Georgia after 1865.[4]

Dominating the Republican delegates were those whose views most closely resembled the sentiments voiced by leaders of the Radical faction within the national party. These men—Bullock, Bryant, Blodgett, and Benjamin F. Conley—were from Augusta. There, they had led in the formation of the Equal Rights Association and one of the strongest Union Leagues in the state. From that starting point they had directed the fusion of the Negro association and the Union Leagues which had resulted in the formation of the Republican party early in 1867. By the fall of 1867, they

based on an analysis of selected votes on relief measures; appointment of Republican state officials in place of Democrats to be removed; franchise qualifications; expulsion of A. A. Bradley, a Negro delegate; resolutions on the impeachment of Andrew Johnson and on Governor Jenkins' prosecution of suits against the Department of the Army; and homestead exemption proposals. For tables giving the vote of each convention delegate on these roll calls, see my doctoral dissertation, "Shaping a New Era: Georgia Politics, 1865–1872" (The Johns Hopkins University, 1966), 143–48.

[2] One hundred sixty-six delegates actually sat in the convention, but J. R. Parrott, the permanent president, did not vote.

[3] Sandersville *Central Georgian*, December 18, 1867.

[4] Candler (comp.), *Confederate Records of the State of Georgia,* VI, 1020–26.

controlled the Republican State Executive Committee. Clearly identifiable as the foremost leaders of the Republican organization, they were immediately dubbed the "Augusta Ring" by Democrats and even by some members of their own party. Their influence, strong in the campaign, carried over into the convention itself.

Members of the Augusta Ring and their followers—the Radicals—supported without reservations the relief, homestead exemption, free schools, and wages and hours planks of the 1867 Republican platform; indeed, in their economic programs, the Georgia Radicals went far beyond reforms urged by their Congressional counterparts in Washington. Precisely what social rights the Georgia Radicals envisioned for the Negro were never clear, but like the most militant of the Congressional Republicans, the members of the Augusta Ring and their followers demanded a program of full Negro suffrage, guarantees of Negro officeholding, and disfranchisement of former Confederates. Throughout the campaign of 1867 and during the convention itself, they sought and cultivated close ties with national Republican leaders. They seemed strangely unaware, however, of shadings of opinion among members of their party in Washington; they sought counsel alike from Radicals such as Thaddeus Stevens and Moderates such as John Sherman.

Not as well organized as the Radicals in the convention were the Republican Moderates. In 1867, their program was largely a negative one: they opposed Radical promises of relief legislation and homestead exemptions, and like many Moderate Republicans in Washington, they had grave doubts about unrestricted Negro suffrage and Negro officeholding. Grouped within the Moderate camp in Georgia were, in fact, all Republicans who had any quarrel with the leadership of the Augusta Ring—whether over specific platform planks or over more fundamental issues like the nature of the Republican party and the groups at which Republicans should direct their appeals. Moderates in Georgia would never achieve more than a transitory organization or agree on a positive program, and not until several months after the constitutional convention would they develop close ties with congressional Moderates. Their disputes with Radicalism arose over issues which seemed to them localized in Georgia, and they did not seek in 1867 to advertise their disagreements with the Augusta Ring beyond state lines.[5] In the constitutional convention, however, they were to prove a powerful force.

Republicans took command of the convention at the outset. At the first session on December 9, Foster Blodgett, chairman of the State Executive Committee, became temporary chairman. His opening remarks did little more than echo the Republican platform of the preceding summer and fall; he demanded action to secure equal rights, relief, homestead exemptions, and public education for all citizens.[6] Not all the Republican proposals should wait until the convention could frame a constitution and Georgians could vote on ratification; temporary ordinances should be passed to meet pressing problems. It was clear that Blodgett—and the Augusta Ring for which he spoke—expected the convention to play a quasi-legislative role.

Balloting for a permanent president resulted in the election of J. R. Parrott. His address, like Blodgett's, reiterated the planks of the Georgia Republican platform. The national party, Parrott reminded the Republican delegates, was watching and waiting for Georgians to accomplish what was expected of them.

[5] For a similar statement of the differences between Radicals and Moderates made by a contemporary observer, see the New York *Times,* December 20, 1867.

[6] Candler (comp.), *Confederate Records of Georgia,* VI, 209–11.

Of all the subjects to engage the convention's attention, the most controversial was relief. On December 11 Rufus Bullock raised the issue by introducing an ordinance providing for a temporary suspension of levies and sales on debtor property until the convention could take final action on a relief measure. His ordinance passed without a roll call test.[7] All further proposals, however, were referred to a special Committee on Relief, which submitted its majority report on January 9. The report, signed by Bullock, five other Republicans, and a lone independent Democrat, called for the insertion of a relief clause in the new constitution. Contracts made before June 1, 1865, would be declared invalid and state courts would be forbidden to entertain suits or enforce judgments founded on them.[8]

On January 13 the minority members of the Committee on Relief, Republicans Amos T. Akerman and Thomas P. Saffold, submitted their report.[9] The only excuse for granting relief, they argued, seemed to be that debtors in 1868 were poorer than they had been when they contracted their debts. But so were the creditors. The proper remedy for the debtors' woes did not lie in adding to the state constitution a clause which would almost certainly violate the sanctity of contracts guaranteed in the federal Constitution. What were needed were amendments to the federal bankruptcy laws. Arguing that relief measures were not a fit subject for debate in the convention, Akerman and Saffold asked that the Committee on Relief be discharged from further consideration of the proposals pending before it.

[7] *Ibid.*, VI, 224–25.

[8] *Ibid.*, VI, 306–308. The same day, the convention voted to call General Meade's attention to the temporary relief ordinance and request that he enforce its provisions. *Ibid.*, VI, 321. See also the correspondence between Meade and Grant concerning debtor relief in Georgia, printed in *Annual Report of the Secretary of War, 1868* (Washington: Government Printing Office, 1868), Pt. 1, pp. 82–83.

[9] Candler (comp.), *Confederate Records of Georgia*, VI, 367–75.

For two weeks the delegates debated the majority and minority reports. Finally, on January 28, Akerman's motion to adopt the minority report came to a vote. Delegate John Harris, speaking for the committee majority and for the Augusta Ring, moved to table Akerman's motion; Akerman demanded a roll call test. The motion to table prevailed, 88–42.[10] Of the Democrats who voted, all sided with Akerman. Most of his support came, however, from delegates who allied themselves with the Augusta Ring on several other issues but who adopted the Moderate Republican position on relief. Of these Republicans, three—Samuel Williams, George Wallace, and Henry M. Turner—were Negroes. The majority of Akerman's supporters represented counties in the central Georgia Black Belt, where relief schemes presumably had less appeal than they did among the debt-burdened farmers in the northern counties and the wiregrass region. The vote on the Akerman report showed clearly the path the convention would follow on relief. The relief clause eventually passed the convention and was incorporated into the new constitution in substantially the same form proposed by the majority members of the Committee on Relief.

On the surface, the fight over relief gained the Radical Republicans more than it cost them. Relatively few delegates bolted the party on the issue, and the relief proposals enabled the Republicans to make further inroads in North Georgia and the wiregrass area. Both regions were traditionally Democratic sections whose support the Republican Executive Committee deemed essential if the party were to dominate the state. Ten Democrats from these rural areas bolted their party and sided with the Republican majority on the relief votes taken in the convention.

In fact, however, the relief victories won by the Radicals were not worth their price, for the issue had bared the split

[10] *Ibid.*, VI, 453–55.

in the party ranks. Those who had led in opposing the Radicals on relief would appear again and again in subsequent months to plague them in their efforts to dominate Georgia's Republican organization.

Equally disastrous for Republican party cohesion were the debates over homestead exemption proposals. On December 16 William A. Fort, a delegate from Floyd County but not a follower of the Augusta Ring, introduced an ordinance "exempting from levy and sale, under any execution, order, or decree . . . the homesteads of citizens or heads of families." Fort's proposal, and others like it, were referred to the Committee on a Bill of Rights.[11] The issue remained quiescent until February 14, when Blodgett suddenly moved to appoint a special committee of seven members to prepare a new homestead exemption measure.[12] Blodgett's motion carried, and convention president Parrott appointed a committee consisting entirely of Republican delegates.[13] Almost certainly, Blodgett's motion and the appointment of the committee were prearranged. The committee wasted little time in deliberation; it submitted its unanimous report on February 20.[14] Each head of a family would be guaranteed a homestead exemption of $2,500 in real estate and $2,000 in personal property; no court in the state could enforce any judgment against it. The committee suggested that the convention leave to the new General Assembly the task of specifying the process by which property would be assessed and exemptions granted.

Debate and voting on the homestead exemption proposals began on February 24, and the tug of war opened between

[11] *Ibid.*, VI, 241, 261.

[12] *Ibid.*, VI, 604–605.

[13] Blodgett, Joseph E. Blount, N. P. Hotchkiss, Samuel F. Gove, William T. Crane, Peter B. Bedford, and H. V. M. Miller. Not all, however, were Radicals.

[14] Candler (comp.), *Confederate Records of Georgia*, VI, 656–57.

Radical and Moderate Republicans. On February 25 a series of amendments offered by Moderate Republicans failed to be adopted, and, on Blodgett's motion, the presiding officer cut off debate. Then came a test vote on a motion to table the entire question of homestead exemptions. On this vote, as on the relief roll calls, Radical Republicans and a small number of Democrats united to defeat a coalition of Moderate Republicans and Democrats. The vote of 73–39 closely paralleled that on the Akerman–Saffold relief report.[15]

After the first test vote, Radical floor leadership faltered. A few Republican delegates, apparently acting independently of the Augusta Ring, attempted to make the homestead exemption measure more palatable to dissident members of their party by reducing the amounts of real and personal property exempted from both levy and sale. The Radicals managed to defeat a proposal by Parrott to reduce the real estate exemption to $1,000. When John E. Bryant bolted the Radical faction and reintroduced Parrott's motion, the Augusta Ring seemed momentarily stunned. Blodgett and other Radicals opposed Bryant's proposal, but Moderate Republicans and a few Democrats united to approve it, 73–43. Before the session of February 25 adjourned, the same coalition of Moderate Republicans and Democrats had also reduced the personal property exemption to $500.[16]

By the next morning, however, the Radicals had once again marshalled their forces. When the convention reconvened, Blodgett moved a reconsideration of the vote to adopt Bryant's proposal, and another Republican demanded a reconsideration of the vote to reduce the personal property exemption. Both motions carried.[17] Clearly, the Radicals once again had sufficient strength to enforce their will, and

[15] *Ibid.,* VI, 699–701.
[16] *Ibid.,* VI., 701–708.
[17] *Ibid.,* VI, 711–12, 713–14.

in a series of test votes throughout the morning of February 26 the Moderate Republicans and Democrats met defeat after defeat. The final vote came at last on Blodgett's proposal to allow exemptions of $2,000 in real estate and $1,000 in personal property. By a vote of 78–53, the measure passed.[18]

The Radicals had successfully appealed once again to North Georgia and the Wiregrass Country—at the cost of party unity. Ten Democrats deserted their party to join with the Augusta Ring on the homestead test votes. That any Democrats should cross party lines on such important questions as relief and homesteads was, of course, encouraging to Radical strategists who counted on North Georgia and Wiregrass Country votes in future campaigns. In fact, so encouraged were they by their limited success in attracting new supporters with their relief and homestead exemption proposals, that they failed to notice the defections or to take them seriously enough.

Despite the Radical Republicans' success in ramming their relief and homestead proposals through the convention, the presence of fifty-nine Moderate Republicans and forty-six Democratic delegates ensured that on most measures the Georgia convention would adopt a conservative stand. The influence of the Moderate Republican and Democratic delegates was nowhere more evident than in the debates over suitable qualifications for voters in state elections.

Before the convention, Radicals like Gudger, Bryant, Bullock, and Blodgett had demanded disqualification of all "Rebels" excluded from federal offices by the provisions of the Fourteenth Amendment and Military Reconstruction Act.[19] They of course insisted that the freedmen be guar-

[18] *Ibid.*, VI, 715–722.
[19] J. Bowles to Samuel Shellabarger, October 11, 1867, in Elihu B. Washburne Papers, Library of Congress. Before the convention elections

anteed the ballot, and they favored strong constitutional protection of the Negro's right to hold political office. Bryant headed the convention's Committee on Franchise, and the committee's report, submitted on January 14, 1868, espoused the Radical program.[20] The report recommended the disfranchisement in state elections until January 1, 1869, of all those politically disabled under the Fourteenth Amendment and the Reconstruction Acts. Only qualified voters would be permitted to hold state office. Negroes, already enfranchised, were guaranteed the right to hold office, for the Bryant report specified that "all qualified electors" would be eligible "to any office in this State."[21]

When debate on the franchise and officeholding sections—the third and tenth sections—of the committee report began on February 10, Moderate Republicans and Democrats made clear their determination to eliminate the more radical features of the proposal. As soon as discussion opened, H. V. M. Miller, who voted Democratic on most issues but who had supported the Radical homestead proposals, offered a substitute for the franchise section. He asked that all mention of disqualifications for participation in the rebellion be deleted; only those convicted of a felony or those judged mentally defective or insane would be barred from voting.[22] Miller's proposal apparently reflected the wishes of most delegates, even of most Radical Republicans. Moderates

took place, Bowles promised that the Republicans would carry Georgia "for a convention and frame a Radical Constitution with a *liberal disfranchising* clause for rebels."

[20] Candler (comp.), *Confederate Records of Georgia*, VI, 388–91. Others who signed the report were N. L. Angier, James L. Dunning, P. B. Bedford, E. S. Cobb, Wesley Shropshire, and Presley Yeates. On most convention votes, Angier, Shropshire, and Yeates sided with the Democrats, and Dunning, Bedford, and Cobb were Republicans of more moderate views than Bryant.

[21] *Ibid.*, VI, 391.

[22] *Ibid.*, VI, 572.

and Democrats opposed sweeping disfranchisement as unnecessary, and astute Radicals knew that vindictive measures
against former Confederates would cost the Republican
party sorely needed white support. When the vote came on
Miller's substitute, it was nearly unanimous—116 for and 15
against.[23] Those opposed included Bryant, Bullock, and a
handful of other white Republicans, and three Negro delegates, Cobb of Houston County, Costin, and Joiner. Twenty-
eight Negroes voted for Miller's proposal.[24]

Discussion of the officeholding clause began on February
13, and the result of the debates was itself to provide the
topic for heated controversy within the state Republican
party. When debate began, a Democratic delegate sought to
limit officeholding to those who had enjoyed United States
citizenship for seven years—an obvious move to disqualify
the freedmen. No Republican, whether Radical or Moderate,
could afford to support a measure aimed at so large and important a group within his own party, and 89 of the convention's Republican delegates joined to defeat the proposal.
John Harris, a delegate from Newton County, promptly
moved to strike out the entire officeholding clause, and thus
to remove from the new constitution any explicit statement
on the freedmen's right to hold office.[25] The convention then
adjourned for the night. When it reconvened on the morning of February 14, a Moderate Republican delegate, H. K.
McCay, called for a vote on Harris' proposal. Only a hand-

[23] After Bryant's committee presented its report, Amos T. Akerman addressed the convention, pleading against sweeping disfranchisement and
against the adoption of the committee's recommendations. On the morning
of February 11, Negro delegate Henry M. Turner moved that Akerman's
"eloquent" remarks be printed by the convention and copies distributed to
each delegate. *Ibid.*, VI, 573, 583–84.

[24] Moses Bentley abstained on the motion, and A. A. Bradley had, by
the time this vote was taken, been expelled from the convention for intem-
perate remarks directed at his fellow delegates.

[25] Candler (comp.), *Confederate Records of Georgia*, VI, 594–96.

ful of Republicans opposed the 126 delegates who voted to eliminate the officeholding clause.[26] Akerman, who favored guaranteeing the freedmen's right to hold office, though he had opposed the stringent franchise measures demanded by the Radicals, voted no. So did Bryant and James L. Dunning, as well as three Negro delegates—Simeon Beaird of Augusta, Bryant's associate on the *Loyal Georgian;* Cobb of Houston County; and Costin. Twenty-nine Negroes, including Henry M. Turner, voted with the majority.[27]

The franchise article as finally adopted, then, omitted the stringent disfranchising clause advocated by many Radicals and feared by many whites.[28] The state of Georgia would disfranchise no whites whatever.[29] Still unsettled, however, and left to haunt Republican campaigners in the months to come, was the question of Negro officeholding.

Many have praised the results of the franchise debates and have credited Joseph E. Brown with engineering the adoption of a moderate program.[30] Brown was not a delegate to the convention, but he remained in Atlanta while the convention was in session, and Republican floor managers came frequently as dinner guests to his home.[31] When debate on the franchise article began, the former governor addressed a letter to the convention delegates, urging against political penalties for former Confederates and against a too speedy elevation of the Negro to full political privileges. In its action on the franchise and officeholding, Brown argued, the convention need move no faster than Congress had moved

[26] The final vote was 126–12. *Ibid.,* VI, 597–99.
[27] See also Thompson, *Reconstruction in Georgia,* 196.
[28] Article II.
[29] Russ, "'Radical Disfranchisement in Georgia," 188.
[30] Thompson, *Reconstruction in Georgia,* 193, 198.
[31] See, for example, the manuscript diary of Brown's teenage son, Franklin Pierce Brown, entry for January 22, 1868, in Joseph E. Brown Papers, Felix Hargrett Collection.

in the Reconstruction Acts and the Fourteenth Amendment.[32]

Unquestionably, Brown threw his influence on the side of moderation. During the debate on the franchise article, the Democratic delegates held a caucus and threatened to bolt the convention should the Negro be guaranteed the right to hold office. Brown at his own request addressed the delegates. "With his oily eloquence," a disgusted Democratic correspondent reported, "he persuaded them to hold on, and immediately slipped out, went to the Radical caucus, and succeeded in persuading that body" to strike out the office-holding clause and thus "to desert the negro."[33]

Though Brown's influence probably swayed a number of Republican votes, the outcome of the franchise and office-holding debates also reflected an attempt by Republican campaigners to save as many votes as possible for their cause. For Republicans seeking to build support for their party among native Georgians, widespread disfranchisement and disqualification of native whites would have seemed remarkably shortsighted. Formal guarantees of the Negro's eligibility to political office, on the other hand, seemed likely to cost votes among the North Georgia and Wiregrass Country whites to whom Republicans had directed their relief and homestead proposals; the animosity between the yeoman whites and the Negroes was deep-seated. Negro freedmen would almost certainly cast Republican ballots whatever the party platform or the new constitution said. Republicans could, therefore, afford to sacrifice ironclad guarantees of Negro officeholding to placate their followers among the white yeoman farmers.

If the relief and homestead measures and the franchise

[32] Atlanta *New Era*, January 11, 1868.

[33] Dawson *Journal*, March 5, 1868. See also the Savannah *Daily News and Herald*, February 20, 1868.

article had occasioned sharp debate within the convention, other features of the Republican program won approval after less heated discussion. The new constitution stipulated that the first session of the General Assembly should establish a system of free schools, to be supported by tax funds.[34] Equally important for the future of the Republican party was Article X, which embodied a Republican proposal to change the capital from the sleepy little town of Milledgeville in Baldwin County to Atlanta. The new capital, fast rebuilding from the devastation of the war, was the center of commerce and transportation for the north central section of the state—the section from which Republicans hoped to draw much of their white support. Not of least importance to party strategists, moreover, was the fact that Atlanta was the headquarters of the Third Military District.

Republican support in the convention of 1867–68 was greatest among delegates who represented counties in central Georgia, where Negroes were often a majority of registered voters, Union Leagues were relatively well organized, and Negro or white party workers had been active since 1865. Republicans had succeeded in electing few convention delegates from North Georgia and the Wiregrass Country, but within the convention itself, they had loosened the Democratic stranglehold on these areas. Whether the Radicals could continue to hold the Moderate Republicans and Negroes to the party while wooing white farmers and laboring men with promises of relief and homestead exemptions would not become fully clear for several months.

II

The meeting of the constitutional convention, meanwhile, had precipitated a renewal of the conflicts between Governor

[34] Article VI.

Jenkins and the military authorities. What in the spring of
1867 had seemed an almost farcical effort by the governor to
evade the operation of the Reconstruction acts now developed into a major confrontation between Democrats and
Republicans.

Jenkins' open opposition to Congressional Reconstruction
made him a prime target for Republican barbs. As early as
October, 1867, the Augusta Ring had demanded his removal
and replacement by Rufus Bullock; when the convention
met, both Radical and Moderate Republicans intensified
their attacks. Bryant and J. H. Caldwell on December 17
introduced a resolution calling for Jenkins' removal and Bullock's appointment.[35] Opposition to Bullock among Moderate Republicans led to the division of the motion into two
parts on December 18. Though the Moderates allied with
Democrats to oppose Bullock's claims to the office, the resolution demanding the removal of Jenkins and the appointment of a new governor passed the convention.[36] Outside the
convention hall, rumors spread that General Pope, still in
command in December, 1867, would soon remove Governor
Jenkins.[37]

Pope's refusal to act failed to end Jenkins' woes. On December 20 the delegates called on the state treasurer, John
Jones, to pay the convention expenses.[38] Jones, like Jenkins,
had consistently refused to acknowledge the legality of a
convention called under the Military Reconstruction Acts,
and on December 21, he refused to comply with the con-

[35] Candler (comp.), *Confederate Records of Georgia*, VI, 261–62, 264–
68.

[36] *Ibid.*, VI, 266–71. The vote in favor of requesting the appointment of
a new governor was 95–59; that in favor of Bullock's appointment was
81–59.

[37] William B. Brown to Howell Cobb, December 19, 1867, in Howell
Cobb Papers, University of Georgia.

[38] Candler (comp.), *Confederate Records of Georgia*, VI, 265–67, 289.

vention's order.[39] Two days later the convention disbursing officer, Nedom L. Angier, reported the state government's refusal to make any payments not regularly authorized by law.[40] All waited, while Pope sought counsel from General Grant in Washington.

Grant's instructions to Pope sealed the fate of the Jenkins regime. The Supplementary Reconstruction Act of July 19, 1867, Grant reminded Pope, authorized the removal of civil officers who obstructed the enforcement of Congressional Reconstruction measures.[41] Pope was removed before he could act, but the change of district commanders at the end of December brought no change in the army's determination to enforce the Reconstruction acts in Georgia. The new commander in Atlanta, General George G. Meade, met with Jenkins early in January to urge that the governor agree to pay the convention expenses. When he met with Jenkins, Meade had apparently decided to remove state treasurer Jones.[42] He had, he reported to Grant, "no alternative" in Jones's case, but he hoped "to avoid making any more changes than . . . [were] required." Jenkins, however, seemed determined to force his own removal.[43] On January 10, he replied to Meade's request, denying once more the legality of the convention and refusing to order the payment of convention expenses.[44] His patience finally exhausted, Meade

[39] John Jones to John Pope, December 21, 1867, in Andrew Johnson Papers.

[40] Candler (comp.), *Confederate Records of Georgia*, VI, 294.

[41] A copy of Grant's reply is attached to John Pope to Ulysses S. Grant, December 26, 1867, in Andrew Johnson Papers.

[42] Meade to Grant, January 9, 1868, in Andrew Johnson Papers. The letter in the Johnson Papers is a copy; the original is in the George Gordon Meade Papers, Historical Society of Pennsylvania.

[43] LaWanda and John Cox, *Politics, Principle, and Prejudice,* 509–10. The Coxes' analysis of Jenkins' removal is one of the very few accounts which assign to the governor a major share of the blame for his difficulties.

[44] Jenkins to Meade, January 10, 1868, in Governor's Letterbooks, Georgia Department of Archives and History.

removed both Jenkins and Jones on January 13. He then detailed two army officers, Brigadier General Thomas H. Ruger
and Brevet Captain Charles F. Rockwell, to serve as acting
governor and acting treasurer, respectively.

At least as vexing to the military authorities and the Republicans as Jenkins' refusal to pay the convention expenses
was his persistent prosecution of suits against the Reconstruction acts before the United States Supreme Court. In
the first case brought by Jenkins in 1867—*Georgia* v. *Stanton*
—the justices ordered at a preliminary hearing that subpoenas be served on all defendents before the case was again
considered by the court.[45] The court adjourned in May, however, before the sixty days allowed for serving the subpoenas
had elapsed. Though it decided on May 16 that it lacked
authority to hinder any officer of the executive branch in the
performance of his official duties, it failed to deliver its
opinion until February, 1868.[46] Meanwhile, of course, Jenkins had been removed from office. On February 12, insisting
that he remained the lawful governor of Georgia, Jenkins
filed another suit against enforcement of the Reconstruction
acts in his state.[47]

The new Georgia case—*Georgia* v. *Ulysses S. Grant,
George G. Meade, Thomas H. Ruger, and Charles F. Rockwell*—was more speedily disposed of. The War Department,
the co-defendants, and the Republican convention delegates,
all sought to prevent the case from coming to a decision before the court.[48] In the Milligan case of 1866, involving a
suspension of the habeas corpus privilege during the Civil

[45] New York *Times,* April 16, 17, 1868.
[46] 6 Wallace, 50.
[47] 6 Wallace, 241, 242.
[48] On February 14, Radical and Moderate Republicans and a few Democrats united to pass a resolution disavowing Jenkins' action in instituting the
suit. The vote was 105–24. See Candler (comp.), *Confederate Records of
Georgia,* VI, 602–604.

War, the Supreme Court had held the imposition of martial law justifiable only if regular courts and civil government were disrupted and unable to act. Now, Congressional Republicans feared, the court might apply the same doctrine to the Reconstruction Acts, but the court, reported Secretary of War Edwin Stanton on March 23, did not want to consider the Jenkins suit at all. It had once again required that subpoenas be served personally on all defendants, and the requirement seemed to offer everyone an easy escape. If Generals Meade and Ruger could arrange to be away when the subpoenas arrived, Stanton hinted, "I think the Court would be glad of it." The two generals should arrange to "take an inspection tour immediately . . . going . . . in different directions" and telling no one of their destinations.[49] Meade and Ruger immediately left Atlanta for parts unknown, but the elaborate precautions were unnecessary. On March 24, Stanton announced triumphantly that the court had dismissed Jenkins' plea.[50]

Jenkins' ouster and the dismissal first of *Georgia* v. *Stanton* and then of *Georgia* v. *Grant et al.* removed potentially serious threats to Republican domination in the state and left Georgia's Democrats more dispirited and disorganized than ever. Republicans, it seemed, could now direct their efforts to closing their own ranks for the election campaign ahead.

III

Before they could unite, however, Republicans had to select a nominee for the gubernatorial elections in April, 1868. Several party leaders aspired to the office, and as early as

[49] Stanton to Meade, March 23, 1868, in Edwin M. Stanton Papers, Library of Congress.

[50] Stanton to Meade, March 24, 1868, in Stanton Papers.

December, 1867, it had become clear that Republicans would not easily agree on a single candidate.

Though Nedom Angier, a convention delegate who sided with the Democrats on most major issues, and Judge Dawson Walker had strong backing for the nomination,[51] the real fight within the Republican party came between Rufus Bullock, the choice of the Augusta Ring, and Henry P. Farrow, who agreed with Bullock on major issues but who was the candidate of the state Union League organization.

Almost nothing can be learned about Bullock's activities during the formative months of the Republican party in Georgia, and the process by which he rose to party leadership remains obscure. There can be little doubt that Bullock, like most of those who became Republicans after 1865, was concerned for the welfare of the freedmen. Much later in his life, he would serve as a trustee of Atlanta University at a time when such service was scorned by most whites. There can also be little doubt that he was politically astute and that he had learned rapidly the techniques of political maneuvering which brought him to the attention of national party leaders. His financial connections with Northern businessmen, developed during his association with the Southern Express Company in the 1850's, perhaps enhanced his value in the eyes of Republican organizers. Yet there seems no entirely adequate explanation for the fact that by the time the constitutional convention met, the handsome, flamboyant New Yorker had supplanted Blodgett and Bryant as leader of the Augusta Ring. In the convention, his leadership of the Radicals in both the relief and homestead debates and the efforts of Radical strategists to have him named governor in

[51] Angier's letter to the Atlanta *New Era*, February 7, 1868, withdrawing his name from consideration. Walker had the powerful backing of Joseph E. Brown.

Jenkins' stead indicated to nearly everyone that Bullock had emerged the foremost spokesman of the Radical faction.

Farrow's backing came from the Union League; he was not a delegate to the convention. As early as November, 1867, Gudger and other Dalton Republicans had urged him to run, and by February, 1868, at least thirty-two meetings had endorsed his candidacy.[52] Farrow himself acted like a candidate, seeking on the slightest provocation to ingratiate himself with national Republican leaders.[53] Parrott and thirty other delegates invited him to address the constitutional convention.[54] Apparently, the league official had state-wide support and the organization needed to win the nomination.

Support of the Union League might well have sufficed for a Republican candidate in 1867, but by 1868 the structure of the party had changed. The Republicans had come into the open, and with the organization of a permanent State Executive Committee in the summer of 1867 control had passed from the hands of the Union League officers. Unhappily for Farrow, the Executive Committee in 1867 and 1868 was dominated by Bullock's backers in the Augusta Ring.

The Executive Committee on January 22 issued a call for a nominating convention to meet at Atlanta on February 19; then, with little or no warning, the committee canceled the call on January 31.[55] On February 19, Republican convention

[52] L. P. Gudger and others to Farrow, November 10, 1867, in Henry P. Farrow Collection, University of Georgia; Shadgett, *Republican Party in Georgia*, 7.

[53] See, for example, Farrow to Edwin M. Stanton, January 15, 1868, in Stanton Papers.

[54] J. R. Parrott and others to Farrow, January 16, 1868, in Henry P. Farrow Collection, University of Georgia.

[55] The convention call appears among the Broadsides in the Henry P. Farrow Collection, University of Georgia. Much later, Farrow recalled, "When Blodgett saw that I would get the nomination over Bullock he withdrew the call and resolved the constitutional convention into a nomina-

delegates met in a caucus instead of a party convention. Farrow and William Markham attended, but both were powerless before the well-organized Radical machine. When the caucus ended, the delegates had voted to transform the constitutional convention into the party's nominating conclave. Convention delegates would vote on the nomination; meetings in counties represented in the convention by Democrats would appoint delegates to the nominating convention. Neither Farrow nor Markham could vote in the caucus; both were invited only to witness Farrow's downfall. Perhaps, too, the Executive Committee hoped by including Farrow and Markham to avoid future charges that Bullock's nomination had been pushed through Star Chamber proceedings.[56] The Executive Committee announced on March 2 that the constitutional convention would convene at noon on March 7 as a nominating convention. A caucus of Moderate Republicans on March 6 resulted in nothing more than a feeble call for a Moderate convention on the twenty-fourth and a vehement protest against the Executive Committee's action.

The nominating convention which met in the convention hall on March 7, then, was only a dreary anticlimax to the maneuvering of the previous six weeks. The proceedings went forward as though rehearsed. Ninety-two delegates, representing 35 senatorial districts, attended. A. L. Harris, now a trusted lieutenant of the Augusta Ring, became convention chairman, and Radicals like Bryant and George W. Ashburn comprised the committee to nominate candidates for permanent convention officers. Harris was chosen president; all save one of the vice-presidents were Bullock supporters. Blodgett continued as chairman of the Executive

---

ting body." This note, in Farrow's handwriting and initialed by Farrow, August 16, 1883, is filed with his papers for 1868.

   [56] For the caucus proceedings, see Augusta *Constitutionalist*, February 24, 1868.

Committee, and all but one of its members were likewise loyal Bullock men. A move by two delegates to require nomination of the gubernatorial candidate by a two-thirds vote failed,[57] and, without further preliminaries, "Mr. Foster Blodgett presented to the Convention as Republican candidate for Governor, Hon. R. B. Bullock, of Richmond" County. At once, "Col. Bullock was nominated by acclamation." Farrow's name was never placed in contention. The Republicans adopted as their platform the new constitution, urged its ratification by the people of Georgia, and then adjourned until evening.[58]

Party leaders devoted the afternoon of March 7 to healing the split in their ranks. Immediately after his nomination, and in full view of the convention delegates, Bullock strode toward Farrow with hands outstretched. Convention reporters thought they heard him offer Farrow anything the defeated candidate wanted.[59] The Farrow, Angier, and Walker men set a high price for their loyalty. Brown, who had urged Walker's nomination, was assured Bullock's backing for a seat in the United States Senate and a share in the control of state and federal patronage in Georgia. To Farrow and Angier, the Bullock men pledged important posts in Bullock's administration, and to Farrow they held out the added sop of a place on the State Executive Committee. Akerman was promised Radical backing for a federal appointment.

In the evening, Farrow, Brown, and other former Bullock

[57] A correspondent of the *New Era* hinted that Brown supported this move, hoping to defeat both Farrow and Bullock and allow the nomination of his own favorite, Judge Dawson Walker, as a compromise candidate. Though the convention was theoretically open only to delegates, Farrow, Brown, and others were present in the hall. Atlanta *New Era*, March 11, 1868.

[58] Atlanta *New Era*, March 8, 1868.

[59] *Ibid.*

opponents addressed the convention. All freely admitted their earlier opposition to Bullock's candidacy, but, despite persistent misgivings, all now pledged to support him as the nominee of the Republican party. Factionalism must be forgotten; unity must be the Republican watchword.[60]

Their show of strength in the constitutional convention and the wide backing anti-Bullock candidates received for the gubernatorial nomination had left the dissident Republicans in a curious position within their own party. Numerically preponderant within the Republican camp, the opponents of the Augusta Ring in the spring of 1868 found themselves thwarted within the party hierarchy by the relatively small Radical faction. The anti-Bullock Republicans could make demands on Radical leaders, but fulfillment of Radical promises, they knew, demanded a victory for the new constitution and the election of Bullock in April. To achieve that victory and to elect their party's candidate, Republicans would have to work with instead of against each other in the coming weeks.

---

[60] *Ibid.*, and March 11, 1868. See also the Augusta *Constitutionalist*, March 12, 1868. Brown continued to have doubts about Bullock—both about his policies and about his ability to win voters to the Republican side. See Brown to William Darrah Kelly, March 18, in Joseph E. Brown Papers, Felix Hargrett Collection. University of Georgia. Brown hesitated to express his doubts publicly, however, and he marked his letter to Kelly "confidential."

CHAPTER IV

Pyrrhic Victory

The 1868 campaign for ratification of the state constitution and for the election of a new governor and seven Congressmen was in nearly every respect a carbon copy of the convention campaign waged the previous fall. Like its predecessor, it was strictly a state affair. Appeals went out repeatedly to national Democratic and Republican leaders, but neither party exerted itself on behalf of its state organization.

Though the national party committees remained indifferent toward the contest, Congress once again acted to ensure a Republican triumph. After the close election of 1867, Georgia's Radical leaders had begged Congress to stipulate that a majority of all those voting, rather than a majority of all registered voters, would suffice to ratify the new constitution and permit the election of a governor and other state officials.[1] Georgians' pleas had little immediate effect, but

[1] See, for example, Foster Blodgett to Edward McPherson, November

the abstention of Democrats from the polls in Alabama and the consequent defeat of that state's Radical constitution on February 4, 1868, spurred Congress to action. The fourth Reconstruction Act, which became law on March 11, 1868, provided that ratification might be accomplished in the Southern states by a simple majority of those participating in the election, no matter how small a percentage they might comprise of the total number of registered voters.[2]

For Georgia's Democrats, the campaign began with a state convention at Macon on December 5. Throughout the fall, individual Democrats had sought a meeting to heal the split in their party, and, by mid-November, the call had won the approval of the influential Atlanta *Daily Intelligencer*.[3] When the convention met, however, the old dispute between those who would denounce Congressional Reconstruction as a crime and take all possible measures for its undoing and those who urged Democrats to remain aloof from politics flared anew.[4]

Benjamin Hill, clinging to the policy he had urged in 1867, demanded that Democrats ignore the forthcoming elections. The Congressional statute changing the basis for voting on the new constitution had not yet become law when Hill spoke in December, so he argued that Democrats could defeat the constitution and overthrow Republican rule by remaining away from the polls.

Other delegates, however, advocated a different course. They accepted Congressional Reconstruction as an accomplished fact, to be combatted as best Democrats could within

29, 1867, in McPherson Papers; W. M. Dunn to John Sherman, November 18, 1867, in John Sherman Papers.

[2] U.S. *Statutes at Large,* XV, 41.

[3] Atlanta *Daily Intelligencer,* November 11, 1867.

[4] Delegates from sixty counties attended the convention, but only a few represented North Georgia. Herschel V. Johnson served as convention president.

the framework of the Sherman and supplemental acts. Looking fearfully to North Georgia, whose traditional Democratic allegiance had wavered because of personal loyalty to Joseph Brown and the lure of Radical relief schemes, they argued that denunciations of Brown and other individual Republicans would alienate that area still further and do irreparable damage to the Democratic cause in the upcoming elections.[5]

On Hill's motion, Democrats referred their differences to a committee, which sought a compromise solution. Avoiding mention of Hill's proposals, and implicitly rejecting his repeated demands that individual Republicans be branded as criminals, the members reported a milksop resolution on which all Democrats could agree. The policy of Congressional Reconstruction, they proclaimed as though discovering a new truth, was a crime.[6]

The Macon convention, however, had failed to gloss over completely Democratic dissensions. Its only constructive action was the appointment of a committee, headed by Herschel V. Johnson, which consulted, debated, and in January published a letter condemning in general terms the Republican program and calling upon Georgians to unite in throwing off the yoke of Radical domination.[7]

If it accomplished nothing else, the Macon meeting did spur Democratic organization. Even before Congress finally swept the ground from under Hill's supporters, the committee letter administered them a damaging blow. By some obscure process, Democrats organized in January and Feb-

[5] I. W. Avery, who as a delegate opposed Hill's policies, recalled these arguments in 1881. Isaac W. Avery, *History of the State of Georgia, 1850–1881* (New York: Brown & Darby, 1881), 373–75. See also the reports of the convention in the New York *Times*, December 10–14, 1867.

[6] Avery, *History of the State of Georgia*, 373–75.

[7] The committee included Johnson; A. H. Chappell, a prominent old-line Whig; Hill; Warren Akin, Brown's opponent for the governorship in 1859; and T. L. Guerry. A copy of the committee letter is in the Herschel V. Johnson Papers, Duke University.

ruary of 1868 with a thoroughness and determination which
contrasted strikingly with their apathy of the previous fall.
By February 20, every Congressional district except the
fourth had a Democratic District Committee, and E. G. Cabaniss of Bibb County had agreed once more to serve as
chairman of the State Executive Committee.[8]

In nominating a governor, however, the Democrats seemed
as pathetically disorganized and divided as ever. Indeed,
they were unable until April to put forward a suitable candidate for the office, and the party's delay and confusion once
more immensely aided the Republican cause.

The first Democratic nominee could not have served had
he been elected. With the feeble justification that the time
remaining before the April elections did not permit the
gathering of a regular nominating convention, the State Executive Committee on March 13 nominated Judge Augustus
Reese, whose defiance of General Pope's jury order had in
1867 made him a martyr to the Democratic faith. Leading
Democratic dailies acclaimed the choice, and Reese accepted
the nomination on March 17.[9] His candidacy seemed a clear
indication that the Democrats had finally rejected non-action
and intended to mount a frontal assault on the Reconstruction measures. But Reese was ineligible under the terms of
the Fourteenth Amendment to hold any political office. As
judge of the Ocmulgee Circuit before 1860, he had sworn to
uphold the federal Constitution, but he had joined with
Georgia in secession and had served the Confederacy. Because Meade urged him to do so, and because he recognized
that his candidacy could only hurt his party's chances, Reese
withdrew his name on March 24.[10]

    [8] Dawson *Journal,* February 20, 1868.
    [9] Augusta *Constitutionalist,* March 15, 1868; Savannah *Daily News and
Herald,* March 16, 1868; Milledgeville *Southern Recorder,* March 17, 1868;
Macon *Georgia Journal and Messenger,* March 18, 1868.
    [10] Avery, *History of the State of Georgia,* 383; Atlanta *New Era,* March
25, 1868.

Meanwhile, a second candidate had entered the race. Although David Irwin had refused after his election as a Democratic delegate to take his seat in the constitutional convention of 1867–68, he had remained strangely silent on the merits of the convention's labors. Now, he advanced his own candidacy for the governorship but refused to take a public stand on the new constitution. Apparently he hoped by remaining uncommitted on the central issue of the campaign to draw dissident Moderate Republicans away from their own party and unite them with Democrats behind his own compromise candidacy.[11]

The Democratic Augusta *Constitutionalist* scored Irwin for his apparent willingness to cooperate with Reconstructionists, but the State Executive Committee, torn by disputes within its membership, stunned by Reese's withdrawal, and desperately searching for a candidate for elections now less than a month away, turned to him as the best available man.[12] Few, apparently, cared to question his ideological or other qualifications. On March 28 the committee urged Georgia Democrats to rally behind Irwin.[13] Almost certainly, he would have been eligible to serve if elected.

But the Republicans feared that his candidacy would divide their party. Joseph E. Brown sensed the Democratic strategy and in what became famous as his "Marietta Speech" of March 18 denounced Irwin and warned Republicans against the easy assumption that silence regarding the proposed constitution implied acquiescence in its provisions.[14] Radicals complained to Meade that Irwin was disqualified by the provisions of the Fourteenth Amendment. Meade

[11] Bloom, "The Georgia Election of April, 1868," pp. 30–33.
[12] Augusta *Constitutionalist,* March 26, 1868.
[13] Milledgeville *Federal Union,* March 31, 1868.
[14] See discussion of this speech, below.

accepted the Radical protest, and Irwin had no choice but to withdraw his name on April 4.[15]

Democrats registered only perfunctory dissent against Meade's decision. Even within his own party, Irwin's candidacy had aroused scant enthusiasm, and whatever usefulness he possessed as a middle-of-the-road, uncommitted nominee had seemingly ended amid demands from both Republicans and Democrats that he clarify his stand on the constitution.[16]

Before again putting forward a nominee, the Democratic Executive Committee sought General Meade's approval of its choice. John Brown Gordon, a Confederate general still proud of his Rebel associations, seemed an unlikely candidate for the military commander's favor, but he met the eligibility tests of the Fourteenth Amendment and the Reconstruction acts. With Meade's blessings, he became the third Democratic nominee in as many weeks.

Gordon's candidacy seemed at first likely to strengthen the Democratic position. A popular war hero whose political and personal credentials appeared impeccable, he stood in sharp contrast to Bullock, whose past was obscure, whose war record was nonexistent, and whose championship of Negroes and yeoman whites rendered him abhorrent to most Georgia Democrats.[17]

Yet, ironically, it was the sharp contrast between his own candidacy and that of Bullock which proved Gordon's greatest weakness. The withdrawal of the moderate, uncommitted Irwin and the nomination of a Democratic candidate unalterably opposed to Congressional Reconstruction had polarized opinion throughout the state.[18] To Republican and

[15] Avery, *History of the State of Georgia*, 383.
[16] See Milledgeville *Federal Union*, March 31, 1868, for a sample of the half-hearted support given Irwin by many Democratic editors.
[17] Bullock had not served in the Confederate army but had acted as a telegraph expert attached to the Quartermaster Corps.
[18] Bloom, "The Georgia Election of April, 1868," pp. 36–37.

Democratic politicians alike, the gubernatorial contest became after Gordon's nomination a struggle between rich and poor and between black and white. Republicans made sporadic efforts to win wealthy Georgians to their side, and Democrats pleaded with Negroes to vote with and for their former masters, but the parties in 1868 were divided and campaigned on economic and racial issues.

Not surprisingly, the chaos of the Democrats' nominating procedures carried over into their campaign itself. Non-action, all agreed, no longer seemed a viable plan; so great, in fact, was popular sentiment against it that former Governor Jenkins, once its staunch supporter, now denied ever advocating such a course.[19] But three other alternatives confronted Democratic strategists. The first was to campaign solely for a vote against the constitution, ignoring other issues and neglecting the gubernatorial contest; the second was to seek defeat of the constitution but work for a meaningless, token election of the Democratic gubernatorial candidate as a show of Democratic strength in Georgia; the third was to permit ratification of the constitution but work for the election of the party's nominees and the restoration of Democratic control in the state. The frantic search for a suitable nominee suggests that Democrats gave little serious thought to the first alternative. Neither the Democratic State Executive Committee nor the party press, however, ever decided which of the last two possibilities would best serve the party's interests.

Divided counsels led some Democratic papers to stress a general, noncontroversial plea to all Democrats to avoid apathy, to organize county committees, and to hold regular meetings.[20] Others, however, took strong—and often con-

---

[19] Macon *Georgia Journal and Messenger,* March 25, April 14, 1868.

[20] Savannah *Daily News and Herald,* March 28, 1868; Augusta *Constitutionalist,* April 22, 1868.

flicting—positions. Both Milledgeville papers, for example, urged the rejection of the constitution, but only one believed it possible. Democrats should direct their best efforts to defeating the constitution, the *Federal Union's* editors urged, but they must not neglect the gubernatorial contest. The election of a Democratic governor, though without meaning in Georgia should the constitution be rejected, would effectively demonstrate the Democracy's strength in the state. To the editors of the *Southern Recorder,* the election of a Democratic governor had a more immediate importance. The constitution would most likely win acceptance; the sole hope of Democratic salvation lay in victory for the party's gubernatorial nominee.[21]

Unable at first to find a suitable nominee or to agree on party policy, Democrats united from the earliest stages of the campaign to denounce a constitution conceived by Radical usurpers "in hate and malignity" and to condemn the Radical relief and homestead exemption measures as swindles.[22] Particularly vehement were their attacks on the relief clause of the proposed constitution. Throwing back at Republican campaigners the arguments advanced by Moderate Republicans in the convention, Democrats charged that even the Radicals opposed relief and had accepted it as a necessary bribe to North Georgia only when assured that the constitutional provision would be struck down by Congress or the Supreme Court. Coming events would, in retrospect, lend plausibility to the Democratic charges, but in the campaign they produced little effect.

[21] For these arguments, see the Milledgeville *Federal Union,* March 17, March 24, April 7, 1868; Milledgeville *Southern Recorder,* April 9, April 14, 1868, quoting the Columbus *Enquirer.* See also R. M. Parks and Lewis Nash, "To the Voters of Gwinnett County!" election broadside in the Reconstruction File, Georgia Department of Archives and History.

[22] Milledgeville *Southern Recorder,* March 17, 1868; Macon *Georgia Journal & Messenger,* March 25, 1868.

Equally futile were sporadic attempts to win Negro support for the Democratic cause. Adhering to their policy of the previous fall and winter—a policy which they had pursued without marked success—Democrats hoped that reasoning with the Negroes "in a dispassionate and sensible manner" would convince the freedmen that Republican promises were blatant lies and that the Democrats were the Negroes' true political friends.[23] Democrats who had consistently opposed any hint of social equality for Negroes now staged barbecues and rallies, inviting the freedmen "to sit down and eat with the whites, if they would only promise to vote the democratic ticket."[24] Democrats readily admitted, however, that the Negroes would probably vote Republican, and it is difficult to see how even the most optimistic party organizer could have expected a little "dispassionate and sensible" reasoning and a few barbecues to undo two years of careful indoctrination and the freedmen's natural ties to the party of Abraham Lincoln.

The Democratic campaign, then, was a lackluster affair, marked by dissensions, indecision, and, for some, continued apathy. It was, moreover, essentially a negative fight. Even after Gordon's nomination its chief objective seemed to most party editors to be the defeat of the constitution, and its loudest battle cries became denunciations of Republican relief and homestead proposals. In some ways, it was a haughty campaign, as Democrats cooly assumed the superiority of their party's methods and motives. Yet it was a strangely hesitant, halting campaign as well, one which seemed especially disappointing after the energetic start Democrats had made in December. Party leaders who scath-

[23] Quotation from Milledgeville *Southern Recorder*, March 17, 1868. See also *ibid.*, April 9, 1868; Savannah *Daily News and Herald*, April 2, April 20, 1868.

[24] Stearns, *Black Man of the South*, 203.

ingly denounced their Republican opponents and their program balked at advancing any proposals of their own. Indeed, the most striking feature of the Democratic campaign was its failure to reflect the political acumen of Hill, Gordon, and the political veterans who made up the State Executive Committee. Democratic leaders seemed cut off from reality —unwilling once they had decided to enter the canvass to accept and abide by the rules laid down by Congress and General Meade, and unwilling even to attempt the formulation of programs which would counteract the defections among their North Georgia and Wiregrass Country supporters. Had the Executive Committee sought to guarantee its party's defeat, it could scarcely have devised a more brilliant strategy than that pursued by the Democrats in the spring of 1868.

II

Republican campaigners concentrated their efforts on the ratification and gubernatorial contests to the neglect of the Congressional and General Assembly races. If the constitution triumphed and Bullock won the election, Republicans felt confident that victories in the other races would follow as a matter of course. And they had ample justification for this view. Voting was by election tickets; every ticket bore the names of all the party's candidates in each county or district. Split ticket voting was virtually impossible. Throughout the campaign, then, the single Republican slogan became "Bullock, Relief & Reconstruction!"[25]

As befitted a party whose leaders believed success hinged on the votes of Black Belt Negroes and former supporters of Joseph E. Brown in northern and south-central Georgia, Republicans in March and April lavished special attention on

[25] Republican election ticket, in Rufus B. Bullock Papers, Georgia Department of Archives and History.

the state's white farmers. Samuel Bard's Atlanta *New Era,* one of the few Republican papers in the state, urged "poor men" to remember that Republican victory would mean "*Relief, Homesteads* and *Schools* for the people." Bullock proclaimed himself the "working man's candidate."[26] And from southwest Georgia, "Dougherty" exhorted "the Poor White Men of Georgia" to let "the slaveholding aristocracy" no longer rule them. "Vote for a Constitution," he wrote, "which educates your children free of charge; relieves the poor debtor from his rich creditor; allows a liberal home-stead for your families and more than all places you on a level with those who used to boast that for every slave they were entitled to three fifths of a vote in Congressional repre-sentation."[27] To Georgia's yeoman whites, a Republican victory would guarantee not only greater economic security, but greater social respectability, as well.

In their travels around the state, Republican campaign speakers virtually ignored the Black Belt and the southern counties. In the former, they confidently expected to poll most of the Negro vote; in the latter, they believed their party safely in the majority. In North Georgia, however, they devoted special efforts throughout the winter and spring to strengthening the Union Leagues and hence, presumably, the party. By February, 1868, Farrow proudly reported a sharp increase in league membership among North Georgia whites.[28]

To Georgia businessmen who might feel neglected, Re-publicans of the Bard—Brown persuasion repeatedly pledged

[26] Atlanta *New Era,* March 22, April 19, 1868.

[27] Campaign broadside, dated March 30, 1868, and printed and dis-tributed by the *New Era* Job Office, Atlanta, in Joseph E. Brown and Elizabeth G. Brown Collection, University of Georgia.

[28] U. L. A., Georgia, Circular, Atlanta, February 5, 1868, in Henry P. Farrow Collection, University of Georgia. At the time, of course, Farrow hoped to use Union League support to win the gubernatorial nomination; he was, therefore, especially zealous in his efforts to recruit new members.

their interest and support. Never satisfied with a Republican coalition comprised chiefly of yeoman whites and Negroes, they now voiced the appeals which they had half-formulated during the convention campaign the previous fall, and they hoped that their voices could attract to the party those groups ignored by the State Executive Committee.

Those who sought a broad Republican coalition in the spring of 1868 had a readymade issue, for particularly important to many Georgians during the gubernatorial campaign was the projected Air Line Railroad. When completed, this road would link Atlanta with Richmond and would open to Georgians potentially profitable markets along the Atlantic Coast. Whether or not to extend state aid to the Air Line had been a subject of sporadic controversy for several months. Railroad promoters throughout the state urged speedy completion of the road and secretly hoped to attach to a state aid bill riders securing subsidies for their own lines.[29] Samuel Bard sought to assure such men that Republican preoccupation with relief, homesteads, and free schools did not indicate insensitivity to their demands. "Let it be known," he proclaimed without authority from the party committee, that Bullock "is a warm and firm advocate of the Air-Line Railroad."[30]

By far the most perplexing problem confronting Republican strategists was that of keeping both Negroes and yeoman whites happy within the same party. North Georgia's antipathy toward the Negro had shown itself in the constitutional convention and had forced the Radicals to withdraw their insistence on constitutional protection of the freedmen's right to hold office. Undoubtedly, however, white Radicals had privately pledged to sustain the freedmen, for Negro

[29] This fact became clear during the debates on the question of state aid to the Air Line Road in the General Assembly session of 1868.

[30] Atlanta *New Era*, March 29, 1868.

delegates had acquiesced in the removal of the constitutional guarantees.

Although Republicans continued their work among the Negroes, organizing meetings and haranguing the freedmen with speeches extolling Republican virtues and exposing Democratic sins, the party throughout the campaign consciously straddled both sides of the officeholding question.[31] In the Black Belt and seacoast counties, where Negroes comprised a majority of the registered voters, where the Democracy's preachings were accepted gospel among most whites, and where, therefore, Negro votes represented the best hope of Republican triumph, Bullock's lieutenants blandly assured the freedmen of their undoubted right to hold office.[32] In the northern counties, Republicans sang a different song. Faced with the prospect of losing hard-won yeoman backing, the party sent the popular Joseph Brown home to North Georgia to reassure his old supporters. In his Marietta Speech on March 18, Brown arrived at the culmination of the strategy which he had so carefully worked out during the convention. Negroes were certainly enfranchised, he declared, but the new constitution nowhere guaranteed them the right to hold office.[33]

As a statement of fact, Brown's remarks were irrefutable. The Marietta Speech, carefully timed to play a major role in the campaign, was also shrewdly calculated to appear to

[31] For the disgusted reactions of a Democratic partisan, see Leigh, *Ten Years on a Georgia Plantation*, 97–98.

[32] Louise Biles Hill, *Joseph E. Brown and the Confederacy* (Chapel Hill: University of North Carolina Press, 1930), 276–77.

[33] *Joseph E. Brown's Speech . . . at Marietta, Georgia . . . March 18, 1868* (n.p.: [1868], pamphlet copy in private possession). See also Hill, *Joseph E. Brown*, 276–77, for the best analysis of Brown's position. My conclusion that Brown's statements on Negro officeholding were carefully contrived is based on circumstantial evidence. No comments on Brown's motivation appear in the various collections of Brown Papers or in other collections of personal papers of Republican politicians which I have examined.

North Georgians an official statement of Republican policy.
So great was Brown's prestige in his home district that his
remarks, artfully couched as his own personal opinions, were
as eagerly and as uncritically devoured by the yeoman whites
as if they had appeared over the signatures of Bullock and
the entire Republican State Executive Committee.

As a short-term strategy in a brief campaign in which
Democrats were divided and ineffectual and newspaper
coverage of events outside each individual editor's domain
remarkably slim, the two-faced Republican appeal was a brilliant device. Chances that the party's duplicity would be
widely exposed long enough before the election to damage
the Republican cause were remote. The Union Leagues and
independent speakers had performed their tasks well, and
there seemed little likelihood that the mass of semiliterate,
politically unsophisticated Negroes would vote Democratic
whatever the Republicans said or did. For a time, at least,
the Republicans had successfully circumvented ancient en-
mities; they seemed well on the way, in the spring of 1868,
to success in their efforts to forge a political union of Negroes
and yeoman whites. Unaware of private letters predicting
the disaster which would overtake the party if the Augusta
Ring maintained leadership, the members of the Radical
State Executive Committee must have been particularly
pleased at their success in using Brown so effectively during
the campaign.[34] Perhaps, after all, they had converted him
to Radicalism—and to support of their plans for building a
Republican party in Georgia.

But the four days of balloting in April, 1868, produced

[34] Brown to William Darrah Kelly, March 18, 1868, in Joseph E. Brown
Papers, Felix Hargrett Collection. Brown feared that a coalition of Negroes
and yeoman whites could not long continue to win elections in Georgia,
and that Republicans must attract to their party the merchants and industrial promoters of the state. Bullock, he lamented, had made no such
plans for building the party's strength.

mixed results. The constitution, supported by Republicans as a party and by a few Democrats who chose to acquiesce in ratification and work for the election of General Gordon, won approval by a majority of nearly 18,000 votes.[35] Bullock won 93 of the state's 132 counties but managed to secure a majority of only 7,171 votes over the better-known and more popular Gordon. The Republicans won the state senate by a comfortable margin and in the Georgia house of representatives obtained but a slim majority whose effectiveness would depend on the maintenance of unyielding party discipline.[36] Democrats won in three of the six Congressional districts holding elections; in the Sixth District, neither party nominated a candidate. Republicans made substantial gains in traditionally Democratic North Georgia. The only major setbacks came in South Georgia, a region which the party had confidently expected to dominate but which it had neglected during the campaign.

Republicans credited their success to the efficiency of the Union Leagues. "The Union League has again saved us," its president, Farrow, exulted.[37] Democrats looked less to matters of organization and more to issues in explaining the Republican victory. The relief issue, the Athens *Southern Watchman* concluded, had made all the difference.[38]

Both analyses were probably partially correct, though so little can be known about the Union Leagues that their in-

[35] *Annual Report of the Comptroller General of the State of Georgia,* 1868, Table A. The actual majority for the constitution was 17, 972.

[36] Thompson, *Reconstruction in Georgia,* 204. For more complete discussion of party alignments in the state house of representatives, see Chapter Five. That the Republicans carried the house is the thesis of Charles Bloom's brilliant M.A. essay. Bloom's conclusions have also been accepted by Wallace Calvin Smith, "Rufus B. Bullock and the Third Reconstruction of Georgia" (M.A. thesis, University of North Carolina at Chapel Hill, 1964), 23–27.

[37] Farrow to [?], April 28, 1868, in William E. Chandler Papers, Library of Congress.

[38] Athens *Southern Watchman,* May 6, 1868.

fluence is hard to measure. Easier to trace are the patterns
Republican strength suggested by examination of the votes
in 1868 and of economic and social characteristics of Georgia's five principal geographic regions.[39]

In the mountain counties of North Georgia, Republican
votes were highest in counties where farms were small and
the land poor. Quite probably, then, the party's support in
North Georgia came from the groups to whom the Radicals
had directed their relief and homestead appeals—the white
yeoman farmers, those who tilled small, unprofitable plots of
land, with little aid from machinery or hired hands. Counties
which gave Republican majorities in 1868 generally had returned majorities for Joseph E. Brown in the gubernatorial
contest of 1857; Brown's conversion to Republicanism almost
certainly had influenced many North Georgia voters to desert the Democracy.[40]

The Upper Piedmont comprises the group of counties situ-
ated between the Blue Ridge of North Georgia and the
Black Belt. This region, though less hilly than the Blue
Ridge, was also in 1868 an area of small farms tilled by
yeoman whites. Negroes here, as in the Blue Ridge, were
only a small minority of the population. Loyalty to Brown
was strong, and Republican campaigners again focused on
the relief and homestead issues. It was a Piedmont Democratic paper which acknowledged the effectiveness of the
relief appeal.[41] It seems likely that Republicans here, too,
made significant inroads in Democratic strength among the
white yeoman farmers.

Georgia's Black Belt and seacoast counties were in antebellum days the residences of such "planter aristocrats" as

[39] See the introduction and Tables A and B, in the Appendix to this
volume.

[40] For coefficients of correlation between Republican votes and various
economic and social indexes, see Tables A and B, Appendix.

[41] Athens *Southern Watchman*, May 6, 1868.

the state could boast and the centers of strength for the powerful Whig organization. But whether relatively early, like Alexander H. Stephens, or relatively late, like Benjamin H. Hill, most Whigs had joined the Democracy during the 1850's—and Democrats they remained after the war. Given the leadership of the remnants of the Democratic party in the fall of 1865, they had little reason to shift their allegiance to a new party whose programs seemed the antithesis of everything they had long believed. Overwhelming support for Republican candidates in the spring of 1868 came from the freedmen who dominated the voter rolls in most Black Belt and coastal counties. Republican votes were high, too, in the counties which produced the most manufactured goods and whose farms and plantations were the most highly developed. Moreover, Republican votes came from areas which had given support to Democratic candidates before the war.[42] Possibly, then, a few commercial planters and merchants who in antebellum days had defied the predominantly Whig orientation of their region and allied with the Democracy sided with the Republicans in 1868. Forerunners of the New South spokesmen of the 1880's, repelled by Democratic invocations of an idyllic plantation South, but indifferent to the Republican relief and homestead measures, these men—if they were Republicans—were most likely party members of the Brown–Bard variety. Their allegiance to Republicanism, however, reflected more than personal loyalty to Brown; they hoped to win from a Republican state administration pledges of state aid to railroads and encouragement of industrial promotion schemes.[43]

[42] In 1857, counties which show high Republican votes in 1868 had supported Brown against Hill in an election which pitted Democrats against old-line Whigs for the last time. Brown was scorned by most Black Belt and seacoast planters for his Democratic affiliations and for his lowly birth and crude ways.

[43] Many merchants and industrial promoters seem to have remained with-

The political situation in the wiregrass region of South
Georgia was anomalous in 1868. Little is available in the
writings or speeches of Republican leaders to suggest the
sources of the party's support. Wiregrass counties which had
supported Whig candidates in antebellum elections probably
voted for Democratic Congressional candidates in April but
gave majorities to Bullock in the gubernatorial contest.
Counties which contained the largest or most profitable manufacturing establishments tended to give majorities to Republican Congressional candidates. But Republicans had
overestimated the strength of yeoman farmers in the wiregrass region, and the support they expected from this group
failed to materialize. Those who voted the Republican ticket
were generally not farmers, but workers or managers in the
small mills which dotted the region. Initially attracted by
Radical promises of shorter working hours, higher wages,
and free schools in the fall of 1867, they did not seem drawn
by the relief pledges that made up the core of the platform
in 1868. They were the forgotten men in the Republican
scheme of things, the victims of the State Executive Committee's miscalculation. Caught between appeals to the
white farmers on the one hand and appeals to wealthy industrial promoters on the other, they were unimpressed by
programs designed for either group. Their wavering, half-
hearted support of Republican candidates in the spring of
1868 bespoke convincingly their resentment of the oblivion
to which Republican campaigners had consigned them.

The campaign and election in the spring of 1868 were
marked by violence and fraud to a degree unprecedented in
Georgia history. The allegations far surpassed the actual in-
cidents, but the night-riders of the Ku Klux Klan and over-

---

in the Republican fold even after Brown and Bard had bolted the party—
Brown to return to the Democracy and Bard to seek in vain confirmation
of his appointment as territorial governor of Idaho.

zealous election managers, both Republican and Democratic, kept agitation in the state at a high pitch throughout March and April.

The existence of the Klan, a Democratic society dedicated in fact if not in theory to the intimidation of Republican voters whom Democrats had failed to win over by more conventional methods, became known early in 1868. Originally organized as a social club in Pulaski, Tennessee, the Klan spread across the state line to North Georgia through "dens" organized by Dudley M. DuBose, son-in-law of Georgia's most vituperative unrepentent rebel, Robert Toombs.[44] Its activities remained secret, however, until a startling act brought it to statewide prominence.

On March 31, 1868, a shot broke the nighttime stillness in Columbus, and carpetbagger George W. Ashburn fell dead. Rumors quickly spread; many whispered that two notorious women of the town had conspired to do away with the Radical leader.[45] More widely accepted, however—at least among Republicans—was the theory that Klansmen had perpetrated the murder. General Meade removed the civil authorities at Columbus, arrested nine prominent young Democrats, and announced his intention to try them before a military court.[46] At once, Meade's action became a party issue. A battery of the state's most experienced lawyers, including Alexander Stephens, volunteered their services for the defense, and Joseph E. Brown became prosecution counsel.[47]

[44] Theodore Barker Fitz-Simons, Jr., "The Ku Klux Klan in Georgia, 1868–1871" (M.A. thesis, University of Georgia, 1957), 29.

[45] Edward T. Shephard to Alexander H. Stephens, June 8, 1868, in Alexander Stephens Papers, Library of Congress.

[46] Meade's reports of the Ashburn murder appear in the *Annual Report of the Secretary of War*, 1868, Pt. 1, pp. 10ff.

[47] For his services, Brown received $5,000. Brown always denied any element of self-interest in his decision to become prosecution counsel; see *Governor Brown and the Columbus Prisoners*, a pamphlet issued in 1880 when Brown was a candidate for the U.S. Senate. I have used a copy in

Because the Ashburn murder and the arrest of the young suspects aroused such excitment during the campaign, Meade delayed the trial until June 29. The constitution by then having been declared in force and Bullock having been installed as governor, Meade apparently doubted the legality of proceeding with a military trial.[48] Confidential dispatches from Washington encouraged him to go ahead, however, and the military court convened on schedule.[49]

Less than four weeks later, Meade seemed eager to withdraw the government from the case. What happened to change his mind about the trial remains unclear. It appeared by July 21, however, that conviction was unlikely, and the military commander was relieved to turn over the prisoners to the newly inaugurated Columbus civil authorities. Democrats during the spring campaign had made political capital out of the military "usurpation," and Brown's appearance as prosecution counsel had further damaged his standing among Democrats and among the moderates of both parties. The new Republican administration skirted uneasily around the Columbus issue, and the trial of the nine prisoners never resumed.[50]

There was certainly a great deal of fraud in the election of 1868, but it is impossible to be sure where genuine cases of wrongdoing leave off and those manufactured by Republi-

---

private possession. The George Gordon Meade Papers, Historical Society of Pennsylvania, contain indisputable proof, however, of the fee Brown exacted for his services. See Brown to Meade, June 27, 1868, J. M. Schofield to Meade, June 27, 1868, Meade to Brown, official copy, June 29, 1868. Copies of the correspondence Meade sent to Brown are in the Joseph E. Brown Papers, Felix Hargrett Collection.

   [48] Ratification of the constitution was proclaimed on May 11; Bullock was installed as governor on June 28.

   [49] John Rawlins to Meade, Washington, July 21, 1868, in George Gordon Meade Papers, Historical Society of Pennsylvania. Rawlins marked his letter "unofficial."

   [50] Hill, *Joseph E. Brown,* 284–85; Thompson, *Reconstruction in Georgia,* 387.

can candidates fearful of being counted out begin. Meade reported to General Grant "many claims of fraud from both sides" and promised full investigations, but the findings of the army's sleuths always seemed to favor the Republican candidates.[51]

The claims of neither side are entirely convincing, but those of the Democrats seem more plausible than those of Republicans who had the active support of Congress and the military government. Election managers, appointed by Meade, were almost always Republicans, and the conduct of the election enabled Republicans to control their own voters, especially the Negroes, and to thwart Democratic efforts to intimidate the freedmen. Voting continued for four days; all knew at the end of each day approximately how each side had fared. Furthermore, balloting took place only at the county seats, and troops were available if requested by the election officials. It was no wonder that the Democrats protested the election results. They could do nothing about the new constitution. Ratification had been by a clear majority. But they claimed that Gordon had been counted out of the governorship by fraud. Multiple or illegal voting by Negroes, Democrats charged, had made all the difference.[52]

Republicans controlled the election machinery in the spring of 1868. Though the returns from fifteen counties which had Negro majorities but which voted Democratic seem questionable, it appears unlikely that all the instances of fraud and violence about which Republicans complained really took place. Most Republican charges, in fact, were

---

[51] See the Reconstruction Files and the miscellaneous County Files, Georgia Department of Archives and History, for numerous affidavits alleging frauds. See also Bloom, "The Georgia Election of April, 1868," pp. 50 ff, and, for the quotation from Meade, the *Annual Report of the Secretary of War, 1868,* Pt. 1, p. 102.

[52] See Thompson, *Reconstruction in Georgia,* 206, for the best summary.

trumped up ten days or more after the election, when it appeared that Democrats would contest Republican seats in the General Assembly or the vote in the gubernatorial or Congressional contests. Ed. Hulbert's circular, sent to Republicans throughout the state, is instructive: "We want affidavits proving force, fraud, intimidation, in violation of general orders. We must have them. Go to work and get them up at once. . . . Please go to work 'sharp and quick'. . . . The election in your county will be contested. Defend yourselves by attacking the enemy."[53]

The "enemy," once again, had made a surprisingly strong showing in the April elections; once again, Democrats had demonstrated that, united, they would be the majority party in Georgia. Divided and apathetic, they had nearly defeated an energetic party, a party supported by the United States Army and by the Congressional Republican organization.

Republicans in Georgia had waged a smart, perhaps even a brilliant, campaign. They had secured their major objectives: ratification of the constitution, control of the governorship, and a majority in the General Assembly. Yet they had won only a Pyrrhic victory. Their ability to maintain themselves in power would depend on their ability to keep their ranks united—and, above all, to maintain the delicate alliance of Negroes, yeoman white farmers, and the few railroad and industrial promoters which made up the party. The support of all three groups was vital to continued Republican success, however much the State Executive Committee might continue to deprecate the importance of anything broader than a coalition of Negroes and yeoman whites. In

[53] This circular, addressed to John M. Duer of Columbus and dated May 8, 1868, appears in Avery, *History of the State of Georgia,* 384–85 and Thompson, *Reconstruction in Georgia,* 207. It and others like it, which were widely reprinted, earned for Hulbert the sobriquet "Sharp and Quick."

the spring of 1868, there seemed a promise that all three groups might work together in a single party. But in gaining their immediate objectives in the spring campaign, Radical Republican leaders had unwittingly set the stage for the breakup of their own coalition and the downfall of Republicanism in Georgia.

CHAPTER V

The Bitter Fruits of Victory

The April, 1868, elections had put Republicans in power, and Georgia had, apparently, complied with the requirements of the Military Reconstruction acts. On June 28, Congress passed the Omnibus Bill, readmitting six states, including Georgia, to the Union. But Bullock, Blodgett, and other leaders of the state's Radical faction could not share the rejoicing of their Republican followers. The April victory had been a costly one, and the burdens of triumph were likely to prove as onerous as the difficulties of defeat.

To ensure support first for his nomination and then for his election, Bullock had involved himself deeply in patronage commitments to Radical and Moderate Republicans alike. To Brown and Blodgett he had pledged Georgia's two Senate seats; disgruntled Democrats and even a few Moderate Republicans charged that Brown had the entire patronage of the new administration at his disposal to guar-

antee his election.[1] Although Bullock's political pledges gave
him a plausible excuse to turn down importunate Democratic officeseekers, they had effectively tied his hands and
prevented him from offering inducements during the summer of 1868 to wavering members of his own party.[2]

Heavy as Bullock's commitments to Brown and Blodgett
were, they represented only the first and most widely known
of the new governor's promises. To his opponent for the Republican gubernatorial nomination, Henry P. Farrow, he had
pledged the state attorney generalship, employment as state
counsel in all claims against the state-owned Western & Atlantic Railroad, and a place on the Republican State Executive Committee.[3] As a reward for faithful service as election manager, Ed. Hulbert received the superintendency of
the Western & Atlantic, a post whose patronage possibilities rivaled on the state level those of the federal postmaster
generalship. Benjamin F. Conley of the Augusta Ring became the Radical nominee for president of the state senate.
Frozen out of the patronage commitments, bitterly resent-
ful, and increasingly restive, were such party stalwarts as
Caldwell and Bryant.[4] Unable to offer suitable rewards to
such loyal partisans, Bullock seemed likely to encounter increasing difficulties in maintaining the unity of his shaky
party coaliton.

Another potential difficulty had been temporarily circumvented by the provisions of the Omnibus Bill. The clause of

[1] Bloom, "The Georgia Election of April, 1868," pp. 83–84; Augusta
Constitutionalist, August 2, 1868; Atlanta *Constitution,* June 18, 1868.

[2] Rufus B. Bullock to Alexander H. Stephens, May 17, 1868, in Alexander Stephens Papers, Library of Congress. Stephens sought an office for
a friend.

[3] Macon *Georgia Journal and Messenger,* March 11, 1868; Contract,
signed August 21, 1868, in Henry P. Farrow Collection, University of
Georgia.

[4] J. H. Caldwell to William Claflin, October 7, 1868, in William E.
Chandler Papers, Library of Congress.

Georgia's new constitution which abrogated all contracts made before June 1, 1865, was as repugnant to Justices Hiram Warner and Isham Harris of the Georgia Supreme Court as it had been to such Moderate Republicans as Akerman in the constitutional convention. Should a test case come before the high court, these justices would almost surely rule the clause in conflict with the contract clause of the federal Constitution. Bullock had, therefore, tentatively determined to remove both Warner and Harris from the bench and replace them with H. K. McCay and another judge known to support the Radical relief measures.[5] The governor was spared this awkward task when Congress, in readmitting Georgia, required that the state strike the relief clause from its constitution.

Democrats during the campaign of March and April, 1868, had thought they sniffed a Radical plot to ensure the rejection of the relief clause by Congress.[6] To the Radicals, such an agreement would have many attractions. It might help conciliate Moderate Republicans angered by the adoption of the clause and chafing under the strains of party loyalty for which they could expect few tangible rewards. At the same time, it might tighten the Radical grip on the yeoman farmers, for Congress, not the Georgia Radicals, would become the villain in the rejection of the relief clause.

If the Radicals indeed entered into a conspiracy with Congressional Republicans, the scheme had lost its utility by May. Republicans owed their election to the votes of white farmers lured away from the Democracy by the bait of relief; to hold these men within their party, the Radicals must do more than plead good intentions. Bullock, therefore, faced in the summer of 1868 the necessity of reopening

[5] Atlanta *Constitution*, June 29, 1868, from the correspondence of the Macon *Georgia Journal and Messenger*, commenting on Bullock's plans.

[6] See, for example, Milledgeville *Southern Recorder*, March 17, 1868.

the relief debate which had so sharply rent party ranks during the constitutional convention.

Of all Bullock's problems, the most pressing was finding effective ways to dominate his divided legislature. Republicans had a clear 27–17 majority in the state senate,[7] but in the house of representatives the parties were more evenly matched. The exact party composition of the house can probably never be known, for that body published no official roster of its own members, and contemporary statements of party affiliations disagree. Both Democrats and Republicans claimed victory,[8] but General Meade's official report announced the election of 95 Republican delegates, whose votes would give the new state administration a comfortable working majority.[9]

There are several ways of testing the conflicting claims—none of them entirely satisfactory. One, chosen by C. Mildred Thompson and accepted until recently, is a study of crucial votes taken during the General Assembly session of 1868. After analyzing the votes on the adoption of the Fourteenth Amendment, the election of United States Senators, the expulsion of Negro members from the General Assembly, and a Radical-sponsored relief bill, Miss Thompson concluded that the Democrats, with eighty-eight delegates, had an absolute majority in the house. There were eighty-four

[7] Thompson, *Reconstruction in Georgia*, 208.

[8] Atlanta *Constitution*, June 19, 1868; Atlanta *New Era*, May, 1868, *passim*, and September 13, 1868. Brown claimed that Republicans had won "a safe working majority" in both houses of the legislature. See Brown to Ulysses S. Grant, May 5, 1868, in Joseph E. Brown Papers, Felix Hargrett Collection.

[9] *Report of Major General Meade's Military Operations and Administration of Civil Affairs in the Third Military District and Department of the South . . . 1868* (Atlanta: Assistant Adjutant General's Office, Department of the South, 1868), 31.

Republican members; seventy-five, according to Miss Thompson, were Radicals, and nine were Moderates.[10]

Miss Thompson's choice of votes, and the small number of roll calls she included, distorted her results. The inclusion of the relief vote in so small a sample and reliance on it as a clear party test was unfortunate, for some Moderate Republicans always voted against Radical-sponsored relief legislation, and a few known Democrats crossed party lines to ally with the Radicals on relief. Miss Thompson's effort to distinguish between Radical and Moderate Republicans represented an important contribution, but the number of Moderates she identified seems suspiciously small. Undoubtedly, the Radicals gained strength within the Republican party during the spring of 1868, and their stranglehold on the nominating machinery led to a disproportionately high number of Radicals among Republican officeseekers. Nevertheless, the strength of the Moderates, so evident in the constitutional convention, could scarcely have dwindled as rapidly between March and April as Miss Thompson's figures suggest.

Charles G. Bloom, however, later offered an imaginative rethinking of Miss Thompson's analysis. Noting that Democratic papers withheld election returns, "perhaps in order to inject an additional element of confusion into the politics of the State," Bloom reasoned that Democrats believed themselves defeated—else they would certainly have published evidence of their victory.[11] He then reexamined the vote of April, 1868. The acknowledged difficulty of split-ticket voting led him to assume that Republican candidates for the state house of representatives won in the ninety-three counties carried by Bullock.[12] Bloom then studied the votes

[10] Thompson, *Reconstruction in Georgia,* 208.
[11] Bloom, "The Georgia Election of April, 1868," p. 92.
[12] *Ibid.,* 64–65.

of representatives from these counties on a series of issues.[13] He found twenty-three who at some time failed to vote with the Republican party. Newspaper lists of party affiliations suggested that four of these twenty-three were indeed Democrats.[14] Two represented counties in the Black Belt and may have won their seats by fraud; one represented a traditionally Democratic county in North Georgia; and the last represented one of the group of counties in South Georgia which went Democratic or returned disappointingly small majorities for Republican candidates.

From split-ticket voting, then, the Democrats gained four seats. "Split voting," Bloom concluded, "cost the Republicans a minimal number of seats for which they were more than compensated by splits in the counties which gave majorities to Gordon."[15] The *New Era* claimed that six Gordon counties returned Republican representatives, and, in five of the six cases, Bloom found the *New Era's* claims valid. He also turned up the name of a sixth Republican elected in a county conceded by the *New Era* to the Democracy.[16]

Bloom concluded, then, that the Republicans carried the Georgia house with a total of ninety-five Republican delegates. Although the point may seem a minor one, the significance of Bloom's work far exceeds the limited satisfaction one finds in overturning a long-accepted interpretation. If the Republicans did carry the house, as they undoubtedly carried the senate, interpretations of events occurring in the

[13] The issues included: ratification of the Fourteenth Amendment; two votes for United States Senators; election of a secretary of state, a comptroller general, a treasurer, and a state printer; a motion to table a report of the Committee on Privileges and Elections; the expulsion of Negro members; and a motion to censure remarks made by Governor Bullock in a message to the General Assembly. *Ibid.*, Appendix I, 90.

[14] Representatives Pepper of Calhoun County, Irwin of Habersham, Mc-Culloch of Jones, and Rainey of Schley.

[15] Bloom, "The Georgia Election of April, 1868," p. 70.

[16] *Ibid.*, 70–71.

summer and fall of 1868 must build upon different premises and lead to different conclusions.

Because Bloom's work calls into question much that has long been accepted about Georgia Reconstruction, I made my own analysis of selected votes taken in the house of representatives during the summer in question, before Negroes were expelled from the General Assembly and Democrats seated in their stead in September.[17] Ninety-three delegates, not including the speaker, voted with the Republicans on one or more roll calls which seem clear party tests. We may assume that they had ties, however tenuous, to the party. Eighty men had consistently Democratic voting records. Apparently, then, Bloom's conclusions are correct—the Republicans carried the house of representatives.

The strength of the Moderate Republicans in the house, therefore, takes on added importance. Of the ninety-three delegates who at some time during the session voted Republican on a clear party issue, twenty-six failed to vote with the party on a majority of roll call tests. Most of these men represented North Georgia or the wiregrass counties. Here, then, is the key to the uncertainty about the composition of the house—the unpredictable voting behavior of some twenty-six Moderate Republicans.

[17] The votes included the following: a vote on July 18, 1868, on a minority report on the eligibility of members (*Journal of the House of Representatives of the State of Georgia*, 1868, pp. 43–44); a vote on July 21, on the ratification of the Fourteenth Amendment (*ibid.*, 50–51); a vote on July 28, for United States Senator in the contest involving Joseph E. Brown, Alexander H. Stephens, and Joshua Hill (*ibid.*, 100–101); a vote on August 1, on a motion to suspend levies and sales of debtor property (*ibid.*, 121–22); a vote on August 4, for state printer (*ibid.*, 148–50); a vote on September 3, on the expulsion of Negro members from the House (*ibid.*, 242–43). Representatives who sided with the Republicans only on ratification of the Fourteenth Amendment or on the suspension of levies and sales of debtor property are not counted as Republicans, since some known Democrats crossed party lines on these roll calls. For tables giving the vote for each Representative, see my doctoral dissertation, "Shaping a New Era," 222–37.

Radical leaders apparently had little control over the Moderates, and perhaps some even recognized that discipline over the party renegades firm enough to produce consistent Republican majorities would prove impossible. The *New Era* stood alone among Republican papers in claiming victory in the house, and Radical leaders in their public pronouncements and private correspondence sounded strangely unlike members of a triumphant party.[18] Undoubtedly, they foresaw clearly the difficulties which would confront them when the legislature organized.

From the moment the General Assembly convened on July 4, Bullock and the Radicals recognized their inability to control the Republican delegates. Accordingly, Bullock attempted to thwart the legislature's efforts to organize and to elect permanent officers. The governor, however, lacked the whole-hearted support both of members of his own faction and of General Meade. Bullock's strategy was to delay or prevent the organization of the legislature—perhaps to gain time more effectively to marshal his own forces, but more likely in the hope that military intervention would result in the unseating of Democratic representatives and the seating of Republican delegates in their stead. He informed General Meade that the legislature had met, but that several of its members, presumably Democrats, were ineligible under the terms of the Fourteenth Amendment to take their seats.[19]

Uncertain of the proper course to follow and suspecting that Bullock's claims stemmed from the governor's acknowledged anxiety to secure the election of a Republican speaker and two Republican United States Senators, the military commander requested instructions from Washington. General Grant's reply dodged the central issue. No one, the

[18] See, for example, Volney Spalding to William E. Chandler, Atlanta, September 1, 1868, in Chandler Papers.
[19] *Annual Report of the Secretary of War*, 1868, Pt. 1, pp. 78–79.

commanding general suggested, should hold office if ineligible to do so—but Meade himself had no authority to
purge the General Assembly of ineligible members.[20] Meade
deliberated for two days and then passed the issue on to the
two branches of the legislature. Each branch, he informed
Bullock, must judge the qualifications of its own members;
he, as military commander, could only await their decision.
He would, he added, refuse to recognize as legally organized
any legislature which failed to comply with the provisions
of the Congressional Reconstruction Acts.[21]

The Republican majority in the state senate was so great
that a united party could obtain for Bullock anything he desired. The governor's purpose in challenging the eligibility
of any Democrat within the senate is uncertain. Perhaps,
however, he suspected from the start of the session the fact
which the votes on eligibility were soon to prove—that even
within the senate, Radical control over the Moderates was
ineffective. The eligibility question was first raised on July
10, when Republicans voted as a bloc against a Democratic
resolution to table the entire subject. Immediately, they
forced the adoption of a substitute resolution, calling for an
investigation into the qualifications of several Democratic
senators.[22] A week later, when two Republicans and three
Democrats reported that the Committee on Privileges and
Elections had found no senator ineligible, Radical floor leaders moved to recommit the report.

What had occurred between July 10 and July 17 to cause
the disaffection of the Moderate Republicans within the committee and on the floor remains unclear. Perhaps Radical

[20] Correspondence between Meade and Grant, July 6, 1868, and John A.
Rawlins and Meade, July 7, 1868, *ibid.*, 108–109.

[21] Meade to Bullock, July 9, 1868, in Executive Minutes of the State of
Georgia, Georgia Department of Archives and History.

[22] *Journal of the Senate of the State of Georgia*, July 10, 1868, pp. 19–
20, 28–30.

leadership faltered. Perhaps Bullock recognized that, lacking Meade's strong support and faced with at best a sharply divided legislature, he could best serve the interests of the Radicals by allowing the "Rebel" legislature to "violate" the Acts of Congress before the world. At any rate, fifteen Moderates broke with their party on July 17 and either abstained or opposed the Radical motion to recommit the committee report.[23] The report was adopted, and no senator lost his seat.

The story in the house was much the same. Moderates and Radicals united on July 10 to force an investigation of the eligibility of several delegates;[24] on July 17, an investigating committee composed of three Republicans and two Democrats submitted several reports. The Republican members found two men ineligible, and two of them concurred that a third should be disqualified. The minority report of the two Democratic members found no representative ineligible. On July 18, Moderate Republicans joined with Democrats to vote acceptance of the Democratic report and defeat for Bullock's plans to purge the General Assembly of his political opponents.[25]

Meade accepted the verdicts of the senate and the house. When word of their decisions reached him, he ordered Bullock formally inaugurated as governor and decreed that the General Assembly should proceed with the election of its permanent officers.[26]

As the eligibility dispute progressed, it must have become clear to Bullock that even should the senate and the house purge themselves of "ineligible" members, the party divisions would be only slightly altered. In the house of repre-

[23] *Journal of the Senate*, 1868, pp. 34–35.
[24] *Journal of the House of Representatives*, 1868, p. 32.
[25] *Ibid.*, 35ff, 43–44.
[26] *Annual Report of the Secretary of War*, 1868, Pt. 1, p. 79.

sentatives—the real target of Bullock's attacks—a purge of
the three members decreed ineligible by the Radicals would
have increased the Republican majority to only sixteen. Had
the governor withdrawn his objections to certain legislators,
few would have expressed surprise. Bullock's chances of securing a purge were meager, and though he would lose face
by a strategic retreat, his prestige—already shaky—would
undoubtedly crumble far more should he sustain a defeat on
a major roll call test so early in his career. Ignoring the
negligible change a purge would have effected in party alignments, he preferred to mask defeats incurred in a divided
Republican legislature behind a screen of abuse for those
who had allowed a "disloyal" assembly to organize.

The key to Bullock's strategy—and to his policies during
the next two years—appeared in a speech delivered at the
governor's old home in Albion, New York, in October of
1868. "The body of legislators," Bullock grumbled, "were
permitted to *decide for themselves* that they were all eligible,
and their decision was accepted by the commanding officer.
. . . While the popular vote was in favor of the Reconstruction Acts, the seating of ineligible members gives an opposite
political complexion to the Legislature."[27]

Despite Bullock's fears, Republicans in July succeeded in
electing their candidates for officers in both the senate and
the house. The choice of Benjamin Conley as senate president surprised no one. Though he had occasionally voted
with the Moderates in the constitutional convention, Conley
was considered the most prominent of the white Radicals in
the senate, and he had served a faithful apprenticeship in
the Augusta Ring. The choice of R. L. McWhorter as speaker
of the house was less expected. McWhorter, a delegate from
Greene County, was studiously noncommittal in his political

[27] Rufus B. Bullock, *Have the Reconstruction Acts been fully Executed
in Georgia?* (Washington: Chronicle Printing Co. [1868]), 3.

pronouncements; at various times, he was claimed by Radicals, by Moderate Republicans, and even by Moderate Democrats. He had never consorted openly with the Augusta Ring, and his candidacy represented a sop to Moderate Republicans on whose votes the election of a Republican speaker would depend. Roll call votes for speaker went unrecorded, but it appears that McWhorter won election only by chance. Several Moderates opposed him, and, after McWhorter had squeaked to victory by the margin of a single vote, a Moderate Republican—himself a minor candidate for the office—asked permission to change his ballot. He didn't favor McWhorter, he explained; he had voted for him only on the understanding that McWhorter would vote for him.[28] Certainly Bullock and the leaders of the Radical faction could find little solace in this narrow and isolated Republican success.

Nor could Radical leaders find more than fleeting encouragement in the ratification of the Fourteenth Amendment. Ratification was one of the conditions for readmission to the Union imposed by the Omnibus Bill. The old pleas from Democratic papers that military rule would prove preferable to life under the Fourteenth Amendment now carried little weight with a people thoroughly sated with military government and convinced that they had an excellent chance of defeating Radical proposals in the legislature. Acceptance of the amendment by both houses on July 21 was nearly unanimous.[29] Moderate Republicans united with Radicals, and Democrats voted with Republicans. In no sense could this vote alone be considered a test of party strength.

The election of state officers also failed to provide a clear indication of party and factional alignments. Republicans on August 6 elected their entire slate of candidates: Farrow

[28] *Journal of the House of Representatives*, 1868, p. 12.
[29] *Ibid.*, 49–51; *Journal of the Senate*, 1868, pp. 44–46.

as attorney general, Nedom L. Angier as treasurer, Madison
Bell as comptroller general, David B. Cotting as secretary
of state, and Samuel Bard as state printer. Farrow had allied
himself with the Radicals, and Bard favored many of Bullock's legislative proposals, even though he disagreed with
the governor's plans for forming a permanent Republican
coalition in Georgia. But Angier, Bell, and Cotting had long
opposed the Augusta Ring. Moderates supported Bard and
Farrow as the price for the other posts they had won in the
pre-election bargaining, and Radicals dependent on Moderate votes to secure election of any Republican officers and
the enactment of Republican-sponsored legislation felt bound
to support the Moderate nominees. Furthermore, the Atlanta *Constitution* reported in ill-concealed disgust, thirteen
Democrats were absent from the General Assembly and
failed to vote for state officers.[30]

Bullock's inability to control his party became abundantly
clear during the elections for United States Senator held on
July 28. His efforts to ensure the choice of Blodgett and
Brown aroused fresh resentment among dissident Republicans and among Democrats who hated Blodgett but now
feared Brown more than any other man in Georgia. Senators
were chosen by joint ballot of the two houses—and on a joint
ballot, a united Republican party would have a clear majority. Having little hope of electing a member of their own
party, therefore, Democrats seeking to defeat both Brown
and Blodgett united with some Republicans to support
Joshua Hill and Dr. H. V. M. Miller.

Blodgett had little personal following outside the Augusta
Ring and the Radical faction. He received no support in
either the house or senate from any but the staunchest Radicals, and his loss to Miller by a vote of 120–72 was swift and
sure.

[30] Atlanta *Constitution*, August 7, 1868.

Defeating Brown proved more difficult.[31] His personal following remained strong, and, although the old Unionist Joshua Hill was carefully selected as the candidate best able to challenge Brown on his home ground, the war governor garnered substantial support from North Georgia legislators. On the early ballots, Alexander H. Stephens, the candidate of the Democrats who had rejected compromise with the Republicans, led Brown, with Hill running a poor third.[32] It became apparent, however, that neither Brown nor Stephens could win. Just before a viva-voce vote of the two combined houses, therefore, managers for Stephens and Hill conferred. Both sides agreed; Brown must be defeated. Stephens' managers swung their candidate's support to Hill, and a few delegates who had supported Brown in the early balloting agreed to cross over. When the final results were tallied, Brown as well as Blodgett had lost by a substantial margin. He received only ninety-four votes. The combined support of dissident Republicans and Democrats gave Hill a majority of sixteen.[33]

All recognized the importance of the Radical defeat. While Republicans maintained a stunned silence, the Democrats gloated over their triumph. Robert Toombs rejoiced to Stephens that beating Brown was "about worth the State."[34] An Atlanta merchant, a Democrat, exulted to Andrew Johnson, "I wish I could see you for an hour to rejoice with you over yesterdays [sic] work here. Radicalism is done for in Geor-

[31] *Journal of the House of Representatives*, 1868, pp. 100–106.
[32] Stephens, apparently, did not seek the Senatorship.
[33] *Journal of the House of Representatives*, 1868, pp. 100–106.
[34] Toombs to Stephens, August 9, 1868, in Phillips (ed.), *Toombs, Stephens, Cobb Correspondence*, 703; the original is in the Alexander Stephens Papers, Emory University. Toombs hated Joshua Hill. He had done his "utmost to elect him"; now he asked of Hill "no other favour" than not to join the Democrats or speak to Toombs.

gia."[35] And in North Georgia the Dawson *Journal* happily bade Brown farewell:

> Georgia Rejoicing!
> Good Times Coming!
> Joe Brown Gone
> To the Devil We Hope![36]

"Let the people of Georgia," the *Journal* added, "thank God for their deliverance." That Brown had often opposed Bullock little concerned those who voted against him or those who cheered his defeat. He was Bullock's candidate; nothing else mattered.

Bullock's defeat in the senatorial contests failed to bring the collapse of the Radical faction and the "deliverance" longed for by the Democratic press. Instead, Bullock and the Radicals during the late summer won several major victories.

The United States Congress had disallowed the relief clause of the Georgia constitution when it readmitted Georgia under the Omnibus Bill, but Bullock in his inaugural message called attention to "the pressing necessity for granting all the relief to the people" possible. Apparently, Bullock and his supporters hoped that a relief measure which scaled down debts but did not cancel them altogether would prove acceptable to the state and federal supreme courts. Lest any Republican forget the platform on which he had won election, Bullock reminded the legislators that "the just expectation of the people . . . is sufficiently well known . . . to make it unnecessary for me to present arguments in their favor."[37]

Action on Bullock's demands for relief legislation came

[35] W. M. Lowry to Andrew Johnson, July 30, 1868, in Andrew Johnson Papers.

[36] Dawson *Journal*, August 6, 1868.

[37] *Journal of the House of Representatives*, July 24, 1868, p. 66.

swiftly. On August 1, with only a few Moderate Republicans voting no, the house concurred in a senate resolution suspending all levies and sales of debtor property until the legislature could take final action on relief. On September 5 the senate passed a relief measure which had been hammered out in sessions of a joint committee. Finally, on September 18, the house also passed the measure.[38] The bill's sponsors believed that it could withstand the scrutiny of those who had held the relief clause of the state constitution a violation of the sanctity of contracts. By the terms of the new legislation, debts would not be cancelled altogether; rather, they would be settled by compromise. All obligations incurred after June 1, 1865, were considered binding, but juries in courts of equity would adjust the terms of contracts made before June 1, 1865.

The leaders of the anti-relief coalition in the constitutional convention, Amos T. Akerman and Nedom Angier, had not sought General Assembly seats; and, lacking leadership, the anti-relief alliance had drifted apart. The April elections, furthermore, had shown the power of the relief issue. Republicans could no longer ignore it with impunity, and Democrats who saw North Georgia slipping from their party's grasp dared not ignore it either. Bullock's final victory on relief, coming after all hopes of an effective Republican majority in the house had been dashed by the expulsion of Negro members, resulted from an alliance of expediency forged for the occasion by Radicals, most Republican Moderates, and a few fearful Democrats.

Strangely enough, the governor refused to sign the bill whose passage he had so strongly urged. Perhaps he feared Congressional displeasure, for the opponents of relief in Georgia had contended that the provisions for the adjust-

[38] *Ibid.*, August 1, 1868, p. 121; August 5, 1868, p. 134; 368–70. For Senate passage, see *Journal of the Senate*, 1868, p. 233.

ment of debts violated the sanctity of contracts as surely as
had the original relief clause of the state constitution. Bullock made no public announcement about the relief legislation; he simply allowed the bill to become law without his
signature on October 6.

An alliance similar to that which resulted in the adoption
of the relief law made possible the enactment of homestead
exemption legislation in September. The constitution directed the General Assembly to indicate the proper means of
assessing property and adjudicating claims under the homestead exemption clause, and Bullock had called for such
legislation in his inaugural address. The perfunctory discussions which took place in the senate and the house failed
to arouse the emotions so evident in the convention debates
the previous winter. Indeed, several members of the house
now declared their preference for homestead exemptions
over relief legislation.[39] The bill as it was finally adopted allowed a homestead exemption of $2,000 in real estate and
$1,000 in personal property. All who claimed exemptions
would list their property, and the land would be surveyed
and the property inspected by the county ordinary. Should
creditors complain of fraudulent claims, boards of appraisers
would investigate the case.[40] The enactment of so liberal a
homestead exemption statute, coming soon after the adoption of the new relief law, marked a major step toward the
achievement of the Radicals' economic program. More important, it seemed likely to weld North Georgia more firmly
than ever to the Republican party.

Equally important were Republican successes in securing
state aid for railroads. Bipartisan support for railroad promotion schemes was in itself scarcely surprising; state aid to

[39] Henri H. Freeman, "Some Aspects of Debtor Relief in Georgia during
Reconstruction" (M.A. thesis, Emory University, 1951), 49.

[40] *Acts and Resolutions of the State of Georgia,* 1868, pp. 27–30.

developing transportation networks had been an accepted policy of both Whig and Democratic regimes in antebellum days.[41] To Georgia Radicals depending on support from the state's small but influential group of industrial promoters and merchants, however, identification of their party as the friend of the businessman seemed all-important. Yet Republicans knew that grants of new corporation charters required a two-thirds majority in the General Assembly and that Democratic votes would be indispensable to the passage of any Republican-sponsored measure. While portraying their party as the ally of Georgia's business interests, therefore, the Republicans had to avoid alienating Democratic members of the legislature. So effective was the Republican strategy that, even when state aid grants became excessive and Republicans were branded with the mark of favoritism and corruption, Democrats who had consistently supported the Republican schemes went free.

The means used by Georgia Republicans in the summer and fall of 1868 to obtain Democratic support for the passage of railroad bills were the timeworn tactics of legislative maneuvering. Almost certainly not employed at this time were such devices as the granting of liberal terms to new corporations founded by prominent Democrats, the placing of Democratic lawyers on liberal retainer fees, and ill-concealed bribery—all of which would eventually form part of the Radical arsenal. Instead, probably, there occurred within the General Assembly considerable logrolling, as legislators quietly agreed to permit the passage of bills of special interest to limited areas of the state. The Air Line bill, which became law on September 21,[42] had been an issue in the

[41] The best study of internal improvements in Georgia before 1860 is Milton S. Heath, *Constructive Liberalism: The Role of the State in Economic Development in Georgia to 1860* (Cambridge: Harvard University Press, 1954).

[42] *Acts and Resolutions*, 1868, Title XVII, No. 109, pp. 143–45.

campaign and was popular throughout Georgia, but other bills had apparently only local support. Yet proposals to grant state aid to the South Georgia & Florida and the Macon & Augusta Railroads passed easily, with Moderate and Radical Republicans combining with Democrats on the roll call votes.[43]

More important for the Radicals than the state aid bills was the defeat in the senate of a proposal to alter the corporate structure of the state-owned Western & Atlantic Railroad. The party which controlled the state administration traditionally appointed the superintendent and hundreds of clerks and subordinate officials of the road. Democrats, however, now planned to remove the Western & Atlantic's vast patronage beyond Bullock's grasp. In this case, the vote was distinctly partisan; only two Democratic senators sided with Bullock, and the governor once again faced substantial defections within his own party.[44] The victory was, nevertheless, regarded by the Radicals as a significant one; their ability to hold the line in the senate perhaps discouraged Democrats from advancing a similar measure in the house.[45]

Bullock's victories, however, diminished in relative importance before the extraordinary event which took place in September. In the constitutional convention of the previous winter, the clause guaranteeing the freedmen's right to hold

[43] Bullock feared that he would be unable to control the legislature even on railroad bills. In November, 1868, when some question arose about the terms of the grant to the Macon & Augusta road, Bullock wrote that he hoped the matter would not again be referred to the legislature; if it were, the road might "fare worse." Bullock to Col.[?] Hazlehurst, November 21, 1868, in Rufus B. Bullock Papers, Georgia Department of Archives and History. The usual terms of state aid bills included a grant of $10,000 for each mile already completed, and an additional $10,000 for every ten miles of new construction. Other state aid bills passed during the session of 1868 appear in the *Acts and Resolutions,* Title XVII.

[44] Five Republicans either abstained or voted against Bullock.

[45] J. R. Parrott to Bullock, Cartersville, September 30, 1868, in J. R. Parrott Papers, Georgia Department of Archives and History.

office had been stricken from the constitution. Negro convention delegates, presumably assured of Radical sustenance, had themselves voted with the majority. Accused at the time of inducing the Republican party to desert the Negro, Joseph E. Brown had seemingly affirmed the truth of the Democratic charges by his Marietta Speech during the 1868 gubernatorial campaign. When the legislature convened in July, a move to unseat the three Negro senators and twenty-nine Negro representatives seemed inevitable.

The attack on the Negro members was not long in coming. As soon as the General Assembly had formally organized, Democratic Senator Milton A. Candler flung Brown's campaign oratory back in the Radicals' faces. In justifying his resolution that the Committee on Privileges and Elections be directed to investigate the eligibility of Negro senators, Candler craftily pointed out that "Ex Governor Joseph E. Brown one of the ablest Lawyers in the Republican party of Georgia, as well as other persons distinguished for their knowledge of Constitutional Law, held during the late election Canvass, that persons of color were not entitled to hold office under the existing Constitution."[46]

In part, the Candler resolution served as a test of sentiment on the Negro question; Democrats expected the defeat it sustained on July 25.[47] Yet in invoking Brown's name and appealing to the long nurtured prejudices of the yeoman whites, the resolution was carefully calculated to loosen the ties that increasingly bound North Georgia to the Republican party. Only three Negroes held senate seats; purging them would not gain for the Democracy control of the upper house. Democratic strategists knew this. Their objective in

[46] Draft copy of Candler's resolution, in unidentified handwriting, in Joseph E. Brown Papers, Georgia Department of Archives and History.

[47] *Journal of the Senate,* July 25, 1868.

July, however, was to breed disorganization and demoralization within Republican ranks.

When Candler's resolution came to a test on July 25, it was tabled by a strict party vote, 21–14. Two of the Negroes absented themselves from the senate chamber, perhaps to avoid sitting as judges in their own case. The other four Republicans who voted with the Democrats or failed to vote were, as Democrats had hoped, Moderates who represented North Georgia constituencies.

The break in the Republican ranks was not yet complete in July, however, and with the defeat of the Candler resolution Democrats turned their attention to other matters. Not until August did the eligibility question again confront the legislature. On August 6, a minority report of a house committee declared mulatto Representative F. H. Fyall of Macon ineligible. C. C. Duncan, a Democrat, at once moved that all Negroes be declared ineligible, and, although the names of four mulatto delegates were later stricken from his list, Duncan's resolution passed the house as a substitute for the minority report. The question carried over into September, but a ruling by Speaker of the House McWhorter that Negro members could not vote on the question of their own eligibility made the outcome inevitable. On September 3, the House voted 83–23 to expel the Negro delegates.[48]

After McWhorter's ruling had made the expulsion of the Negroes a certainty, Moderates and especially North Georgia representatives found themselves free to vote their own

[48] *Journal of the House of Representatives,* 1868, pp. 220–24, 229, 242–43. Hearsay evidence suggests that the names of the mulattoes were stricken because they were so nearly white that no one could prove they were Negroes. Among those voting to expel the Negroes or abstaining were three delegates who sided with the Radicals on every other roll call test analyzed. Nineteen others who voted against the freedmen or abstained had allied with the Radicals on all except one other test vote. Of the twenty-three delegates who voted to sustain the Negroes' right to office, one was a Moderate Republican.

convictions or those of their constituents with impunity. Several abstained; others voted with the Democracy. In all, forty-six Republicans implicitly or openly sustained the expulsion from the General Assembly of members of their own party.

In the senate, the procedure paralleled that of the house. The eligibility question arose anew on September 7 and was debated until the sixteenth. On that day, the senate declared Tunis G. Campbell and George Wallace "not eligible to office by the Constitution and laws of Georgia nor by the Constitution and laws of the United States."[49] In the Senate, the final vote of 24–11 represented a Democratic gain of ten votes and a Radical loss of ten as compared with the July roll call on Candler's resolution.[50] Five Democrats who failed to vote on the Candler motion voted in September, and the Democrats had gained a sixth vote when Rufus E. Lester was seated after the expulsion of Negro Senator Aaron Alpeoria Bradley on August 13. The other four votes which made up the Democratic majority came from three Moderates, J. Griffin, M. C. Smith, and W. C. Smith, and from a fourth senator, J. C. Richardson, who represented the North Georgia counties of White, Dawson, and Lumpkin. Seven other Republicans—all members of the Moderate faction or North Georgia delegates who on other issues had allied with the Radicals—refused to vote.

In the house, then, a decision by a Republican speaker had sealed the Negroes' doom; in the senate, defections from the Republican ranks had played a major role. Radical strategy in the spring elections had turned against the Republican party; though the freedmen's natural allegiance was to the Republican cause, Radical leaders would find it increasingly

[49] *Journal of the Senate*, 1868, pp. 243–44, 273, 277–78. A. A. Bradley, the third Negro Senator, had already been expelled because of his criminal record in the State of New York.

[50] Thompson, *Reconstruction in Georgia*, 213.

difficult in subsequent campaigns to convince the Negro
that his interests had not been sacrificed.

Democrats rejoiced in the success of their maneuvers, and
they prepared to take advantage of their new majority in the
house of representatives.[51] In response to a request that he
submit to the assembly the names of those who had received
the next highest vote for the seats formerly held by Negroes,
in order that these men—all Democrats—could be seated,
Bullock issued a "respectful" but vituperative objection to
the purge. "No, gentlemen!" he expostulated, "the framers
of the Constitution made no distinction between electors or
citizens on account of race or color, and neither can you."
But the house, now firmly under Democratic control, cen-
sured Bullock for his remarks and refused to receive any
part of his message except that giving the names of the
Democratic claimants.[52] In both the house and senate,
Democrats took the places of the expelled Negroes. Even
had they wanted to prevent the seating of these Democrats,
Radical leaders could not have done so.

Stung by their defeat, the Negro legislators offered a protest to the house of representatives. Under the leadership of
Henry M. Turner, they then met in an all-Negro convention
at Macon on October 6. One hundred thirty-six delegates
from eighty-two counties joined in condemning the actions
of the Democrats and of those Republicans who had deserted
the freedmen in the General Assembly.[53] Seemingly, a major
breach between the Negroes and the white Republicans had
opened. But the formation of Negro Civil and Political Rights
Associations throughout Georgia never led to the organiza-

[51] Dawson *Journal*, September 10, 1868; Augusta *Chronicle and Sentinel*,
September 11, 1868; Augusta *Constitutionalist*, August 28, 1868.

[52] *Journal of the House of Representatives*, September 9, 1868, p. 301,
303. The vote was 71–32.

[53] The most accessible account of the Negro convention appears in
Coulter, *Georgia Historical Quarterly*, XLVIII (December, 1964), 385.

tion of a separate Negro political party. Negro leaders like Turner knew that Radical strategists, still dependent on Negro votes, would be forced to grant the freedmen patronage and other concessions which an independent Negro party could not claim. They had no natural ties to the Democracy, and remaining within the Republican fold promised them much. Almost certainly, a Republican administration would take control of the national government in March, 1869, and it would support and strengthen the Bullock regime in Georgia. As the 1868 election returns would prove, the freedmen's allegiance to Radicalism was severely shaken by the expulsion of the Negro legislators, but the majority of Negroes still remained within the Republican party.

Democrats whispered that Bullock had allowed the expulsion of the Negro legislators.[54] There is no direct proof that he did so. That twenty-two white Radicals in the house and three in the senate abstained from voting on the expulsion issue, however, seems more than a mere coincidence. Certainly Bullock did nothing to halt the march of events in either the house or senate. Whether or not he agreed to the purge, the expulsion of the Negroes—the culmination of his other difficulties with his legislature—became for the Radical governor a most convenient "outrage." Having failed in his early attempt to delay the organization of the General Assembly, having secured the organization of the legislature for the Republicans and the election of minor state officials by only a narrow margin, unable to control substantial elements of his own party, and unable even to fulfill the most important of his pre-election patronage commitments, Bullock by September seemed in a most unenviable position.

Whether Bullock sanctioned the expulsion of the Negroes or not, he maneuvered quickly and adroitly to capitalize on Northern outrage at the event. His actions and policies

[54] Macon *Georgia Journal and Messenger*, September 8, 1868.

during the next two years were his response to the bitter
experiences of his first two months in office; their object was
to guarantee by outside support the Radical ascendency in
Georgia which state leaders had proved unable to maintain
on their own. Of more immediate importance to the governor, however, was the necessity of uniting his party and his
state behind the presidential candidacy of General Ulysses
S. Grant.

CHAPTER VI

Inevitable Defeat

Rufus Bullock's troubles with his party and his legislature coincided with others which the Republicans faced in their efforts to carry the state for Ulysses S. Grant and Schuyler Colfax. Their short-sighted strategy for dealing with the question of Negro officeholding in the April elections added to Bullock's difficulties, as did their seeming desertion of the Negro in the legislature. And the governor's efforts to delay the organization of the General Assembly and his attempts to control the election of United States Senators in July further created popular distaste.

The campaign began auspiciously enough. The convention which nominated Bullock for governor in March also expressed the hope that Grant would lead the national ticket in November; some weeks later, the State Executive Committee instructed its delegates to the national convention, which would meet at Chicago in May, to back Grant. By

June 25, shortly after Grant's nomination, the *New Era* reported the organization of a Central Grant Club of Georgia, with Foster Blodgett as its chairman, but with officers drawn from among Moderate as well as Radical Republicans.[1]

The hierarchy of the Georgia Republican party during the presidential contest functioned more efficiently than ever before, and the party developed new and closer ties with the Union Republican Executive Committee in Washington. In financing the campaign, the Georgia party drew heavily on the resources of the national organization. Though Blodgett directed each Congressional district to provide $1,000 for the state treasury, party coffers in Georgia were nearly empty, exhausted by the demands of the April elections.[2] The Republicans, therefore, repeatedly pressed for aid from Washington—for the money and documents which the Georgia party could not itself provide. In August, John H. Caldwell, the former Methodist missionary now serving on the State Executive Committee, suggested that the national committee contribute between $2,000 and $3,000 to each Georgia Congressional district, and, a month later, Blodgett urged that the national organization at least match the funds contributed by the state's Republicans.[3] The Union Republican Executive Committee never provided all that the Georgia leaders asked,[4] but, throughout the summer and fall, the national party did give substantial support to its Georgia

[1] Atlanta *New Era*, June 25, 1868.

[2] Circular enclosed in John H. Caldwell to William Claflin, July 4, 1868, in Chandler Papers.

[3] John H. Caldwell to William E. Chandler, August 19, 1868, and Foster Blodgett to John T. Johnson, September 11, 1868, *ibid*.

[4] See, for example, James Atkins to William E. Chandler, August 12, 1868, and C. W. Arnold to Horace Greeley, September 19, 1868, *ibid*. Atkins, refusing a request from the national committee that he contribute $100 to the Grant and Colfax campaign fund, pleaded that, with the Georgia campaign treasury exhausted, he had himself been obliged to finance a mass meeting in support of the state and national tickets.

organization. Early in September, Blodgett thanked the national committee for "fifty Grant and Colfax Club books, and . . . six thousand badges," and, at the end of the month, Caldwell acknowledged the receipt of $1,500.[5] On October 27, the national executive committee approved spending $5,000 in Georgia.[6]

The campaign, then, seemed on the surface well organized and well supported—and likely to proceed smoothly. All minor considerations and factional disputes must bow, the *New Era* proclaimed on July 14, before the task of electing Grant and Colfax in November.[7]

The shrewdest of the Republican politicians, however, readily perceived the dangers to their party in Georgia. Declining an invitation from the national Executive Committee to tour the North, Joseph E. Brown pleaded the greater need of the party in his own state. "Could not the Committee send us some speakers, [who know] the character of our people and who could be of service here?" he begged. "We need help very much. We have but three presses in the State. . . . We therefore have to reach people by pamphlets and documents, which must be prepared [to be] sent [to] our people here. Can we expect any . . . aid?"[8]

The difficulties of which Brown spoke were only the most minor to plague the Georgia Republicans during the summer and early fall. A more pressing problem was the new division within the state organization itself. No longer did Republicans publicly divide only along the old, familiar lines of Radicals and Moderates, and no longer did threats of

[5] Blodgett to John T. Johnson, September 11, 1868, and Caldwell to William E. Chandler, September 30, 1868, *ibid.*

[6] Leon Burn Richardson, *William E. Chandler, Republican* (New York: Dodd, Mead & Company, 1940), 113.

[7] Atlanta *New Era*, July 14, 1868.

[8] Brown to Thomas L. Tullock, June 29, 1868, in Chandler Papers.

retaliation by the governor suffice to keep dissidents in line. The Radical faction itself began splintering dangerously.

When Bullock had made his major patronage commitments soon after his nomination in March, 1868, two prominent Radicals, John E. Bryant and John H. Caldwell, had inexplicably failed to receive a share of the booty. Disgruntled, possessing a measure of independent power, and held by no special obligations to Bullock, Bryant and Caldwell retaliated for the slight by rebelling against Bullock's choice of Blodgett for one of Georgia's two Senate seats. The Republican state chairman, Bryant explained to national party secretary William E. Chandler, was a *"very bad* man." Blodgett had "done almost nothing to build up the Republican party in Georgia"; the real work of organization had fallen to others. Calling Blodgett "a *drunkard* and a *liar*," Bryant insisted that Blodgett had received the senatorial nomination at a caucus attended by only 89 of the 113 Republican members of the house and senate.[9]

Blodgett's defeat in the Senate contest, his consequent loss of prestige, and Bryant and Caldwell's rebellion combined to work a revolution within the Radical hierarchy. Bullock did not desert Blodgett; he promised his trusted lieutenant the lucrative superintendency of the Western & Atlantic Railroad.[10] The governor, however, offered no opposition when dissident Radicals staged a coup within the State Executive Committee. In mid-August, Blodgett reluctantly relinquished the chairmanship to Bryant.[11] The reorgani-

[9] Bryant to [William E. Chandler], October 5, 1868, *ibid.* There is no evidence to support Bryant's charge that Blodgett was an alcoholic.

[10] Blodgett could not, however, receive the Western & Atlantic post immediately, for Ed. Hulburt had only recently been appointed superintendent, in recognition of his faithful service as election manager in the April contests.

[11] John H. Caldwell to William E. Chandler, August 19, 1868, in Chandler Papers. Caldwell reported that the reorganization had rid the party of "all discouraging and hurtful elements."

zation of the state committee came relatively late in the campaign, and it widened rather than healed the split in the Radical faction. It did, however, stave off what might have been serious defections in the November elections.

Of greatest concern to Georgia's Republicans was the problem of effectively controlling the Negro vote. Radical leaders blamed the party's failure to sweep the predominantly Negro counties of southwest Georgia in April on the section's remoteness from military posts and on the fact that Republicans there had "no organization, no efficient canvassers, [and] no men of influence" on their side. But the defeat in the southwest had demonstrated that the Democrats could influence, in various ways, many blacks to go with them. The presence of United States troops in the area was essential to prevent fraud and violence. Should the troops be withdrawn, the state could organize no adequate militia to protect the freedmen at the polls, and the inevitable intimidation and violence would result in another Republican defeat.[12]

The underlying problem was that many Republicans feared the consequences of their seeming desertion of the freedmen. Although the Radicals had earlier concluded that the Negroes would automatically vote the Republican ticket rather than join the Democracy, the spring elections had taught them otherwise. Furthermore, their contradictory statements on the eligibility issue had long since been exposed and Republicans had acquiesced in the expulsion of Negro delegates from the General Assembly. The consistent Democratic plea that the former slaveholders were the Negroes' best friends might, when coupled with threats of economic sanctions, draw many freedmen away from the Republican camp. So, too, for different reasons, might the activities of

[12] John H. Caldwell to William Claflin, July 4, 1868, *ibid.*

the Ku Klux Klan, whose midnight rides and terrorism struck fear into Negroes and whites alike.[13]

Even if Republicans managed to retain their control over the Negro vote, they faced problems in holding a firm grip on the former Democrats of North Georgia. The appointment of Joseph E. Brown as chief justice of the Georgia supreme court after his defeat in the Senate contest had satisfied Bullock's obligations to the former governor, but at a heavy cost. For the appointment removed from the campaign trail one of the Republican party's most effective propagandists.[14] North Georgia had secured its desired relief and homestead measures, but as yet the free schools promised by Radical campaigners had failed to materialize. Unable again to capitalize on Brown's personal popularity in North Georgia, Republicans feared substantial defections from their party in that section.

Before the expulsion of the Negro members, when Republicans still controlled the General Assembly on a joint ballot, some party leaders wistfully suggested allowing the house and senate to choose presidential electors. Such a course, they believed, would avoid the necessity for a party convention and perhaps prevent the airing of Republican squabbles which could best be settled within the party

[13] On the activities of the Klan, see Volney Spalding to William E. Chandler, September 1, 1868, and Joseph E. Brown to Chandler, October 8, 1868, *ibid.*; the testimony of the Rev. Thomas M. Allen, a Negro, in *Ku Klux Conspiracy,* VII, 609; Stearns, *Black Man of the South,* 233, 247; and a proclamation issued by Governor Bullock, Atlanta, September 14, 1868, in Rufus B. Bullock Papers, Georgia Department of Archives and History.

[14] Volney Spalding to William E. Chandler, August 6, August 14, 1868, in Chandler Papers. It is, of course, possible that Bullock recognized in Brown a potential challenger for control of the Republican party and hoped by appointing him chief justice to remove him from the political arena. I have, however, found no evidence to suggest that Bullock entertained such thoughts, and there seem other, more pressing, reasons for granting Brown the appointment.

committee.[15] The national organization rejected the plan, however, and on August 4 the Republican state convention met at Atlanta to choose an electoral ticket.[16] Of the nine electors selected, only four—Akerman, Bryant, Farrow, and Dunning—could be called prominent Republicans.[17] Clearly, the choices reflected the dissensions which before the reorganization of the state committee threatened to wreck the party. Akerman and Bryant were the choice of the Moderates and the rebellious Radicals; Farrow, the state attorney general, and Dunning represented the Bullock forces.

Though Republican campaigners held the usual number of county meetings, organized the customary county committees, sponsored statewide "Grant Clubs," and made properly partisan speeches, the air of defeat hung over all their efforts. Caught in a trap of their own making, and not wishing openly to advocate what many now urged privately— the remanding of Georgia to military rule—Republican leaders waged a half-hearted campaign. The watchword remained "unity," but the party appeared thoroughly demoralized. Not even the *New Era*, once a strong supporter of Bullock but now allied with the rebellious Radicals, could muster any enthusiasm for the fall campaign.[18] Georgia Republicans mouthed the old slogans of debtor relief, railroad promotion and state aid, support for the Negro, and, above

[15] John H. Caldwell to William E. Chandler, August 7, 1868, *ibid.*
[16] Caldwell to William Claflin, July 14, 1868, *ibid.*
[17] A list of Republican electors appears in the Henry P. Farrow Collection, University of Georgia, and more conveniently in Shadgett, *Republican Party in Georgia*, Appendix B, 164–65.
[18] The *New Era's* editor, Samuel Bard, remained strangely silent throughout the campaign. A sampling of editorials taken from every third edition of the *New Era* indicates that, in a majority of the issues, Bard failed editorially to mention the campaign at all. The other major Republican papers published in Georgia during the fall of 1868, the Augusta *Republican* and J. Clarke Swayze's *American Union*, were unavailable to me.

all, Grant's pledge that a Republican ballot in November would be a vote for peace and prosperity. But the campaign clichés no longer seemed to stir even the party faithful.[19]

Privately, state leaders confessed to the national committee their premonitions of defeat.[20] They ignored their own strategic mistakes and apparently believed that, by professing themselves to be firm advocates of the Negro's right to office, they could counteract the effects of Brown's Marietta Speech and the expulsion of the freedmen from the General Assembly.[21] Disaster would come to the Republican party in Georgia, they predicted, but it would arise from the Klan outrages and other Democratic attempts at fraud and intimidation.

The Democrats seemed little more optimistic than did the Republicans. As divided in defeat as they had been in April when victory seemed within reach, and campaigning without assistance from their party's national organization, Democrats continued to debate among themselves the merits of strong opposition to the execution of the Congressional Reconstruction Acts.[22] Though the party leaders publicly predicted overwhelming victory in November, their private correspondence betrayed their fears.[23] Even the knowledge that Congressional Republican strategists had "despaired of Georgia" and were "preparing to reject her vote in the Presidential election" failed to encourage the Democratic leaders.

[19] This statement is based on an admittedly limited number of campaign editorials which appeared in the *New Era* between August 1, 1868, and the November election.

[20] Volney Spalding to William E. Chandler, September 1, 1868, and Foster Blodgett to [Chandler], September 6, 1868, in Chandler Papers.

[21] John E. Bryant to William E. Chandler, October 5, 1868, *ibid.*

[22] Atlanta *Constitution,* October 30, 1868.

[23] See, for example, Herschel V. Johnson to Alexander H. Stephens, October 8, 1868, in Alexander Stephens Papers, Library of Congress.

The party, Linton Stephens mourned, was too "dispirited" to take proper advantage of Republican difficulties.[24]

Once again, dissensions within the party stemmed from differences over the proper kind and tone of opposition to Republican rule. Benjamin Hill had now determined to fight Congressional Reconstruction with every means at his command, and by the fall of 1868 he and Robert Toombs constituted the nucleus of a small group of extremists—men who condemned scalawags and carpetbaggers as *"white negroes,"* who denounced Republican government in all its forms, and who would willingly support its overthrow by virtually any method short of direct violence.[25] Although no Democratic leader seriously advocated the terrorism of the Ku Klux Klan, Georgians knew well that the Klan's state-wide organizer, Dudley M. DuBose, was a son-in-law of Toombs, and they generally agreed that the Grand Dragon for Georgia was the Democratic candidate for governor in the spring elections, General John Brown Gordon.[26] In a speech at Elberton, Toombs himself, reportedly drunk at the time, exhorted his listeners to "clean up their muskets, rifles and *shot* guns to shoot Yankees and negroes." Some Georgians, a horrified Democrat feared, were "just big enough

[24] Linton Stephens to Alexander H. Stephens, September 25, 1868, in Alexander Stephens Papers, Manhattanville College of the Sacred Heart.

[25] William H. Hidell to Alexander H. Stephens, August 22, 1868, in Alexander Stephens Papers, Library of Congress; Benjamin H. Hill's speech at the "Bush Arbor" meeting, Atlanta, July 23, 1868, reported in the Atlanta *Constitution*, July 24, 1868, and included in a flyer in the Benjamin H. Hill Papers, Georgia Department of Archives and History.

[26] Gordon's testimony, in *Ku Klux Conspiracy*, VI, 304ff, and especially 341. The General acknowledged that others had suggested his connection with the Klan, but he denied the charges in testimony which is singularly unconvincing. Gordon's most recent biographer takes no clear position on the issue of Gordon's Klan activities. See Allen P. Tankersley, *John B. Gordon: A Study in Gallantry* (Atlanta: The Whitehall Press, 1955), 248–49.

fools to imagine *they* [could] *of themselves be an army and wage successful war.*"[27]

What Hill and Toombs promised often seemed peaceable enough. The consequences of Democratic victory they described in idyllic terms: "Confidence will return, harmony between the races will be restored, war and strife will then certainly be avoided; capital and a better class of immigrants will then come among us from the North; business will revive, the price of our property will enhance, and we can afford to increase *the wages* of labor."[28] Again, Democrats invited the freedmen to barbecues and meetings, and Hill himself was ready to promise 50 percent higher wages to his Negro employees in 1869 should the Democratic presidential and vice-presidential candidates, Horatio Seymour and Francis P. Blair, be elected.[29]

But the other side of the Democratic extremists' oratory received more publicity, and many prominent party members objected strongly to the vituperation of Hill's attacks on the Bullock regime.[30] "Why should we use the weapons of abuse," queried Herschel Johnson, "when argument and facts are all on our side?"[31] Johnson's hopes that Democrats would prove "mild, but firm: powerful, in argument, but courteous to our oppressors" had a practical object—such a course would help the national Democratic party to attract the Conservative Republican vote of the North, and would

[27] William H. Hidell to Alexander H. Stephens, August 4, 1868, in Alexander Stephens Papers, Library of Congress.

[28] See Benjamin H. Hill's public letter in Augusta *Chronicle and Sentinel,* August 25, 1868.

[29] Handbill inviting Negroes to a Democratic meeting, Washington, Ga., October 1, 1868, in Broadsides, Duke University. On Hill's promise of higher wages, see Haywood Jefferson Pearce, Jr., *Benjamin H. Hill: Secession and Reconstruction* (Chicago: University of Chicago Press, 1928), 185.

[30] See Pearce, *Benjamin H. Hill,* 181, and summaries of editorial opinion which he cites from the Columbus *Daily Sun,* July 28, 1868.

[31] Johnson to Alexander H. Stephens, August 5, 1868, in Alexander Stephens Papers, Library of Congress.

help the state organization to lure back to the Democracy
those men who had "honestly, but mistakenly, sustained the
reconstruction acts and had voted ratification of the Constitution, under the influence of its relief provisions." Hill's
"stupendous folly," his eternal "bleating," tried the patience
of Democrats like Alexander H. Stephens, Johnson, and a
former Whig Congressman and governor, Martin J. Crawford.[32] Yet nothing could induce these men, and others like
them, to publicly denounce either Hill or Toombs.[33]

Even Alexander H. Stephens, usually to be found near
the center of Democratic activities, remained secluded at
Liberty Hall, his modest Crawfordville home. In July, he
wrote for the Augusta *Chronicle and Sentinel* a series of
articles urging Georgians to accept the fact of Republican
ascendancy and to work for change only through political
channels. When some Democrats joined the Ku Klux Klan,
Stephens voiced his disapproval—but privately, to his friend
Augustus Reese.[34] So far was Stephens removed from the
mainstream of his own party's campaign, that in September
he received an invitation to speak in Atlanta signed by
thirty-nine Democrats and endorsed by Bullock, who trusted
him "to address the people [of Atlanta] in such a manner
as to promote harmony and peace within our State."[35]

Democratic editors, like the party itself, seemed once
again divided over which course to follow. None, however,
disagreed about the tasks facing the party in November.
Democrats must win a share of the Negro vote in the face
of Republican pledges to redress the freedmen's grievances,

[32] Martin J. Crawford to Alexander H. Stephens, August 4, 1868, *ibid.*
[33] The Democratic state committee took no clear stand in favor of either
position.
[34] Martin J. Crawford to Alexander H. Stephens, August 4, 1868, in
Alexander Stephens Papers, Library of Congress, reporting that he had
relayed to Reese Stephens' views about secret political organizations.
[35] Invitation, dated Atlanta, September 19, 1868, *ibid.*

and they must convince whites seduced by Radical promises of higher wages, relief, homesteads, and free schools that Democratic victory alone could bring renewed prosperity to Georgia.[36]

If the strategy of the Democratic editors seemed sensible, however, their tactics for winning the renewed loyalty of the yeoman whites and a share of the Negro vote seemed strange, indeed. Not all editorials in such papers as the *Georgia Journal and Messenger* and the *Chronicle and Sentinel* were as tactless as one addressed to the freedmen and designed to "convince" the Negroes that the Democrats were their true friends, but all had similar overtones: "Stupids, will you never learn anything? Will even experience, in the shape of practical kicks and cuffs, fail to teach you on which side your bread is *really* buttered?"[37] The Atlanta *Constitution* on October 23 lashed out at "Radical vengeance and hate";[38] the Savannah *News and Herald* proclaimed that the only choice in November would be between "Restoration" and "Despotism" and resurrected the old cry of non-actionists who in 1867 had professed infinitely to prefer military to Radical Republican rule.[39]

That the violence of Democratic campaign oratory and of much of the Democratic press would foment overt strife before election day seems, in retrospect, almost inevitable. Indeed, the Democrats anticipated riots—though of course

[36] Analysis of Democratic press opinion is based on a sample of editorials taken from every third edition of the Macon *Georgia Journal and Messenger*, the Milledgeville *Southern Recorder*, the Augusta *Constitutionalist*, the Atlanta *Constitution*, the Augusta *Chronicle and Sentinel*, and the Savannah *News and Herald* published between September 1 and election day.

[37] Macon *Georgia Journal and Messenger*, September 8, 1868. For more moderate appeals to the freedmen, see the Augusta *Constitutionalist*, October 2, October 23, 1868.

[38] Atlanta *Constitution*, October 23, 1868.

[39] Savannah *Daily News and Herald*, October 20, 1868. No prominent party spokesman, however, endorsed non-action in the fall of 1868.

they would be riots instigated by Negroes and carpetbaggers, not by stalwart and respectable Democrats.[40] The Camilla riot of September 19 was nothing more than a predictable outgrowth of the summer's campaign, an occurrence for which both sides must be held responsible.

A Republican candidate for presidential elector, John Murphy, had circulated a call for a Republican conclave at Camilla, the county seat of predominantly Negro Mitchell County, on September 19. Somehow, word spread that those who attended the rally should come armed, and on the nineteenth a group from Albany marched toward Camilla, gathering recruits from farms and towns along the way. As the crowd, headed by Murphy and Congressional candidate W. P. Pierce, approached Camilla, it consisted of "some three hundred [men], a majority carrying guns and pistols."[41]

Governor Bullock had earlier issued a proclamation forbidding armed assemblies, and Sheriff Munford Poore, accosting Murphy and Pierce at the edge of town, demanded that the group disperse.[42] But the crowd refused to scatter and pushed on toward Camilla. Poore retreated to summon a posse, but firing began when a drunken onlooker, James Johns, grappled with the leader of the band hired for the rally. During the struggle, Johns fired his own pistol. The shot—perhaps an accidental one—buried in the dirt a few feet from where Johns stood. Nobody was struck, but the marchers, panic-stricken, returned the fire. In the ensuing melee, seven Negroes were killed and several freedmen and bystanders wounded.[43]

[40] Theodore B. Fitz-Simons, Jr., "The Camilla Riot," *Georgia Historical Quarterly,* XXXV (June, 1951), 118. See also Conway, *The Reconstruction of Georgia,* 168–71.

[41] *Senate Executive Documents,* 57th Cong., 2nd Sess., No. 209, p. 126, quoted, Fitz-Simons, "The Camilla Riot," 120.

[42] A copy of Bullock's proclamation is in the Rufus B. Bullock Papers, Georgia Department of Archives and History.

[43] Fitz-Simons, "The Camilla Riot," 121–22.

Both sides sought to take political advantage of the Camilla affray. To Bullock, the disturbance was only the latest indication that without further Congressional action Georgia would remain rebellious and unreconstructed. Accordingly, the governor demanded an immediate investigation by the General Assembly, charging that Sheriff Poore had violated the right of the Negroes "peaceably to assemble" and that, as a result of the riot, no adequate protection for life or property existed in Camilla.[44] Federal troops, the governor believed, should be sent immediately to Mitchell County. Plainly, Bullock based his charges on a partisan view of the evidence. The investigating committee of the General Assembly, equally partisan but strongly Democratic, quickly reported that it found no fault with Poore's conduct. No need existed, it concluded, for federal troops.[45] Probably the most accurate observation of all came from Linton Stephens. From everything he had seen and heard about the riot, he informed his half-brother Alexander, it appeared that both sides must share the responsibility.[46] Republicans had provoked the outbreak by entering the town armed—in direct violation of a proclamation issued by their own governor. Democrats, on the other hand, had tried to disrupt the Republican rally, and it was an intoxicated Democrat who had fired the first shot.

In any other year, the Camilla riot might have passed virtually unnoticed. In itself, writes a recent student, it was nothing more than a local skirmish between ardent advocates of diametrically opposed views. But in the fall of 1688,

[44] *Journal of the Senate of the State of Georgia*, September 21, 1868, p. 353.
[45] *Ibid.*, 364–65. Meade, who still commanded troops garrisoned in Georgia, accepted the committee report and sent no troops to Camilla, although he later in the campaign sent a detachment to Albany. Fitz-Simons, "The Camilla Riot," 123.
[46] Linton Stephens to Alexander H. Stephens, September 25, 1868, in Alexander Stephens Papers, Manhattanville College of the Sacred Heart.

violence was "almost a logical . . . climax" to the ideological struggles between native white Democrats and those whom they believed the usurpers of all they had known and cherished.[47]

As election day approached, Bullock and the Republicans realized that they probably could not hold enough voters to their party to carry the state for Grant and Colfax. The only hope seemed to lie in retaining the allegiance of a solid phalanx of Negro voters, for it appeared that Democratic efforts to lure wavering North Georgia antebellum Democrats back to their party would prove at least partially successful.

Accordingly, Bullock turned to a final, desperate device to save the election for the Republicans. The 1868 constitution provided that voters must have paid all taxes due in the past year in order to participate in elections. Many Negroes had failed to pay their poll taxes, however, and they would be ineligible to vote in November. On October 20, Bullock issued an order suspending the collection of poll taxes until the next regular meeting of the General Assembly in 1869.[48] The governor's intention, and the practical effect of his proclamation, was to eliminate the payment of poll taxes as a requirement for voting in the presidential election.[49] Grateful Negroes would, presumably, flock to the polls to cast their ballots for Grant and Colfax.

Immediately, the Democratic press struck out at Bullock.

[47] Fitz-Simons, "The Camilla Riot," 116.

[48] Order that a proclamation be issued, in Rufus B. Bullock Papers, Georgia Department of Archives and History. The proclamation appears in the Executive Minutes of the State in Georgia, Georgia Department of Archives and History. The Savannah *News and Herald,* noting on October 23, 1868, that Bullock had been in New York on October 20, thought it detected Joseph E. Brown's hand behind the proclamation. There is no evidence to support this contention.

[49] J. H. Caldwell to William E. Chandler, October 26, 1868, in Chandler Papers.

The proclamation, the editors insisted, was illegal; the governor had no power to suspend the collection of taxes. Furthermore, even should the proclamation be considered lawful, it would not accomplish Bullock's purpose; it suspended the collection of taxes, but it failed to eliminate the requirement that taxes must be paid before a citizen could vote.[50]

The Democratic editors wasted their ink and their words. Bullock and the Republicans ignored the opposition's protests, and the proclamation accomplished its partisan purpose. The only qualifications for voters in November, then, were that they be citizens of the United States, residents of Georgia for six months, and residents of the county in which they intended to vote for the ten days immediately preceding the election.[51]

The last-minute confusion which Bullock fomented over voting requirements matched the confusion which persisted throughout much of the campaign about the holding of Congressional elections to choose delegates to the Forty-first Congress. Most Georgians apparently understood that the three Democratic and three Republican Congressmen elected in April, 1868, would serve for both the Fortieth and Forty-first Congresses.[52] Many expected that no Congressional elections would take place in the fall of 1868. But Democrats hoped that Bullock would intervene in favor of electing new Congressmen, and that he would urge the General Assembly to provide for Congressional balloting. The governor, however, refused to urge his legislature to early action.[53] After the expulsion of the Negroes, the legislature passed completely beyond Bullock's control, and any recommendations he could have made in September or Oc-

[50] See, for example, Augusta *Chronicle and Sentinel,* October 27, 1868.
[51] Atlanta *New Era,* October 30, 1868.
[52] Shadgett, *Republican Party in Georgia,* 17.
[53] Macon *Georgia Journal and Messenger,* October 13, 1868.

tober would have been ill-received. Probably the governor realized, too, that the fall Congressional elections would result in further Democratic gains. Although Georgia Republicans talked openly of asking Congress to reject Georgia's electoral vote and refuse to seat her Congressmen or Senators in the Forty-first Congress well before the presidential contest, Bullock undoubtedly understood the insurance value of failing to authorize elections in November. Regular elections resulting in Democratic victories would provide the governor with more "evidence" that Georgia remained unreconstructed, but they would confront Congress with the immediate necessity of finding plausible grounds on which to reject the Georgia delegates properly accredited to the new Congress.[54] By keeping the status of Georgia's Congressional elections—and, indeed, the status of Georgia's Congressmen-elect—ambiguous, Bullock hoped to leave Congress completely free to deal with Georgia when and how it saw fit.

Despite the confusion over the holding of Congressional elections, both parties early nominated Congressional candidates. In the November election, Richard Whiteley, Marion Bethune, and Jefferson Long won election as Republicans from the Second, Third, and Fourth Districts, and William W. Paine, Stephen A. Corker, W. P. Price, and Pierce M. B. Young were chosen as Democrats to represent the First, Fifth, Sixth, and Seventh Districts. So slight was the attention paid to the Congressional contests, however, that no Georgia paper or government publication printed complete election returns. Presumably, there was little split-ticket voting, and the results in the Congressional canvass paralleled those in the presidential election.

The votes for President, however, provided striking evi-

[54] The Fortieth Congress, elected in 1866, would end on March 4, 1869; the Forty-first Congress would be elected in 1868 and sit until 1871.

dence of the sharp decline in Republican strength.[55] In the gubernatorial election, the party had won just over 52 percent of the total vote; now, six months later, it could win only 32 percent. Thirty-eight counties which had given majorities to Bullock in April went Democratic in November; of these, twenty-seven showed Negro majorities on the 1867 registration rolls.[56]

In the mountain counties of North Georgia, where Brown's ability to campaign had so aided the Republicans in April, the party apparently lost strength among the white farmers disillusioned by the Bullock administration's failure to fulfill all its campaign promises.[57] Republicans continued to attract voters in counties where farms were small and the land poor, but Democrats between April and November had labored successfully to woo many of their former supporters back from their temporary alliance with the Republican party.

In the Black Belt, the Negro vote fell off sharply. So, most likely, did Republican support from merchants and planters who had backed Bullock in April. Along the coast, patterns of Republican support remained relatively stable, although again, in individual counties, Negro voters fell away sharply from the Republican party.

The wiregrass region was the only one in which Republicans registered substantial gains. There, the counties which produced the most valuable manufactured goods gave the highest votes to Grant and Colfax. Perhaps lured by programs of state aid to railroads running through their area, Wiregrass Country voters who had withheld their support from Republican candidates in the spring elections apparently swung over to the party by November. Republican cam-

[55] See Appendix. Grant and Colfax received 57,134 votes in Georgia; Seymour and Blair received 102,822.

[56] Thompson, *Reconstruction in Georgia*, 205.

[57] Shadgett, *Republican Party in Georgia*, 14–15.

paigners had labored long in southern Georgia, determined not again to misinterpret the needs of the people there or to allow the region to go Democratic by default. Their efforts had brought striking results, the sole Republican success in what was otherwise a devastating defeat.

Charges of fraud and intimidation came immediately, once the election returns were in. Undoubtedly, many were justified. In Oglethorpe and Columbia counties, the Republicans polled about one thousand fewer votes in November than they had in April, and eleven counties reported no votes at all for Grant and Colfax. The Radical Charles Stearns collected reports from Taylor, Muscogee, Marion, Chattahoochee, Richmond, and Lincoln counties; all charged Democratic partisans with frauds, intimidation, and violence. Every observer of the election noted a sharp drop in the numbers of Negroes who voted. "There was no change," Stearns asserted, "in the political opinions of the blacks."[58] Democratic skulduggery alone had cost Grant and Colfax Georgia's electoral votes.

There was fraud, there was intimidation, and there was violence in 1868. But there were other reasons for the Republican losses. New dissensions had split the party. Its legislative accomplishments had failed to match its April campaign pledges, and its short-sighted strategy on the Negro officeholding question had been skillfully exposed. The Union League, its main task apparently accomplished and its chief now preoccupied with the duties of high state office, had loosened its grip on the mass of Negro voters. The freedmen were no longer the well-disciplined, unquestioning Republican regulars they had been in April. Then, too, the Democrats had waged a more skillful campaign. Their party, like that of the Republicans, was handicapped by internal squabbles. But the dominant faction had suc-

[58] Stearns, *Black Man of the South,* 247–55.

ceeded in rousing the passions of voters in a campaign which contrasted sharply with the apathetic, chaotic canvass they had conducted in March and April. Although few reliable facts can be learned about the activities of the Ku Klux Klan, it seems clear that it operated as an effective adjunct to the Democratic party, securing by intimidation and violence at night whatever the party orators might have failed to win by day. And finally, the November elections marked a return, albeit an exaggerated one, to the normal Democratic majority in Georgia.

The elections signaled, too, the start of a desperate new campaign by Georgia's Republican party. Out of the wreckage of their party in November, Georgia Republicans of all persuasions hoped to find new strength. That strength, most of them believed, would have to come not from within the state itself, but from outside—from the national Congress. As soon as the election returns were in, John H. Caldwell urged further legislation to "rectify the disorder[ed] condition of affairs" in Georgia. "Fraud, violence, intimidation and coercion were employed to cheat General Grant out of the vote" in the state, he said. Congress should reject the vote for Seymour and Blair, Caldwell added. "It ought not to be counted. In all fairness & honesty it belongs to Grant. It is not necessary to his election . . . but the moral effect of throwing out this vote will be good for our party in this State."[59] In the months to come, Bullock himself would make the "fraudulent" election of November, 1868, a prime example of the failure of Georgians to accept Reconstruction. His goal, and that of others in the Georgia party, was to secure by Congressional fiat the Republican ascendancy in the state which Radical leaders had proved unable to maintain by themselves.

[59] John H. Caldwell to William E. Chandler, November 23, 1868, in Chandler Papers.

CHAPTER VII

Salvation

As November turned into December, Rufus Bullock grew increasingly desperate. The crushing defeat inflicted on his party in Georgia during the 1868 presidential elections provided only the latest and most striking evidence of what astute observers had long recognized. Republicans had failed in their efforts to build a strong party. Indeed, Bullock, as governor and presumably party leader, had contributed to the difficulties by his inability to control his own coalition. Shunning the difficult and time-consuming task of broadening their party's base in Georgia, Bullock and his closest advisers had already decided to seek Congressional aid to save the state organization.

Ever since the General Assembly had organized in July without purging itself of members "ineligible" under the terms of the Fourteenth Amendment, and especially since the expulsion of the Negro members and the censure of his

147

protest message, Bullock had been formulating an argument
and a plan which would return Georgia to military rule and
place the state Republican party once more under direct
federal protection. The presidential election, with its apparent frauds, provided the governor with a long-sought
opportunity.

Almost immediately after the election, representatives of
the various factions of Georgia's Republican party appeared
in Washington. Akerman, one of the ablest lawyers in the
state and an ardent supporter of Grant during the campaign, journeyed northward as the spokesman of the anti-
Bullock State Executive Committee.[1] His sole purpose was
to secure the rejection of Georgia's electoral votes, but his
presence in Washington and the evidence he presented in
behalf of the committee pointed unerringly to the same
political strategy Bullock was advocating. Joining Akerman
in the spring of 1869 was the representative of the Bullock
forces, state Attorney General Farrow.[2] In the winter of
1868–69, and again in December, 1869, Bullock himself
travelled to the North to lobby in his own behalf.

The arguments used by Radical lobbyists never changed;
only new "evidence" and new "proof" were added during
1869 to bolster the case. Bullock and his colleagues de-
fended their leadership of the Republican party in Georgia
and laid their troubles to the failure of the General Assembly
to purge itself of men ineligible to seats under the provisions of the Fourteenth Amendment.[3] Expulsion of Negro
members from the assembly, they asserted, was clearly

[1] J. H. Caldwell to William E. Chandler, November 23, 1868, in
Chandler Papers.

[2] H. K. McCay and others to Henry P. Farrow, April 7, 1869, in Henry
P. Farrow Collection, University of Georgia.

[3] See especially the Macon *American Union*, April 9, 1869, copying
from the Washington *National Republican* Bullock's public letter on
conditions in Georgia, Washington, March 26, 1869.

unconstitutional; Negroes were entitled to full enjoyment of their rights as citizens—including the right to hold office.[4] Although General Meade had not required the stringent test oath of members of the General Assembly in 1868, Bullock now claimed that, since the expulsion of the Negroes, the house had contained at least forty and the senate fifteen or eighteen men who could not take the oath.[5] In failing to require the test oath of its members, the legislature had failed legally to organize. The Fourteenth Amendment, Bullock blandly assured the Congress, had won acceptance only because it came to a vote before the expulsion of the Negro delegates. Its adoption by an "illegal" legislature was, however, void; technically, therefore, Bullock argued, Georgia had yet to ratify the Fourteenth Amendment.[6] Not until she did so legally could she be readmitted to the Union under the terms of the Omnibus Bill.

Truly, the difficulties in Georgia seemed overwhelming, but the governor—or "provisional governor" as Bullock now styled himself, since he claimed that Georgia had yet to fulfill the requirements for readmission—offered a ready solution. The "commanding general" should order the reassembling of the legislature elected in April, 1868, and provide for administering the test oath as a qualification for membership.[7] The Negro delegates would thus regain their seats; Democrats would fall victim to the unflinching words of the iron-clad oath; and, the long-desired purge of Democratic legislators accomplished, Republicans would control

[4] *House Miscellaneous Documents,* 40th Cong., 3rd Sess., No. 52, Pt. 2, p. 3.

[5] Those swearing to the test oath were required to affirm that they had never taken an oath to support the Constitution of the United States and then served the Confederacy. The test oath, therefore, went considerably beyond a pledge of future loyalty.

[6] *House Miscellaneous Documents,* 40th Cong., 3rd Sess., No. 52, Pt. 2, pp. 2 and 5.

[7] *Ibid.,* 2.

both houses of the General Assembly without fear that factional disputes within their own party would destroy their majority. Though his trusted lieutenants had spoken openly of the possibility,[8] Bullock avoided suggesting directly that Georgia be remanded to military rule.[9] So clear were the governor's wishes, however, that friends and foes alike recognized his purpose.

In December the "provisional governor" and his followers urged and secured an investigation into the "condition of affairs in Georgia"; the evidence, taken by the Joint Select Committee on Reconstruction, appeared on January 6, 1869. The investigators collected testimony from Bullock and his aides and from Democratic Congressman Nelson Tift. Bullock, it became clear, had planned his attack well. Much of the evidence introduced by the Georgia Radicals purported to show that no adequate protection existed for life and property in rebellious Georgia; not even the ballot box remained sacrosanct. Bullock testified fully concerning the organization of the General Assembly, and Congress received a memorial signed by stalwart Republican members of the legislature and by other Radicals.[10]

What appeared the most convincing testimony, however, was that concerning the November elections. Unintentionally, the anti-Bullock chairman of the state committee, John E. Bryant, had contributed to the governor's storehouse of atrocity tales. Soon after the November elections, Bryant had employed the time-worn strategy of a defeated party chairman in letters to his district managers asking for evi-

[8] Foster Blodgett to William E. Chandler, September 13, 1868, in Chandler Papers. See also Richardson, *William E. Chandler*, 115.

[9] *Journal of the House of Representatives of the State of Georgia*, 1869, pp. 5–18, giving the text of Bullock's annual message; *House Miscellaneous Documents*, 41st Cong., 1st Sess., No. 34, pp. 2–3.

[10] Memorial dated Atlanta, September 18, 1868, received in Washington December 8, 1868, and referred to the Committee on Reconstruction. See *House Miscellaneous Documents*, 40th Cong., 3rd Sess., No. 6.

dence of fraud and the names and depositions of witnesses.[11] This evidence, Bryant, Caldwell, and Akerman hoped to use to secure the rejection of Georgia's vote in the electoral count on the grounds that widespread voting frauds in the state had rendered the election results there invalid. All three men strongly disapproved Bullock's scheme to remand Georgia to military rule.

Bullock, however, used the evidence collected by Bryant and the State Executive Committee to telling advantage. A trusted Negro Republican, James M. Sims, swore that in Savannah intimidation and violence prevented a Republican victory. Attempting to show that all freedmen would vote Republican if given fair opportunity, the Negro leader declared, "I never met a single [Negro] man . . . of any intelligence, who expressed himself openly to me as a democrat. Those who did so express themselves were either acting under the degrading influence of pay, or else were driven to it from circumstances of home and family." Sims claimed personally to know of fifty Negroes threatened or actually fired from their jobs for voting Republican.[12] Colonel A. W. Stone termed the Savannah voting a "perfect farce"; Democrats controlled the ballot boxes and prevented Negroes from freely casting their votes.[13] Dr. S. P. Powell of Augusta reported that "below Americus" in Early, Randolph, Clay, Baker, Calhoun, Stewart, Dougherty, and some other adjoining counties, Negroes were "compelled to vote the democratic ticket."[14] Radical partisan Charles Stearns introduced his own evidence, drawn chiefly from affidavits executed by Freedmen's Bureau personnel.[15] In all, Bullock and his aides

[11] Bryant to "Dear Sir," November 17, 1868, in *House Miscellaneous Documents*, 40th Cong., 3rd Sess., No. 52, pp. 48–49.

[12] *Ibid.*, 7, 9.

[13] *Ibid.*, 45.

[14] *Ibid.*, 35.

[15] *Ibid.*, 102–10.

introduced evidence of election frauds in at least thirty-seven Georgia counties.

Not all Georgia Republicans, however, were ready to accept Bullock's use of the executive committee's evidence, and once again the old split between Radicals and Moderates and between pro-Bullock and anti-Bullock Radicals raised its head. Akerman, the official representative of the anti-Bullock State Executive Committee, acknowledged that whites had committed outrages against Negroes and that Congress should step in to correct injustices, but he believed the Reconstruction Acts had been fairly executed in Georgia.[16] From Bullock's standpoint, Bryant's testimony proved even more disappointing. On the whole, the committee chairman now asserted, the election had been a fair one. He had heard of frauds in the Black Belt, especially around Augusta, but he knew of these only through affidavits. Reimposition of military rule in the state was unnecessary. Georgia required only a little "straightening out."[17] Such unmistakable evidence that his party was splintering behind him failed, however, to impress Governor Bullock.

Not even the prospect that Negro members would regain their seats in the General Assembly stayed Bullock's hand. Indeed, the governor seemed encouraged in his course by evidence that his campaign had cowed the legislature into submission. In February, 1869, the assembly passed a joint resolution, clearly intended by Democrats to placate both Congress and the pro-Bullock Radicals, asking the state supreme court to hear and decide a test case on Negro officeholding and pledging the legislature's acceptance of the high tribunal's decision.[18] Justice Hiram Warner, a Democrat, would probably decide against the freedmen; Republican

[16] *Ibid.*, 12–13.
[17] *Ibid.*, 27–28, 31.
[18] *Journal of the Senate of the State of Georgia*, 1869, pp. 252–54.

Justice H. K. McCay would doubtless sustain the Negroes' claims. What position Chief Justice Brown would take remained in doubt—whether he would hold to the views expressed in his Marietta Speech of 1868, or officially adopt those which since September had become a *sine qua non* for Republican politicians. Bullock was unwilling to wait for the decision. Recognizing that a mere reinstatement of the Negro members could not give him the control he wanted over the state, the governor vetoed the joint resolution. Congress, he argued, had two complaints against Georgia. The legislature had permitted ineligible men to take their seats, and it had expelled the Negro delegates. The joint resolution proposed no remedy for either grievance.[19]

Despite Bullock's veto, the court decided a test case in June, 1869. In *White* v. *Clements,* two of the three justices held that Negroes were entitled to hold office.[20] By this time, the General Assembly had adjourned, but the governor's veto of the joint resolution in February seemed in any case to relieve the legislature of any obligation to act on the court's decision. Press and citizens divided over what practical results the decision would produce, and the question was never answered.[21] Before the assembly reconvened for the 1870 session, Congress had removed all decisions from the hands of the "rebellious" Georgians.

Bullock's veto of the joint resolution was not the only indication of the governor's unwavering determination to have his state remanded to military rule. Before the General

[19] Woolley, *Reconstruction of Georgia,* 92.

[20] *White* v. *Clements,* 39 *Georgia Reports,* 232 et seq. Brown and Mc-Cay declared the freedmen eligible to hold office. The chief justice based his opinion on Georgia statute law, which since antebellum days had declared all citizens eligible to hold office.

[21] Thompson, *Reconstruction in Georgia,* 215–16, gives a summary of press opinion, drawn from excerpts appearing in the Macon *Telegraph,* June 18, June 20, 1869.

Assembly adjourned in the spring of 1869, he had tried in both houses and succeeded in the senate to secure the defeat of the Fifteenth Amendment.[22] The strategy seemed obvious. Many Democrats, eager to avoid a second military reconstruction, were preparing to swallow Negro suffrage as a necessary concession to Congressional Radicals. They knew, as did Bullock, that ratification of the amendment would explode the governor's argument that Georgia remained unreconstructed. Should even a few Democrats, as well as all Moderate and Radical Republicans, vote in favor of the amendment, it would easily pass both houses. To Bullock, therefore, it became a matter of the utmost urgency that the General Assembly Republicans should either abstain or actually vote against the Fifteenth Amendment. When the final house vote was taken on March 16, only twenty-one Republicans voted for passage. Two voted against it, and the rest abstained. Bullock's efforts in the house, however, proved futile, for enough Democrats voted for ratification to secure approval of the amendment by a 64–53 vote. In the senate, the governor was more successful. On March 18, seven Republicans—including four Radicals—and six Democrats voted for the amendment. Seven other Republicans, all loyal Bullock followers, joined the nine Democrats who voted against ratification. Nine Republicans, all Bullock men, and six Democrats abstained. The Senate rejected the Fifteenth Amendment by a three-vote margin.[23] Georgia failed, therefore, to ratify the amendment, and Bullock could still claim that the state had yet to accept Reconstruction.

[22] For the complete, complex story of the votes on the Fifteenth Amendment, see Thompson, *Reconstruction in Georgia*, 260–62, and William Gillette, *The Right to Vote: Politics and the Passage of the Fifteenth Amendment* (Baltimore: The Johns Hopkins Press, 1965), 101–103.

[23] The votes appear in the Georgia house and senate journals for March 16 and March 18, and more conveniently but with minor errors in party designations in Edward McPherson, *A Hand Book of Politics for 1870* (Washington: Philip & Solomons, 1870), 489–90.

Throughout the spring and summer and into the fall, Bullock continued to bombard the Congress with tales of atrocities occurring in Georgia, and the new Atlanta military commander, General Alfred Terry, appeared eager to cooperate.[24] Disorders in Savannah during May brought a hint from Washington: were not troops needed in Chatham County?[25] In June, Bullock reminded General Terry that the sheriff of Warren County, a loyal Republican "who took active steps to secure to the colored people a fair, free vote in the . . . presidential election," had fallen, crippled, before a would-be assassin's bullet.[26] Also in Warren County, Republican state Senator Joseph Adkins had been murdered—and his murderers had gone unpunished. Proclaiming that a state of unrest and disorder existed in Warren, Terry on June 4 ordered federal troops into the county.[27]

Other Georgians, too, did their bit to convince Congress of the truth in Bullock's testimony. From Macon, an obscure Radical campaign worker, James Fitzpatrick, warned Representative Benjamin F. Butler and Secretary of the Treasury George Boutwell against making a planned trip to Georgia to attend the state agricultural fair. "The Rebel democracy of this State," Fitzpatrick assured Butler, "would contribute liberally to any party who would take your life."[28]

[24] Terry had relieved Meade as commander of United States troops in Georgia in the spring of 1869. For a summary of his views, see James E. Sefton, *The United States Army and Reconstruction, 1865–1877* (Baton Rouge: Louisiana State University Press, 1967), 200.

[25] J. M. Schofield to [Terry], June 2, 1869, in War Department Records, Telegrams Sent, R. G. 107, National Archives.

[26] *House Executive Documents*, 41st Cong., 2nd Sess., No. 288, pp. 16–18. The letter was published after Congress had decided to remand Georgia to military rule, but Bullock's intentions were widely known in the summer of 1869.

[27] *Ibid.*, 2ff.

[28] James Fitzpatrick to Benjamin F. Butler, September 17, 1869, in Benjamin F. Butler Papers, Library of Congress.

Undoubtedly Bullock, like many of his colleagues, was sincerely concerned that bloodshed be prevented in Georgia. But the governor took telling advantage of the violence which did occasionally erupt. Only by portraying a state in a condition of anarchy, unable to afford its citizens protection of their lives and property, could Bullock and his followers persuade Congressmen to reimpose military rule in Georgia. To the disgusted editor of the Democratic Athens *Southern Banner,* "the outrage business in Georgia" bore "so many evidences of being a 'put up job' . . . that it ought not to [have] convince[d] anybody."[29]

One whom it failed to convince was Congressman Tift. Almost singlehandedly throughout the bleak months of 1868 and 1869, the Democrat fought Bullock and the Radicals on their own ground—before the committees of Congress. Lacking funds from his state party committee, Tift himself financed a circular letter in the winter of 1868–69, requesting from Georgia Democrats information on the same topics touched upon by Bullock and his supporters. The replies he received to the circular letter, of course, told him exactly what he wanted to hear, but his testimony came close to the truth.[30] Tift conceded that atrocities had occurred, but he contended that there was little violence and disorder, that the laws had been faithfully executed, and that all Georgians were anxious for peace and restoration to the Union. In no way were Republicans persecuted, Tift asserted. In

[29] Athens *Southern Banner,* December 17, 1869.

[30] See, for example, H. F. Russell, the mayor of Augusta, to Tift, December 31, 1868, in Broadsides, Duke University. Tift's testimony appears in *House Miscellaneous Documents,* 40th Cong., 3rd Sess., No. 52. Bullock replied, *ibid.,* Pt. 2. Tift then issued a rejoinder, printed as *House Miscellaneous Documents,* 41st Cong., 1st sess., No. 34. He also issued an "Address to the People of Georgia," published in the Albany *News,* April 23, 1869; a copy appears in the Nelson Tift Papers, University of Georgia.

short, no justification existed for Congress to intervene in the affairs of the state of Georgia.[31]

In Georgia, the Republican party divided more sharply than ever over Bullock's quest for a return to military rule. The first to break publicly from the governor was his most indispensable supporter, Joseph E. Brown. Georgia, Brown admonished the governor, had executed the Reconstruction Acts and the Omnibus Bill fully and in good faith, "in accordance with Genl Grants views, and instructions." Congress should now "take no step backward;" it should not "undo what . . . [had] been done by destroying the . . . State Government." Georgia, in short, should not undergo a second period of military rule.[32]

Salvation for Georgia's Republican party, Brown thought, could be attained without recourse to Congressional intervention. Georgia Republicans must act to mend their own fences. In particular, they must win greater white support from among members of the Democracy, who possessed "most of the intelligence and wealth of the state." Brown would divide the Democracy by appealing to the moderate Stephens–Johnson wing, leaving Toombs, Hill, and their followers to go their own way. In effect recognizing the permanent minority position of the Republican party as it was constituted in 1868, Brown proposed a fusion of all Republicans and conservative Democrats.[33] All could, presumably, unite for the economic recovery of Georgia and for her quick return to prosperity within the Union. By December 8,

[31] *House Miscellaneous Documents,* 40th Cong., 3rd Sess., No. 52, pp. 140–236, *passim.*

[32] Brown to Bullock, December 3, 1868, draft copy in Joseph E. Brown Papers, private possession. For a different view, see Hill, *Joseph E. Brown,* 288–89; she did not have access to the letter of December 3. I have been unable to locate the copy of the letter which Bullock presumably received.

[33] Brown to Bullock, December 3, 1868, draft copy in Joseph E. Brown Papers, private possession.

1868, in what indeed seemed a preliminary move to conciliate a prominent moderate Democrat, Brown wrote openly to Alexander H. Stephens of the breach between Bullock
and himself.[34]

Other Republicans deserted Bullock that winter. In his
statement before the Reconstruction Committee, John E.
Bryant made his own break with the governor official. Amos
T. Akerman's testimony, too, manifested an ever-increasing
coolness toward Bullock and his policies. During the presidential campaign, *New Era* editor Samuel Bard, who held
the state printing contract, had proved noticeably unwilling
to exert himself for the Republican nominees. On January
6, 1869, Bard formally announced his opposition to Bullock's
plans for a second military reconstruction,[35] and, after the
rejection of the Fifteenth Amendment in the state senate, he
again lashed out at the governor and his schemes. The future
of the Republican party in Georgia, the editor warned, would
be bleak indeed should Congress yield to gubernatorial
pleas for a reimposition of military rule.[36]

Serious as they were, however, these defections paled in
significance beside the formal split in the party ranks which
occurred at Augusta on March 1, 1869. There, in the birth-
place of Georgia Republicanism, the district convention
met to nominate delegates to the Republican state convention scheduled for March 5. Inevitably, the issue of Bullock's policies arose—with Blodgett supporting and Bryant
attacking the governor. A bitter exchange between the two
factions culminated in victory for Blodgett and defeat and
repudiation for Bryant. On their home grounds, the Bullock
forces had once more seized control of the state party ma-

[34] Brown to Alexander H. Stephens, December 8, 1868, in Alexander
Stephens Papers, Library of Congress.
[35] Atlanta *New Era,* January 6, 1869.
[36] *Ibid.,* March 27, 1869.

chinery. Branded by the Bullock men as a renegade, Bryant yielded the state chairmanship and his place on the State Executive Committee. The break between the Bullock and the Bryant men was now complete and irreparable. Bullock had succeeded in alienating not only the Moderate wing of of his own party, but an important element of the Radical faction, as well. The defection of Bryant and his followers was to prove more costly to Bullock than the governor could ever have imagined.[37]

II

Within Congress during the twelve months following the 1868 presidential election, action on the Georgia imbroglio took two distinct forms. Throughout the closing weeks of the Fortieth Congress and the first and second sessions of the Forty-first, the legislators debated various proposals designed to meet in one way or another Governor Bullock's demands. As the Fortieth Congress drew to a close, the members faced a more pressing problem: whether or not to count the electoral vote of Georgia.

The counting of votes was disposed of after sharp but relatively brief debate. On February 6, 1869, Senator George F. Edmunds of Vermont introduced in the Senate a concurrent resolution that the electoral votes be counted first with, then without, Georgia's votes included.[38] An objection by Lyman Trumbull of Illinois forced postponement of the question until February 8. On that day, after debate, Edmunds' resolution passed, with Radicals and a few Moderates voting for it, and Democrats and Trumbull opposed.[39]

[37] For reports of the convention from a Democratic standpoint, see the Augusta *Chronicle and Sentinel,* March 2, 1869.

[38] *Congressional Globe,* 40th Cong., 3rd Sess., XL, Pt. 2, p. 934.

[39] *Ibid.,* 796–98. The vote was thirty-four in favor of the resolution, eleven opposed, and twenty-one, including men of all parties and factions, not voting.

In the House, debate centered around the objections made by Massachusetts Representative Benjamin Butler to counting the Georgia vote at all. How Butler and Bullock became acquainted remains a mystery, but by the winter of 1868–69, the two men had developed warm personal as well as political ties, and Butler now emerged the most consistent champion of Bullock's wishes in the halls of Congress. On this occasion, however, his efforts to secure passage of a resolution protesting the counting of Georgia's votes failed, and, when the House watered down his measure, Butler himself joined with other members of his party to table it.[40]

In accordance with the Edmunds concurrent resolution, then, the presidential ballots were opened and counted on February 10; results were announced first with Georgia's vote included and then with her vote omitted.[41] The inclusion of Georgia's nine electoral votes for Seymour and Blair, of course, would have made no difference in the outcome of the presidential contest; Grant had won easily. The Edmunds resolution merely placated Georgia Republicans who wanted the state's vote rejected entirely. More important, it allowed Congress to delay for a while longer any decision on the status of Georgia under the Reconstruction Acts.

Congress could no longer avoid a decision, however, when the Forty-first Congress convened and Georgia's "Congressmen-elect" presented their credentials. To seat these men would imply the rejection of Bullock's pleas and would be tacit Congressional admission that Georgia had complied with the terms of the Reconstruction Acts. Several bills for the remanding of Georgia to military rule had died in committee at the close of the Fortieth Congress. Almost certainly, they would be reintroduced in the Forty-first, and the legislators were unwilling so soon to doom them to defeat. In the

[40] *Ibid.*, 1064, 1065–67, 1094, 1097, 1106, 1107, 1144, 1148.
[41] *Ibid.*, 1050ff.

Senate, the Judiciary Committee recommended that the credentials of Joshua Hill and H. V. M. Miller be tabled until action could be taken on the pending Georgia Reconstruction measures. The Senators accepted the report, and, to no one's surprise, Hill and Miller remained without seats.[42] The House had on March 5 more easily disposed of the Georgia delegates who had been elected in April, 1868, and who believed themselves chosen for both the Fortieth and Forty-first Congresses. An eagle-eyed representative noticed a flaw in their credentials; the documents failed to stipulate to which Congress the men had actually been elected. Falling back gratefully on this technicality, the House Republicans found themselves able to accommodate Bullock and exclude the Congressmen-elect, and yet to avoid premature discussion of questions best left until the various Georgia bills should come up for debate.[43]

In both the House and Senate during this period, several Georgia bills went down to defeat. In the House, Bullock's faithful friend Butler introduced in December, 1868, a bill which met all of the "provisional governor's" demands. The House referred it to the members of the Committee on Reconstruction, and the bill died in committee as the Fortieth Congress ended.[44]

Undaunted, Butler tried again in the Forty-first Congress. As before, his bill met all of Bullock's demands. Troops would be stationed and used in Georgia to enforce the Reconstruction Acts; the "provisional governor" would summon the legislature elected in 1868, reseat the Negro members, and reorganize the General Assembly after administering

[42] *Congressional Globe*, 41st Cong., 1st Sess., XLI, 102.
[43] *Ibid.*, 16.
[44] *Congressional Globe*, 40th Cong., 3rd Sess., XL, Pt. 2, p. 74. The House did, however, agree in January, 1869, to a resolution calling on the Reconstruction Committee to investigate fully conditions in Georgia. *Ibid.*, 25–29, 587, 674, 675.

the test oath to all members-elect.[45] This time, however, Butler encountered stiff opposition from Democrats who had perceived the alliance between the Massachusetts Representative and the Georgia governor and had seen through some, though not all, of Bullock's tactics. Bullock, Democrats alleged, had engineered the defeat of the Fifteenth Amendment, had misused state funds to finance his lobbying activities, and had schemed eventually to have himself elected Senator from Georgia should a new, Radical-dominated legislature convene. Such allegations went far to prolong debate on the Butler bill.[46] It never passed the House.[47]

In the Senate, two prominent Republicans espoused Bullock's cause. On December 9, Massachusetts Radical Charles Sumner introduced a measure which, like Butler's bill in the House, adopted Bullock's argument that the Georgia legislature had failed properly to organize. Georgia remained, therefore, unreconstructed—and a fit subject for Congressional attention.[48] The Senate referred Sumner's measure to the Judiciary Committee. Then, a week later, George Edmunds introduced a measure designed to repeal the clause of the Omnibus Bill providing for the readmission of Georgia and to set up a new, provisional government for the state. Edmunds' bill, too, went to the Judiciary Committee.[49] So did a proposal by Senator Samuel C. Pomeroy of Kansas to reconvene the Georgia constitutional convention and force the addition to the constitution of a clause guaranteeing the Negro's right to hold office.[50]

---

[45] *Congressional Globe,* 41st Cong., 1st Sess., XLI, 591. The bill, introduced on April 7, 1869, became H. R. 259.

[46] *Ibid.,* 595–98.

[47] *Ibid.,* 600ff.; see also the Appendix, 2–13, 17.

[48] *Congressional Globe,* 40th Cong., 3rd Sess., XL, 27–28.

[49] *Ibid.,* 144.

[50] *Ibid.,* 157–58. Also referred to the Judiciary Committee was a measure introduced by Senator William M. Stewart of Nevada. *Ibid.,* 171. Pomeroy's measure failed to meet Bullock's demands, for it failed to provide for

All but the Sumner bill died in the Judiciary Committee. Sumner's measure, reported out of committee without any recommendation, never came to a vote.[51] Neither did a new measure Edmunds introduced on March 5, as the Forty-first Congress convened.[52]

Though the Republicans could have secured the passage of any measure they desired, they seemed unwilling in the spring of 1869 to again assume control of Reconstruction in Georgia. The causes of their unaccustomed inactivity fail to appear in their correspondence or in the letters and papers of Georgia Radical leaders. Nor is it entirely clear why Bullock's propaganda failed in 1868 and early 1869 to impress either Congress or Ulysses S. Grant, but impressed both mightily scarcely nine months later. The Democratic explanation—that Republicans resorted to bribery after their failure to secure what they wanted by more conventional methods—is unconvincing.[53] Quite probably, however, General Terry's report of conditions in Georgia, submitted in August, 1869, seemed to confirm much of Bullock's testimony and carried for many legislators an authority which the presentations of the Radical governor and his followers had lacked.[54] And a few Congressmen and the President himself may by the fall of 1869 have seen in a second military reconstruction of Georgia their chance to guarantee ratification of the Fifteenth Amendment.

---

the unseating of General Assembly members who could not take the test oath.

[51] *Ibid.*, Pt. 3, p. 1056.

[52] This bill, S. 3, provided for the use of troops to "enforce the fourteenth amendment . . . in the State of Georgia." *Congressional Globe,* 41st Cong., 1st Sess., XLI, 8. See also *ibid.*, 30, 102, and 176.

[53] Nelson Tift to John Screven, December 12, 1869, in Arnold–Screven Papers, University of North Carolina.

[54] Terry's report, dated Atlanta, August 14, 1869, appears most conveniently in the *Report of the Secretary of War for 1869–70,* 89–95. See also Sefton, *United States Army and Reconstruction,* 200.

By December, 1869, President Grant had determined to remand Georgia temporarily to military rule. Grant's first annual message, delivered on December 6, suggested the enactment of a law "authorizing the governor of Georgia to convene the members originally elected to the legislature, [and] requiring each member to take the [test] oath prescribed by the reconstruction acts."[55]

Grant's proposal came as no surprise to Georgia Radicals. Everyone knew that the President and Butler were good friends, and Grant quite likely discussed his message with the Massachusetts Representative before he submitted it.[56] Butler, in turn, remained in close touch with Georgia leaders. As early as November 5, Blodgett wrote begging information about the President's plans. He had called a secret caucus of the party for November 24, he confided, and hoped then to "place the [Georgia] party . . . in full accord and sympathy with . . . the probable action of congress."[57] Bullock men controlled the state party machinery. Therefore, even though substantial groups within their own party opposed them, they were able to ram through the caucus a resolution urging that Georgia be remanded to military government.[58]

Members of Congress had also anticipated Grant's proposals regarding Georgia, and members of both houses were ready with bills which met the President's request. On December 16, the Senate took up and debated and on December 17 passed Indiana Republican Oliver Perry Morton's

[55] James D. Richardson (comp.), *A Compilation of the Messages and Papers of the Presidents, 1789-1907* (Washington: Bureau of National Literature and Art, 1896-1909), VII, 28.

[56] William D. Mallam, "The Grant–Butler Relationship," *Mississippi Valley Historical Review,* XLI (September, 1954), 259-76.

[57] Foster Blodgett to Benjamin F. Butler, November 5, 1869, in Butler Papers.

[58] Avery, *History of the State of Georgia,* 420; *Atlanta Constitution,* November 25, 1869.

measure embodying all of Grant's proposals.[59] In the House, Butler urged a similar measure but agreed to accept the Senate version, which passed the House on December 21 despite a desperate Democratic revival of the old charges of corruption and duplicity against Bullock.[60] The bill directed Bullock to reassemble the legislature elected in April, 1868. Members of the General Assembly must then take the iron-clad test oath or must swear that disabilities imposed on them by the Fourteenth Amendment had been removed by Congress. Only after its members had properly qualified, might the assembly transact regular business. Before Georgia's Senators and Representatives-elect would be seated in Congress, the legislature would have to ratify the proposed Fifteenth Amendment to the federal Constitution. Upon the application of the governor of Georgia, the President of the United States was ordered to "employ such military or naval forces . . . as [might] . . . be necessary to enforce and execute the provisions" of the bill.[61]

Bullock, in Washington to savor the victory he had won at last, carried the Georgia bill to Grant. The President, reported an embittered Democrat, signed the measure without reading it.[62] On Christmas eve, he appointed General Alfred Terry, who already commanded federal troops at Atlanta, to "exercise the duties of commanding general of the District of Georgia."[63] At least until the legislature reconvened, civil government would again be only provisional, and Terry would exercise the same authority which had

[59] *Congressional Globe*, 41st Cong., 2nd Sess., XLII, 165–77, 201–32.

[60] *Ibid.*, 244–62, 275–92. The final vote in the House, p. 293, was 121–51, with 39 Representatives not voting. The Senate version was thus accepted by the House.

[61] *Statutes at Large*, 41st Cong., 2nd Sess., Chap. 3, pp. 59–60.

[62] Avery, *History of the State of Georgia*, 423.

[63] Richardson (comp.), *Messages and Papers*, VII, 93; General Orders No. 83, December 24, 1869. See also Sefton, *United States Army and Reconstruction*, 201–203.

been granted to Generals Pope and Meade under the Reconstruction measures of 1867.

The second military reconstruction of Georgia had begun. Republicans, a party worker reported to Butler, rejoiced at the prospects before them.[64] Well they might. The devastating defeat of the previous winter, it appeared, had now changed, at a single stroke of a pen, into almost certain victory. Georgia Radicals had developed firm ties with powerful Congressional leaders and with a stalwart Republican in the White House. If Bullock's policies had cost his party dearly in defections among Moderate leaders and even among some Radicals, they appeared to have produced gains which far outweighed the losses. Bullock and his friends spent an unusually joyous Christmas in 1869. What they did not know, and perhaps could not foresee, was that their efforts and those of their Congressional allies were doomed to failure.

[64] C. W. Chapman to Benjamin F. Butler, December 20, 1869, in Butler Papers.

CHAPTER VIII

The Politics of Desperation

The Reorganization Act of December 22, 1869, drawn by the Congressional Republicans and signed by Ulysses S. Grant in conformity with Bullock's wishes, ordered that the governor summon all those elected to the legislature in April, 1868, to meet at Atlanta and there organize themselves in accordance with the instructions contained in the bill. All delegates must take the test oath or swear that Congress had removed the political disabilities imposed upon them by the Fourteenth Amendment.[1] All who thus qualified for the General Assembly must be seated; exclusion for any other reason, notably for race or color, would violate the terms of the act. Before Georgia could be readmitted to the Union, her legislature must ratify the Fifteenth Amendment,

[1] After July 11, 1868, southerners were provided with an alternative to the stringent, ironclad oath. They could now take a modified oath which pledged only future loyalty, provided that Congress had relieved them of their political disabilities.

protecting the right of individuals to the ballot in federal
elections against infringement by the states on grounds of
race, color, or previous condition of servitude. Nothing in
the act of December 22, however, explicitly remanded
Georgia to military rule.[2]

Whether Congress had intended to impose military rule
on the state was never entirely clear. There is little in the
debates of either the House or the Senate to suggest that
most Congressmen intended to again establish a military
government.[3] But the statute did provide for the use of federal troops in Georgia if requested by the governor. Grant,
in appointing General Terry to "exercise the duties of commanding general" in Georgia on December 24, appears to
have believed that, until the legislature reconvened, Georgia's civil government would remain subordinate to military
authority.[4]

Bullock and Terry followed the President's interpretation
of the statute. Although Bullock had signed bills passed by
the General Assembly in 1868 and had issued certificates of
election to the United States Senators chosen by joint ballot
of the two houses, both he and Terry now claimed that the
state government had always remained provisional. With
Bullock's enthusiastic approval, Terry ruled Georgia during
the early months of 1870 much as Generals Pope and Meade
had done—removing civil officers and supplanting civilian
with military authority. To the legislature, he dictated sub-

[2] *Statutes at Large,* 41st Cong., 2nd Sess., Chap. 3, pp. 59–60; Sefton,
United States Army and Reconstruction, 203.

[3] *Congressional Globe,* 41st Cong., 2nd Sess., Pt. 1, pp. 165–67, 169–
77, 244–62, 275–84, 285–92. For the views of one of the few Congressmen who apparently wished full military rule reimposed in Georgia, see
the remarks by Republican Representative John Coburn of Indiana, *ibid.,*
252–62.

[4] Richardson (comp.), *Messages and Papers,* VII, 93.

jects for discussion, granting or withholding his permission for the General Assembly to deal with specific topics.[5]

As soon as Grant signed the Reorganization Act, Bullock summoned his legislature to meet at Atlanta on January 10, 1870.[6] Summoning the legislature was all that the statute authorized Bullock to do; Sections 2 through 5 clearly indicated that the legislature would reorganize itself within the limits set forth by Congress. But from his authority to call the assembly, Bullock claimed to derive authority to supervise its organization. When the delegates gathered, therefore, they found two Bullock henchmen, J. G. W. Mills and A. L. Harris, ready to oversee the organization of the senate and the house of representatives.

In the senate, with its clear Republican majority, there was little difficulty. The two expelled Negroes, Campbell and Wallace, readily regained their seats; the whites who could do so took the test oath or swore to the removal of their political disabilities.[7] Republicans re-elected Bullock's faithful ally Benjamin F. Conley president of the senate. Conley's opening address gave further indication, if any was needed, of the motive behind Bullock's reorganization. "In this republic," Conley proclaimed, "Republicans shall rule."[8]

Establishing firm control over the house presented greater problems, for, even before the expulsion of the Negro members, Bullock's inability to muster the support of all Moderate as well as Radical Republicans had become clear. Now, two years later, the formal defection of John E. Bryant and J.

[5] Woolley, *Reconstruction of Georgia*, 74.

[6] Bullock's proclamation, December 22, 1869, in Executive Minutes of the State of Georgia, Georgia Department of Archives and History.

[7] Only one Senator, W. T. Winn, could not take the oath and was disqualified.

[8] See Bullock's remarks to the legislature, *Journal of the Senate of the State of Georgia*, 1870, pp. 1ff., and the quotation from Conley's address, *ibid.*, 26.

H. Caldwell and their followers from the Bullock camp
threatened to make Radical domination impossible. Bullock
recognized the difficulties, however, and he thought he could
surmount them. In all his presentations before Congress and
in all his messages to the legislature, he had stressed the
"illegal" seating of Democratic members under the terms of
the Fourteenth Amendment and the Omnibus Bill. Now,
assuming the law authorized him and not the legislature itself to judge the qualifications of its members, he planned
to restore to their seats the Negro delegates expelled from
the assembly in 1868 and to purge the house of members
ineligible to seats under the terms of the Reorganization Act.
The result would be to ensure a Republican majority. In
his plans, he had the uneasy but nonetheless powerful support of General Terry. Not surprisingly, he incurred the
desperate opposition of Democrats, of Moderate Republicans, and of the Bryant–Caldwell clique.

Within the house, action during the reorganization struggle
gave little indication of events occurring behind the scenes.
Before the General Assembly met, some Democratic leaders
had once again briefly raised the possibility of non-action—of
a refusal by Democratic members to recognize the validity
of the Reorganization Act by taking their seats. So thoroughly discredited had this policy been during the early months
of Congressional Reconstruction, however, that few now
gave it serious consideration.[9] The Democrats appeared with
their Republican counterparts on January 10; with them
they came forward, took the oath, and then adjourned, as
Bullock maneuvered to organize a Republican-dominated

[9] Milledgeville *Southern Recorder*, January 18, 1870, reporting a meeting held January 5; Rome *Courier*, January 1, 1870; Dawson *Journal*,
January 13, 1870; Joseph E. Brown to Alexander H. Stephens, January 5,
1870, in Alexander Stephens Papers, Library of Congress. But see the
Rome *Courier*, December 24, 1869.

house. Over the proceedings in the legislative chamber presided "Fatty" Harris, who, declared Benjamin H. Hill, "enthroned like another Falstaff acting the part of King Henry IV before his profligate son overawed and thundered into silence the representatives of the people."[10]

Outside the legislative halls, all lay in readiness for Bullock's purge. The eligibility of many members would hinge upon the interpretation of a single word, for, under the terms of the Fourteenth Amendment and the reorganization statute, state "officers" who had sworn to uphold the Constitution of the United States and who had later voluntarily supported the Confederacy could hold no position in the postwar government unless Congress removed their political disabilities. On January 8, therefore, Bullock had requested from his attorney general, Henry Farrow, a written opinion defining "officers" under the December 22 bill.[11] Farrow submitted a long document, contending that Bullock might interpret the law to include all those "whose duties are the execution of a general law or the administration of justice," but not those "who administer local law alone." Specifically, Farrow held, "officers" included notaries public, constables, railroad assessors, and state librarians.[12] By remarkable coincidence, these were the positions held before the Civil War by Democratic legislators whom Bullock now sought to remove.

At the behest of anti-Bullock Republicans, former Governor Brown wrote out a more narrow opinion, excluding from among the officers who fell within the purview of the Fourteenth Amendment and the Reorganization Act such minor

[10] Ellis Paxon Oberholtzer, *A History of the United States Since the Civil War* (New York: The Macmillan Company, 1917), II, 264 n3.

[11] Bullock to Farrow, January 8, 1870, in *Journal of the House of Representatives of the State of Georgia*, 1870, Pt. 1, pp. 9–10.

[12] Farrow's opinion, *ibid.*, 10–16. The quotation is from p. 11.

functionaries as state librarians.[13] His opinion, however, had no legal force, and Bullock paid no heed to his chief justice's arguments.

The first hint that Farrow's opinion had set the stage for a sweeping executive reorganization of the General Assembly came on January 13. As soon as the house met, A. L. Harris presented a communication from Bullock, countersigned by General Terry. The clerk *pro tempore* should declare a recess as soon as the roll had been called in order "that an investigation . . . [might] be made into the right of certain persons to hold seats in the House of Representatives."[14] Quickly and efficiently, Terry and Bullock convened a board of military officers to pass upon the eligibility of Democratic members of the house.[15]

Immediate political chaos was the result. Democrats and Republicans alike appealed once again to Washington. To Senator Simon Cameron, Radical W. C. Morrill reported that, if Terry held firm and refused to seat delegates "known to be disqualified," all would be well. But, Morrill added, he had "never seen a more desperate effort made to nullify the acts of Congress except the actual use of armed force." Indeed, "some few who . . . [had] heretofore acted with the Republican party . . . [seemed] to be the prime movers" in the revolt against Bullock's schemes.[16] Bullock himself sensed the danger. Calling the situation "critical," and protesting that he was "wholly without any personal ends to secure or any personal ambitions to gratify," he urged Congress and the President to support Terry's investigation of

[13] Brown's opinion, manuscript copy in Joseph E. Brown Papers, Georgia Department of Archives and History. See also Allen Candler Smith, "The Republican Party in Georgia, 1867–1871" (M.A. thesis, Duke University, 1937), 189–90.

[14] *Journal of the House of Representatives,* 1870, Pt. 1, pp. 22–23.

[15] *House Executive Documents,* 41st Cong., 2nd Sess., No. 288.

[16] W. C. Morrill to Simon Cameron, Macon, January 15, 1870, in Simon Cameron Papers, Library of Congress.

the General Assembly.[17] Foster Blodgett rushed to Washington to argue the case of the Bullock regime. For their part, anti-Bullock Republicans and Democrats sent representatives to the national capital to plead their own cause.[18] The real battle over reorganization, however, was fought not in Washington, where Democrats, Moderate Republicans, and even a few Radicals had tired of the Georgia confusion, but in Georgia, where, as "Terry's purge" progressed, dissident Republicans and Moderate Democrats labored to forge the political alliance whose creation Joseph E. Brown had urged over a year before.[19]

Throughout the second and third weeks of January, Terry's board of officers debated the eligibility of over thirty members of the legislature. Behind the scenes, Bullock directed the operations, forwarding to Terry for his perusal documents concerning the past careers of individual delegates.[20] Sixteen members of the assembly, all Democrats, could not take the test oath and had not yet been relieved of their disabilities by Congress. They claimed that Bullock had assured them that they could submit applications for pardon to General Terry, and he would consider each case on its merits. Somewhat naively, all sixteen accepted Bullock's plan; Terry, they believed, would forward their applications to Washington for action. On January 26, they learned that the military commander would regard their applications for

[17] Bullock to Judge William Lawrence [Representative from Ohio], January 20, 1870, in Butler Papers.

[18] The best description of the lobbying activities appears in the manuscript diary of Edward Clifford Anderson, Democratic mayor of Savannah, who was in Washington during January and February, 1870. The diary is in the Edward Clifford Anderson Papers, University of North Carolina.

[19] Brown to Rufus B. Bullock, December 3, 1868, draft copy in Joseph E. Brown Papers, private possession.

[20] See, for example, Bullock to Terry, January 13, 1870, January 15, 1870, and January 24, 1870, all in Rufus B. Bullock Papers, Georgia Department of Archives and History.

pardon as *prima facie* evidence that they were ineligible for legislative service.[21]

Terry's board effectively accomplished its partisan purpose. It failed to sustain the governor in all matters. It declared one senator, W. T. Winn, and three representatives, R. A. Donaldson, E. M. Taliaferro, and J. H. Nunn, ineligible, but it rejected Bullock's and Farrow's contention that notaries public and state librarians fell within the provisions of the Fourteenth Amendment.[22] In the house, twenty-one Democrats lost their seats—nineteen by decisions of Terry's board, and two because they failed to take the test oath.[23] All, in the months of their service, had voted consistently against the Bullock regime. In the senate, the unseating of Winn increased an already strong Republican majority.

The mere unseating of Democratic members, however, was itself no guarantee that Bullock's supporters would dominate the legislature. Only when the pro-Bullock Radicals overcame the opposition of Democrats and anti-Bullock Republicans and adopted the old trick of seating the candidates who had garnered the second highest vote in the April, 1868, election was the composition of the legislature settled.[24]

The strong Republican majorities in the General Assembly, which now included a plurality of about thirty-three votes in the house, ill concealed the continuing division in Georgia

[21] *Journal of the House of Representatives,* 1870, Pt. 1, January 26, 1870, and Congressional Globe, 41st Cong., 2nd Sess., XLII, Pt. 2, p. 1926.

[22] *Journal of the House of Representatives,* 1870, Pt. 1, pp. 35–39.

[23] The list of those disqualified from the House includes those purged on Bullock's alleged deception, Burtz, Brinson, Bennett, George, Goff, Hudson, D. Johnson, Kellogg, Meadows, Penland, Surrency, J. R. Smith, H. Williams, Drake, J. T. Ellis, and Rowse; those declared ineligible after full investigations of their cases by the board, Donaldson, Taliaferro, and Nunn; and those failing to take the oath, Crawford and McCulloch.

[24] *Journal of the House of Representatives,* 1870, Pt. 1, pp. 35-39.

politics.[25] During the early months of 1870, the rift between the Bullock Republicans and the dissidents led by Bryant and Caldwell widened, and that between the Moderate Republicans and Democrats showed signs of narrowing.

In their hostility to Bullock, the Bryant and Caldwell followers, the Moderate Republicans, and the Democrats tried to subordinate their differences and form a united opposition to the governor. The dissident Republicans and Democrats protested the purge of the legislature, but they could do little to halt it. More threatening was their opposition in the house of representatives to Bullock's choice for speaker, R. L. McWhorter.[26] Early in January, it became apparent that the strongest opposition to McWhorter would come from Bryant. The former member of the Augusta Ring had drifted closer and closer to alliance with the Democracy since his formal break with Bullock early in 1869. His "National Republican Club," an informal organization founded to combat Bullock's attempts to preserve the Radicals in power, had mobilized such dissident Republicans as State Treasurer Nedom L. Angier, J. H. Caldwell, Joseph E. Brown, Joshua Hill, and Thomas P. Saffold.[27] These men, stigmatized by Bullock men as the Bryant Democracy,[28] hoped to work with Democrats to thwart the governor's schemes. The test which came in January, 1870, however, found the Democratic members of the potential alliance unready and, in some cases, unwilling to cooperate.

The Rome *Courier* noted on January 21 the reluctance of

[25] Peterson Thweatt to John Screven, February 7, 1870, in Arnold–Screven Papers, University of North Carolina.

[26] J. W. Alvord, *Letters from the South* (Washington: Howard University Press, 1870), 20.

[27] Bloom, "Georgia Election of April, 1868," p. 80.

[28] Atlanta *New Era*, January 27, 1870. By this time, Bullock, Blodgett, and Radical carpetbagger Hannibal I. Kimball had purchased the *New Era* from Samuel Bard and made it once more the official voice of the Radical administration.

many Democrats to abandon traditional party ties for temporary alliance with so recent a Radical as Bryant. These men, *Courier* editors feared, would back McWhorter for speaker. Such a policy would prove "suicidal." The editors deplored, as did all true Democrats, Bryant's Radical past. But being new to the state in 1865, he might have been led astray, and his recent conversion to moderation might prove sincere. Swallowing its pride, the *Courier* gave "three cheers" for Bryant and announced that it would support him for the speakership.[29]

More typical of the attitude of front-rank Democrats was the opportunistic, cynical position taken by former Confederate Secretary of War Robert Toombs. The old fire-eater reported to Alexander H. Stephens that "Bryant is the candidate of the Democrats for speaker of the House, and I and Joe Brown are trying to elect him! Rather a strange conjunction is it not? But you know my rule is to use the devil if I can do better to save the country."[30] Despite the urging of such stalwarts as Toombs, however, the Democratic caucus which met on January 8 failed to make support of Bryant a party requirement.[31] Democratic leaders might be willing to join with the Republicans, but the party's rank and file failed to see the wisdom of the alliance.

Both sides viewed the speaker's election as a crucial test of strength, and both sides spent money freely in support of their candidates. During the long recess while the Terry board debated the eligibility question, Bullock began his

[29] Rome *Courier*, January 21, 1870. Less open-minded was one of Stephens' correspondents, James R. Randall, who opposed alliance with the Bryant men under any circumstances; see Randall to Alexander H. Stephens, February 17, February 20, 1870, in Alexander Stephens Papers, Library of Congress.

[30] Robert Toombs to Alexander H. Stephens, January 24, 1870, in Phillips (ed.), *Toombs, Stephens, Cobb Correspondence*, 707. The original is in the Alexander Stephens Papers, Emory University.

[31] Rome *Courier*, January 10, 1870.

campaign. By mid-January, he had several assistants lobbying for McWhorter. The governor, a Democrat noted ruefully, "pays well."[32] To aid Bryant's cause, the state's oldest and most prominent politicians, including Toombs and Brown, brought all their influence to bear, and the publishers of the Atlanta *Constitution*, the propaganda organ of the Bryant group, allegedly offered wavering legislators $1,000 apiece for their votes.[33]

The vote for speaker, however, was less a test of party alignments than either group had anticipated. McWhorter received seventy-six votes, all from Radical Republicans or Moderates who usually adhered to the Radical caucus position on important party tests. Bryant's support came from anti-Bullock Republicans and a few Democrats. Other Democrats scattered their ballots among minor candidates; most failed to vote at all.[34] Temporarily, at least, the dream of a Moderate Republican–Democratic coalition had indeed, as the Bullock supporters gloated, "gone up in smoke."[35] Republicans had carried off all the offices in the legislature, and the end of January found dissidents like Brown sobered and saddened. The alliance they had so long urged had failed to work, and who could hope that it would work better in the future? Perhaps by now there was no chance for a broad-based Republican coalition in Georgia. Perhaps the stigma of Republican rule was now too great for any politician or any program to overcome.

Even the most optimistic of Bullock's opponents conceded

[32] Peterson Thweatt to Alexander H. Stephens, Atlanta, January 20, 1870, in Alexander Stephens Papers, Library of Congress.

[33] *Ibid.*; Atlanta *New Era*, January 27, 1870.

[34] In the balloting for speaker, W. P. Price received four votes and John Smith, one. The final vote, taken on January 26, was: McWhorter, seventy-six; Bryant, fifty-two; Price, four; and Smith, one. Forty Representatives were absent or abstained. *Journal of the House of Representatives*, 1870, Pt. 1, pp. 33–34.

[35] Atlanta *New Era*, January 30, 1870.

by February that in the senate and in the house on major bills the governor seemed invincible.[36] With most Democrats refusing to vote, the Radicals pushed through the ratification of the Fifteenth Amendment and then, because they contended that the legislature of 1869 had never properly organized, they re-ratified the Fourteenth Amendment as well.[37] They then turned virtually unopposed to the task of choosing United States Senators.

Bryant Republicans and Democrats had long charged that one of Bullock's goals in securing a reorganization of the legislature was the election of Foster Blodgett as Senator. Events on February 16 seemed to confirm such suspicions. The anti-Bullock men offered only token opposition as the Radicals chose Blodgett for the Senate term ending in 1877, Farrow for that ending in 1873, and Richard H. Whiteley for the term expiring in 1871. In fact, Joshua Hill and Dr. H. V. M. Miller had already been elected to the seats now given Farrow and Whiteley, though neither had ever been admitted to the Senate, and state law called for no balloting for the 1877 term until 1871. Bullock and his friends argued that, because the legislature of 1868 had failed to achieve a legal organization, the elections of both Hill and Miller were invalid.[38] But for the election of Blodgett, not even Bullock's supporters could find the slightest legal justification.

In other matters, the reorganized legislature faithfully clung to the view that Georgia remained under military rule and that the General Assembly could transact business only

[36] Peterson Thweatt to John Screven, February 7, 1870, in Arnold–Screven Papers, University of North Carolina. Thweatt reported Brown's views. See also Thweatt to Screven, February 19, 1870, *ibid.*

[37] *Acts and Resolutions of the General Assembly of the State of Georgia,* 1870, pp. 492–93. The Senate ratified the Fifteenth Amendment by a vote of 26–10 and the Fourteenth Amendment by a vote of 25–10. The House accepted the Fifteenth Amendment, 55–29, and the Fourteenth Amendment again, 71–0.

[38] *Journal of the House of Representatives,* 1870, Pt. 1, pp. 95–97.

with General Terry's permission. On February 17, it passed a stay law similar to those enacted in 1866 and 1868; on May 2, it enacted the necessary revenue and appropriation statutes. Otherwise, the assembly accomplished little. In fact, it stood adjourned throughout most of the spring. It recessed in February, after the election of Senators, not to meet again until April. On April 18, it reconvened, to sit for only two weeks before again adjourning to await Congressional action on the status of Georgia. After the initial flurry of activity at Atlanta, then, the drama of Georgia Reconstruction in 1870 shifted to Washington, as Bullock supporters and anti-Bullock men girded themselves for their final efforts to influence Congressional legislation on the readmission of the state.

During the controversy over the reorganization of the General Assembly, both sides had carried their case to Washington. In addition to the usual appeals to Congressional leaders—to Butler for the Radicals and to Lyman Trumbull for the Moderates and Democrats—lobbyists for both factions pleaded with the President to espouse their cause. In December and early January, it appeared that most influential Congressmen and the President himself would sustain Bullock, and anti-Bullock men despaired. "While the President and Congress aid and abet our home-made rascals," the Augusta *Constitutionalist* complained, "it is not quite clear how the salvation of Georgia is to be managed."[39] At about this time, however, politicians prominent in the national administration began to doubt the sincerity of Bullock and his friends. In late January and February, Congress and the President retreated from their support of the governor and his schemes. Their withdrawal of support sealed the doom of Bullock's administration in Georgia.

The immediate cause of Congressional discontent was the

[39] Augusta *Constitutionalist*, January 16, 1870.

construction Bullock, Terry, and, in fact, the War Department had attached to the Reorganization Act of December
22, 1869. Bullock and Terry, of course, contended that the
act remanded Georgia to military rule until Congress should
take further action to readmit the state to the Union.
Though Congress did not debate Georgia affairs during the
reorganization of the General Assembly, several Senators
and Representatives asserted privately that they had never
intended Georgia to remain under military government.[40]
Moreover, they were disturbed that Bullock and Terry—
rather than the members of the General Assembly—were
directing the legislative reorganization. On January 19, the
House of Representatives adopted without debate a resolution offered by Democrat James Brooks of New York, calling upon the commanding general of the United States
Army, William Tecumseh Sherman, to inform the House by
what authority military officers were sitting as a board to
judge the qualifications of General Assembly delegates.[41]
Similarly, the Senate on February 4 adopted Matthew Hale
Carpenter's resolution seeking information about the proceedings in Georgia since the enactment of the reorganization statute.[42] On February 19, after the information requested had been made available, the Senate ordered the
Judiciary Committee to investigate whether the Georgia
legislature had reorganized as directed by Congress.[43]

The Judiciary Committee reported on March 2. Congress,
it declared, had intended only that the Georgia legislature
be reorganized in accordance with the provisions of the
Fourteenth Amendment, that the Negroes be reseated, and

[40] Edward Clifford Anderson Diary, January 28, 1770, in Anderson
Papers, University of North Carolina; Dawson *Journal,* February 10, 1870,
reporting a communication sent from Washington by N. L. Angier.
[41] *Congressional Globe,* 41st Cong., 2nd Sess., XLII, Pt. 1, pp. 575–76.
[42] *Ibid.,* Pt. 2, p. 1029.
[43] *Ibid.,* 1128.

that the Fifteenth Amendment be ratified. The assembly had accomplished these things; the terms of the act of December 22 had been met, and the reorganization measure should cease to operate in Georgia. Furthermore, the committee asserted, Terry and Bullock in convening the military board had "misconstrued" and misapplied the act. On the other hand, the Judiciary Committee acknowledged, no substantial injustice had resulted from the board's activities, for all those disqualified from the General Assembly were unquestionably ineligible to take their seats.[44]

Other Republicans now spoke out against Bullock's maneuvers. Georgia State Treasurer Angier reported that John Sherman and George F. Edmunds, the sponsor of one of the Georgia reorganization bills of 1869, opposed Bullock and condemned Terry's interpretation of the reorganization statute.[45] To this condemnation E. C. Anderson added the names of Ohio Representative John A. Bingham and Secretary of the Interior J. D. Cox.[46]

Most important, of course, was the attitude of the President himself. Grant's friendship with Butler and his seeming readiness to cooperate with Bullock in 1869 had obscured for many several equally important considerations. Before his nomination and election to the Presidency, Grant had always sought a prompt end to the Reconstruction process, and from the beginning of Reconstruction, he had been skeptical of Southern atrocity stories.[47] Furthermore, he had more than a passing acquaintance with Amos T. Akerman, a Georgia Republican, to be sure, but a long-time opponent of Bullock and now a prominent member of the Bryant

[44] *Senate Reports of Committees,* 41st Cong., 2nd Sess., No. 58.
[45] Dawson *Journal,* February 10, 1870.
[46] Anderson Diary, entries for January 14 and January 24, 1870, in Anderson Papers, University of North Carolina.
[47] *Senate Executive Documents,* 39th Cong., 1st Sess., No. 2.

faction.[48] Grant, it seemed, lacked any strong ideological commitment to either side in the Georgia struggle. His only apparent wish in 1870 was to see order and stability restored in the South.

Reports of Grant's attitude during the reorganization crisis of January and February, 1870, are partisan and conflicting. Unquestionably, the President believed Georgia temporarily under military rule and expected Terry to exercise the duties of a military commander. On the other hand, he doubted the necessity for and the wisdom of the reorganization policies pursued by both Terry and Bullock. John E. Bryant's supporters heard indirectly that Grant had expressed indignation at Terry's actions and had transmitted to Georgia "positive orders to break up the Military Commission and to forbid [A. L.] Harris from any further intrusion of his presence as presiding officer" of the house.[49] Grant, the Bryant men rejoiced, was so displeased with Bullock's interference with the legislature that he had in exasperation even authorized Terry to remove the governor, should such a step be necessary "to promote harmony in the General Assembly and to remedy what had been done." No record remains that Grant personally sent any such dispatches. But Bullock seemed to acknowledge that new orders had reached Georgia when he complained that "the Rebels" had "dispatches from Washington that the powers of the District Commander [were] limited to the last reconstruction act" and did not extend to the sweeping authority granted military governors under the first Military Reconstruction Act of March 2, 1867.[50]

48 Bloom, "Georgia Election of April, 1868," p. 80.

49 Anderson Diary, January 28, 1870, reporting an interview with Trumbull, during which Trumbull in turn reported on an interview he had had with the President two weeks earlier, in Anderson Papers, University of North Carolina.

50 Bullock to Judge William Lawrence, Atlanta, January 20, 1870, in Butler Papers.

Grant was certainly not acting like an ardent backer of Bullock's regime, but the anti-Bullock forces probably overstated the case and placed a false construction on the President's motives. A report of a cabinet meeting held on January 20 is instructive, for the reporter, Secretary of State Hamilton Fish, had little partisan interest in Georgia affairs. Fish read to the Cabinet a telegram from Bullock to Butler, begging assistance for the Georgia Radicals. Secretary of War William Worth Belknap also reported receiving several messages from Terry; the general had been "telegraphing continuously for orders, instructions and opinions." Grant apparently wanted nothing so much as to extricate the federal government from the entire affair. Within the Republican party, opposition was mounting to sustaining corrupt Radical regimes in the South, and all Republicans were painfully aware of charges of malfeasance which had been brought against Bullock and his colleagues during the debates of 1869. Moreover, the President knew that, within the Congress, powerful members of his party doubted the legality of the reorganization proceedings. He proposed to "telegraph to Terry that all previous orders & instructions to him . . . [were] withdrawn . . . and that he must decide and act upon his best judgment; [and that] the Administration . . . [had] confidence in his discretion, and [would] sustain him in all matters when it . . . [could] consistently do so."[51] Whether Grant saw and approved the telegram actually sent by General Sherman on January 22—a telegram ordering Terry to "decide all questions as they arise" and assuring him that "the Attorney-General thinks you are the only power there other than that reserved to itself by Congress"—is unclear.[52] Certainly Sherman's telegram went

[51] Hamilton Fish Diary, January 20, 1870, in Hamilton Fish Papers, Library of Congress.

[52] *American Annual Cyclopaedia & Register of Important Events of the*

beyond Grant's proposed message—and it pointedly avoided assuring Terry of the President's backing.

Probably, as the Athens *Southern Banner* speculated, Grant agreed fully with neither the Bullock nor the anti-Bullock men.[53] But his failure to give Bullock the active support which the governor expected came as a distinct shock to Georgia Radicals, and it gave the governor's opponents the encouragement they sorely needed.

The desire of high government officials to be rid of the Georgia question gave a foretaste of things to come. The state had complied with the provisions of the Reorganization Act, and, seemingly, Georgia awaited only the formal admission of her members-elect to Congress. But in Atlanta, Governor Bullock and his allies had other ideas. Should the state now be readmitted and military control withdrawn, the Radicals would certainly meet a crushing defeat in legislative elections scheduled to take place in the fall of 1870. Bullock and his faction, bolstered by Congress and the army, could maintain themselves as long as a friendly legislature could stave off investigations of financial wrongdoing. Already, State Treasurer Angier had charged the governor with misuse of state funds, and Democrats were grumbling about excessive state aid to Republican-owned railroads, the failure of Superintendent Blodgett to pay the proceeds of the Western & Atlantic's operations into the Georgia treasury, and soaring state expenses.[54] The

---

Year 1870 (New York: D. Appleton & Company, 1871), 334. Apparently basing their conclusions on the Sherman telegram, the writers of the *Annual Cyclopaedia* asserted that Grant was at first unhappy with but later acquiesced in the proceedings of the military board. I do not believe this to have been the case. See also Sefton, *United States Army and Reconstruction,* 203–204.

[53] Athens *Southern Banner*, February 18, 1870.

[54] For the most convenient recent summary of corruption in Georgia during the Bullock administration, see Conway, *Reconstruction of Georgia,*

election of a hostile General Assembly would inevitably mean for Bullock searching investigations and—so the governor feared—impeachment. In the spring of 1870, Georgia's Radicals made their last bid before Congress, a bid to prolong the term of the General Assembly delegates elected in 1868 by postponing the regularly scheduled elections. The bid failed—not because Bullock and his lobbyists suddenly failed to present their pleas before Congress, but, in part at least, because Congress and the Administration had tired of sustaining a corrupt faction in Georgia and were willing to see the Bullock regime end.

The complex legislative history of the Georgia bills which came before the House and Senate in 1870 would confound the most expert parliamentarian. In the House, Bullock's old friend Butler introduced a measure embodying the governor's proposals, which permitted the postponement of Gen-

202–15, which is, however, more favorable to Bullock than is Thompson's *Reconstruction in Georgia*. James Houston Johnston, *The Western and Atlantic Railroad of the State of Georgia* (Atlanta: Stein Publishing Company, State Printers, 1931), contains excerpts from reports of committees investigating mismanagement of that road during Reconstruction. For a report of a friendly Republican committee investigating railroad corruption in 1870, see *Journal of the Senate*, 1870, Pt. 1, pp. 920–30; a hostile Democratic investigation of the same subject resulted in a report printed as *Evidence Taken by the Joint Committee of the Legislature . . . Appointed to Investigate the Management of the State Road, Under the Administration of R. B. Bullock and Foster Blodgett* (Atlanta: J. Henly Smith at the Daily Sun Office, 1872). For Angier's charges against Bullock, see his letter to the Finance Committee of the Georgia House of Representatives, Atlanta, January [1869], in Rufus B. Bullock Papers, Georgia Department of Archives and History. The charges appear more conveniently in *Ku Klux Conspiracy*, VI, 149ff. The House of Representatives commended Angier for his zeal and honesty; see the *Journal of the House of Representatives*, 1869, pp. 260–66. But the Republican-dominated Senate was more sympathetic to Bullock, and charged that Angier himself had diverted state funds to his own personal bank account; see *Journal of the Senate*, 1869, pp. 319–21. Bullock tried, without success, to have Angier removed from office in 1870; see the resolution and articles of impeachment against Angier, in Nedom L. Angier Papers, Georgia Department of Archives and History.

eral Assembly elections until November, 1872.[55] This time,
however, the Radicals were not to have things entirely their
own way. Bullock's accounts of outrages in Georgia convinced fewer Congressmen in 1870 than they had in 1869.
As one Representative put it, "There have been disorders in
Georgia, I know, but in my judgment they have been gross-
ly exaggerated. I have always noticed, the moment Georgia
affairs are to come up, we read in the [Washington] Chronicle . . . of outrages; then we have Governor Bullock and his
staff here with more outrages, then an act of Congress."[56]
On March 7, Representative Bingham of Ohio offered an
amendment to Butler's bill, stipulating that elections must
take place in Georgia at the time required by the state
constitution.[57] Although Butler, speaking for Bullock and
the Radicals, protested that the sole purpose of prolongation
was to allow those elected in 1868 but seated only in 1870
to serve out a full term, few were deceived. "It is very well
understood what this bill is for," a disgusted Democrat
retorted. "It is to prolong the tenure of office of a certain
gentleman in the State of Georgia."[58] On March 8, with the
support of a coalition of Moderate Republicans and Democrats, the House passed the Butler bill—with the crippling
Bingham amendment attached.[59]

In the Senate, the first real action on the Georgia problem
came on March 18, when Charles D. Drake, a Republican
from Missouri, sought to attach to the House bill an amendment permitting the President to send troops to any state
to quell disturbances which were beyond the control of the

[55] *Congressional Globe*, 41st Cong., 2nd Sess., XLII, Pt. 2, pp. 1570,
1704, 1705.
[56] *Ibid.*, 1710.
[57] *Ibid.*, 1743–44.
[58] *Ibid.*, 1706.
[59] *Ibid.*, 1770. Butler abstained from voting on the Bingham amendment.

state administration.[60] Then, on April 7, Kansas Republican Samuel Pomeroy offered another amendment, declaring the government of Georgia provisional under the Reconstruction acts of 1867.[61] Not even the most experienced Senators could completely understand the proceedings when the House bill and the Senate amendments were debated in Committee of the Whole on April 19. Despite the reported objections of President Grant,[62] the Senate accepted the Pomeroy amendment and acquiesced in the Drake amendment as well.[63] Also offered during the all-night session were two new proposals. One, introduced by Senator Henry Wilson of Massachusetts, would have permitted the postponement of the fall elections.[64] Pomeroy immediately advanced a substitute for Wilson's amendment, declaring Georgia's state government provisional, but ordering elections held as scheduled in the fall of 1870.[65] Perhaps Pomeroy believed that under federal protection the Georgia Radicals could carry the fall election. The adoption of his substitute left the House measure amended beyond recognition, and the Senate's decision later to strike out the entire bill only complicated matters. The measure finally passed by the Senate and sent to the House declared the government of Georgia provisional and decreed that the state remain under military rule. Elections, however, would be held in the fall for members of the General Assembly, and the newly-elected members would meet in December to "organize, preparatory to the admission of the State to representation in Congress."[66]

[60] *Ibid.*, Pt. 3, pp. 2088–89.
[61] *Ibid.*, 2491.
[62] Rome *Courier,* April 29, 1870.
[63] *Congressional Globe,* 41st Cong., 2nd Sess., Pt. 4, pp. 2817ff.
[64] *Journal of the Senate,* 41st Cong., 2nd Sess., 515–16.
[65] *Ibid.*, 516–17.
[66] *Ibid.*, 516–17, 521.

Not until June 23 did the House again debate the Georgia
bill. On the twenty-fourth, it voted to reject the Senate mon-
strosity and to insist on the House bill as originally passed.
In the conference committee the Senate delegates gave way
before their counterparts from the House, and the bill for
the readmission of Georgia, with the Bingham amendment
attached, became law on July 15.[67]

By far the most entertaining part of the debates over the
Georgia bill took place not in the halls of Congress but in
the hearing rooms of Lyman Trumbull's Senate Judiciary
Committee. On April 18, George Edmunds, now thoroughly
disgusted with Bullock, had risen in the Senate to demand
an inquiry into alleged attempts to purchase the vote of
Senators on the Georgia bill.[68] The ensuing investigation
probably did little to alter the final result in the Georgia
case, for by the time the committee reported its findings,
both houses had already voted to reject Bullock's demands.
Nonetheless, the hearings revealed much about Bullock's
lobbying tactics and the desperation with which he and his
colleagues had worked to postpone the fall elections.

To the usual supply of atrocity stories, it appeared, Bullock had on this occasion added several new elements. The
governor summoned thirty-three or thirty-four Negro members of the legislature to Washington to play on the sympathies of Radical Congressmen. To pay their expenses, he
himself advanced between twelve and fourteen hundred
dollars.[69] During the course of the debate on the Georgia
bill, the governor paid to John W. Forney, editor of the
influential Washington *Chronicle*, $4,228, ostensibly for
"printing expenses." Although Bullock and Forney agreed

[67] *Congressional Globe*, 41st Cong., 2nd Sess., XLII, Pt. 6, p. 4727.

[68] *Ibid.*, Pt. 3, p. 2740.

[69] *Senate Reports of Committees*, 41st Cong., 2nd Sess., No. 175, p. ix,
and Bullock's testimony on the expenses of the Negro lobbyists, 136.

on the proper charges for the printing of propaganda material supplied by Bullock,[70] no witness, not even the governor himself, could give an exact account of the services for which Forney received payments. Much of the money, the committee hinted, must be considered a bribe—a payment to Forney to guarantee editorials favorable to Bullock's position.[71]

Also a part of the picture were the extensive railroad interests of the Georgia Radicals. The state-owned Western & Atlantic, of which Blodgett was superintendent, was only the most visible of these interests, for Hannibal I. Kimball, a northern entrepreneur and close ally of Bullock, controlled the Brunswick & Albany and the Cartersville & Van Wert, both recipients of large state aid grants and both allegedly awarded payments from state funds before completion of the track mileage required by law. Wild tales of bribery and corruption circulated in Washington. Bullock himself reported learning that, should he arrange the sale of the Western & Atlantic to a group of New York capitalists, a certain Senator—later identified to him as Samuel Pomeroy—might vote for prolongation.[72] The governor self-righteously denied considering the offer.

In other cases, only the refusal of prominent Congressmen to accept bribes seems to have prevented Georgia Republicans from spending large sums to secure votes against the Bingham amendment. P. J. Avery, a director of the Brunswick & Albany, admitted saying that defeat of the Bingham amendment would be worth $10,000 to the Radical faction. Though he acknowledged visiting with Edmunds, however, Avery denied making any effort to influence senatorial

[70] *Ibid.*, 138.

[71] *Ibid.*, vi, and Atlanta *Daily Intelligencer*, July 5, 1870.

[72] *Senate Reports of Committees*, 41st Cong., 2nd Sess., No. 175, pp. 143–48.

votes.[73] But one Lewis Porter, an assistant postmaster in Georgia and a Bullock partisan who had apparently acted as a go-between for Georgia Radicals and certain Senators, claimed that Avery had suggested spending money to influence the votes of Senators Howe, Conkling, and Matthew Hale Carpenter.[74] Porter had $10,000 in Georgia railroad bonds at his disposal; he suggested to James Hughes, an Indiana lawyer, the Bullock group's willingness to pay such a sum to sway the vote of Senator Carpenter. Others, including Joshua Hill, had also heard that bribes of $10,000 in railroad bonds were available.[75] Despite all the rumors, however, not a single case of bribery could be proved.

When the Georgia bill finally passed, many Georgians remained uncertain as to whether the state would hold an election in the fall.[76] Though the Bingham amendment should have swept away any doubts, the issue remained unsettled throughout the summer, while the Radicals made one final attempt to prolong their administration. General Terry had announced that, even should Congress readmit Georgia, the state government would remain provisional until after Georgia's Senators and Representatives took their seats in Congress.[77] Military rule would continue, and no elections need be held. In a message to the General Assembly on July 18, announcing the passage of the Georgia bill, Bullock adopted Terry's arguments. The General Assembly might proceed with legislation, he conceded, but in reality

[73] *Ibid.*, 31.

[74] *Ibid.*, iii.

[75] *Ibid.*, i, 22–23.

[76] See, for example, Milledgeville *Southern Recorder*, July 19, 1870; J. R. Sneed to Lyman Trumbull, Savannah, July 22, 1870, in Lyman Trumbull Papers, Library of Congress.

[77] Terry to William Tecumseh Sherman, Atlanta, July 2, 1870, in William Tecumseh Sherman Papers.

the state government remained subject to military authority.[78]

Republicans in the House and Senate immedately took
Bullock's hint. On July 26, a resolution postponing the fall
elections was offered in the Senate; on the twenty-ninth, the
Radical majority secured passage of a slightly altered version.[79] Bullock's control over his party in the House, however, was as shaky as ever. The anti-Bullock Representatives
massed their forces to defeat the Senate resolution when it
came to a vote in the House.[80]

Prolongation had met its final defeat. Elections in the fall
of 1870 now seemed inevitable, and elections were sure to
mean defeat for the Bullock faction. Bullock's period of
domination in Georgia politics seemed to have ended as it
had begun—with the governor's inability to hold together
and control the warring factions of the state's Republican
party.

[78] Bullock's message "To the General Assembly," July 18, 1870, in Rufus
B. Bullock Papers, Georgia Department of Archives and History.
[79] *Journal of the Senate,* 1870, Pt. 2, pp. 29, 50.
[80] *Journal of the House of Representatives,* 1870, Pt. 2, p. 343.

CHAPTER IX

Too Little, Too Late

The defeat of the prolongation resolutions in the General Assembly had by August of 1870 removed what little hope Governor Bullock could have retained of avoiding a fall election. Even members of his own faction now turned against him and demanded elections. The state attorney general, Henry Farrow, so zealous in his efforts for the Bullock administration in January but now, as a Senator-elect, equally zealous in guarding his reputation with the Congress, pronounced the governor's arguments for prolongation specious. Republicans, he asserted piously, must not seek to advance their own cause by depriving Georgians of their constitutional right to hold elections.[1]

Moreover, no longer could the governor appeal from the state to the national party. Disillusionment with Bullock's

[1] Atlanta *Constitution*, July 18, 1870, quoting Farrow's address upon his election as Senator from Georgia.

regime and with corrupt Radical rule in general, the ambitions of Moderate Republicans like Trumbull and their increasing power, and a President who wavered between Radical and Moderate factions—all these had discredited ultra-Radicals like Butler in Washington and had diminished their influence. Moreover, there seemed in the summer of 1870 a pervasive desire finally to dispose of the Georgia issue.[2]

Soon after the bill for Georgia readmission became law on July 15, but while discussion of the prolongation resolution was yet proceding in the General Assembly, rumors spread that President Grant himself favored the holding of regular fall elections in the state. The new United States Attorney General, Georgia Moderate Republican Amos T. Akerman, also urged that elections take place.[3] He and the President apparently joined forces to put pressure on the Georgia Republicans. "Just before the President left . . . [Washington]," Akerman wrote Secretary of War W. W. Belknap on August 6, "he desired me to request you to write an unofficial letter to Genl Terry, urging that officer to exert his moral influence in favor of the holding of an election in Georgia this year, unless he shall be satisfied that a fair election cannot be had."[4]

In the fall, Akerman himself returned to Georgia and supervised the drafting and enactment of an election bill calling for balloting to take place in December. No ordinary statute, the Akerman election bill seemed brilliantly cal-

---

[2] Patrick J. Riddleberger, "The Radicals' Abandonment of the Negro during Reconstruction," *Journal of Negro History,* XLV (April, 1960), 91.

[3] Augusta *Constitutionalist,* August 14, 1870, quoting a letter from Akerman, dated August 8.

[4] Amos T. Akerman to W. W. Belknap, August 6, 1870, in William Worth Belknap Papers, Duke University. A copy of this letter also appears in the Akerman Papers, Georgia Department of Archives and History, quoted in full in Philip Fitzhugh Stryker to Mrs. Mary G. Bryan, December 29, 1962.

culated to save the Georgia Republican party—if not the Radical faction—from what had seemed an inevitable defeat. The election would begin on December 22 and continue for three days. Election managers would be appointed by the governor and confirmed by the legislature—the Republican legislature. No election need be held in any county for which Bullock should neglect to appoint election managers. No voters could be challenged at the polls. The balloting, in short, would take place under the direction of Republicans, under rules which in the past had helped ensure Republican success.[5] The votes on the Akerman bill—62–57 in the house and 17–10 in the senate—reflected the divided loyalties of the dissident Republicans. A few joined Democrats in voting against the measure or abstaining. Others, including Bryant, who still professed themselves Republicans and opposed only Bullock and his faction, voted for the bill as the only means of saving the Republican party in the state. Bullock signed the measure on October 3, 1870.[6]

That a President who only weeks before had seemed willing to permit the removal of Governor Bullock, and an attorney general who had consistently opposed Georgia Radicalism, should now seem to reverse their positions and act to guarantee a Republican victory in Georgia is scarcely surprising. Democratic papers in the state thought they saw

[5] The Atlanta *Daily True Georgian*, edited in 1870 by the *New Era's* former editor, Samuel Bard, charged on August 20, 1870, that Bullock had held a caucus of the Negro members of the General Assembly and assured them that no elections would take place in the fall. Defeat of prolongation resolutions in the assembly, Bullock assured them, made no difference; he would veto any election bill passed by the legislature. I have found no evidence to support Bard's charges, but if his allegations were true, Bullock obviously found the Akerman bill so attractive that he was willing to sign it.

[6] *Acts and Resolutions*, 1870, Title VII, No. 55, pp. 62–66. See also *Journal of the Senate of the State of Georgia*, 1870, Pt. 3, pp. 274–75, and *Journal of the House of Representatives of the State of Georgia*, 1870, pp. 874–75.

behind the sudden conversion of both Grant and Akerman a scheme to win Senate seats for Akerman and Bullock. They believed their suspicions confirmed when Grant in November ordered fresh troops to Georgia, to remain until after the elections.[7] The "grand design" of the national administration, these papers reported, was to effect a reconciliation between Radical and Moderate Republicans in Georgia and the election of a Republican General Assembly. Should the strategy be successful, the unpopular and questionable election of Foster Blodgett to the Senate term ending in 1877 would be abrogated and new Senators chosen. Bullock himself would take one Senate seat.[8] Had the Democratic editors known during the fall campaign of Bullock's insistent demands that Congress avoid seating the Georgia Representatives until after the Christmas recess, they would doubtless have raised even louder cries of foul play.[9]

It is entirely possible that Bullock ardently desired the Senate seat, but most unlikely that either Akerman or the President acted solely to further the governor's personal ambitions. Whatever their factional affiliations, both Grant and Akerman, as prominent members of the national Republican party, had a heavy stake in maintaining a Republican administration in Georgia—particularly in the face of a rising tide of reform which threatened to sweep Grant from the White House in 1872. A Republican victory in Georgia in 1870 would enhance Akerman's influence within the Administration and would greatly strengthen the party in Georgia in anticipation of the 1872 elections. Whether Bullock continued as governor was probably unimportant to

[7] See, for example, Augusta *Constitutionalist,* November 30, 1870.

[8] *Ibid.;* Augusta *Chronicle and Sentinel,* December 29, 1870.

[9] Bullock to Simon Cameron, December 1, 1870, in Cameron Papers. Bullock told Cameron that he had sent similar letters to Oliver Perry Morton of Indiana and to Butler. He would willingly "leave the matter with the friends of the nation and the state administration."

the national leaders; in fact, they would likely have preferred the state in the hands of a reform administration.
But one-half the members of the Georgia senate and house
of representatives and all delegates to Congress had to face
election campaigns in the fall of 1870. The Akerman bill
seemed an attempt to salvage for the Georgia party, and its
members of whatever faction, as much from these contests as
possible.

The Akerman bill could not help the Republicans until the
voting actually began, and in waging a campaign during the
fall of 1870, the Georgia party encountered what in retrospect seem overwhelming problems. The party received
only half-hearted support from the national Union League
organization and virtually none from the Republican committee.[10] Republicans had difficulty in finding candidates
for even local positions,[11] and, although the usual round of
meetings and speeches took place, prominent Bullock men
freely predicted another disastrous Republican defeat.[12]

In their desperation, Republicans in Georgia could not
fall back, as could the party in so many other Southern
states, on a state-organized and Republican-controlled force
of Negro militia. In other states, governors used the militia
to counteract the activities of the Democratic-dominated Ku
Klux Klan—to protect Republican voters during election

[10] J. H. Edmunds to Zachariah Chandler, Union League of America,
National Council Chamber, October 16, 1870, in Zachariah Chandler Papers,
Library of Congress. There is no correspondence concening the fall elec-
tions in the papers of William E. Chandler, Secretary of the Republican
Congressional Campaign Committee.

[11] In Atlanta, Republicans asked H. I. Kimball, H. C. Holcombe, William
Markham, and J. W. G. White to run for mayor. All refused; Republicans
finally nominated an independent Democrat. See Clarence A. Bacote, "William Finch, Negro Councilman and Political Activities in Atlanta During
Early Reconstruction," *Journal of Negro History*, XL (October, 1955), 345
and 351.

[12] Richard H. Whiteley to Henry P. Farrow, August 15, 1870, in Henry
P. Farrow Collection, University of Georgia.

campaigns and at the polls. While the Georgia legislature remained under Democratic control in 1869, Bullock and the Radicals had successfully sought Congressional prohibitions on the organization of a state militia force; not until July 5, 1870, was Georgia allowed to organize her own militia.[13] Even then, however, it was unlikely that the Republicans could put together an organization effective enough to assist in the fall elections. Since the Democrats had retained control of most of the county offices in the state, they could prevent Republicans from using a state militia to the fullest extent in the areas where it was most badly needed to support wavering Republican voters.[14]

In the fall campaigns, Bullock's Republicans belatedly changed their strategy. Gone were the direct, polemical appeals to Negro voters. In the columns of the *New Era,* purchased by the administration from Samuel Bard early in 1870, and in their speeches and campaign broadsides, the Bullock men sought a new alliance of "progressive" men— of old-line Whigs whose support they had spurned in earlier contests, of conservative Union men of 1861, of broad-minded Democrats, and even of anti-Reconstructionists of 1868.[15] The "new" Republican party, the Bullock supporters hoped, would be a broad-based coalition of all who had backed Grant, of merchants and industrial promoters interested in internal improvements and in Republican state aid programs, and of Negroes and yeoman whites who de-

[13] Otis A. Singletary, *The Negro Militia and Reconstruction* (Austin: University of Texas, 1957), 9.

[14] *Ibid.,* 11–12; Thompson, *Reconstruction in Georgia,* 365.

[15] *The Campaign Speech of Hon. Foster Blodgett, on the Issues Involved in the Georgia Campaign, Delivered at Augusta, November 3, 1870* (Atlanta: *New Era* Printing Establishment, 1870). See also Dawson *Journal,* December 24, 1870, reporting a speech by Henry M. Turner. Turner claimed before the election that many white Democrats in southwest Georgia would vote Republican.

sired to secure at long last a system of free public schools.[16]
Even the Bullock men, apparently, recognized the loss of
prestige the Georgia Republican party had suffered. By
minimizing their appeal to the Negro, by soliciting support
from dissident Democrats, and by concentrating their efforts
on dividing the white vote, they hoped to restore to their
party its dignity and respectability.[17] Their program for
1870, in short, was the program Joseph E. Brown had urged
the party to adopt since 1867.

Dignity and respectability were official watchwords, but
they could not break the habits of two years, and many Republican speakers proved unable to abandon the rhetoric
of previous campaigns. Lacking a state militia, lacking a
statewide Republican press, and above all, lacking the strong
Congressional support which had long played so important
a role in Georgia politics, Bullock and the Radicals fell back
in the fall of 1870 on the time-worn technique of ex-
ploiting the disturbances and violence which occasionally
erupted in every Reconstruction political campaign.[18] Condemnation of Democratic "outrages" against Negro and
white Radicals seemed out of place in a campaign directed
at dissidents within the Democratic party, for they might
alienate many party members who were otherwise disposed
to heed Bullock's pleas. Almost certainly, the atrocity propaganda would attract few new voters to the Republican camp,

[16] *The Campaign Speech of Hon. Foster Blodgett.*

[17] Richard H. Whiteley to Henry P. Farrow, Bainbridge, August 15, 1870,
in Henry P. Farrow Collection, University of Georgia; Matthew Hale
Carpenter to Farrow, Milwaukee, August 30, 1870, *ibid.*

[18] Democrats reacted swiftly and angrily when Radicals renewed their
charges of atrocities, alleging that Bullock had once again manufactured
tales of violence. The Dawson *Journal* on September 29, 1870, went so
far as to suggest that Bullock and his supporters planned "to have murdered,
in each county of the State, a prominent colored man, and to accuse the Ku
Klux Klan with [*sic*] the outrage."

and resorting to it during the canvass seems a major tactical blunder.

As the campaign progressed, Bullock's personal unpopularity, the mounting evidence of graft and corruption throughout his administration, and the incontrovertible fact that Georgia had a normal majority of Democratic voters all seemed to foreshadow a Democratic triumph in the December elections. Even the frankly partisan Akerman election bill seemed more of a nuisance than an insurmountable obstacle to Democratic victory, for the Democrats, like the Republicans, never hesitated during the Reconstruction period to manipulate election returns to their own advantage. Only some irreparable division within their own ranks, Democratic leaders believed, could cost their party the elections of 1870.

Such a division in fact threatened during the first weeks after passage of the Georgia bill. The fear that dissident Republicans led by Bryant, Bard, and Brown would offer a ticket which would woo many old-line Whigs from their alliance with the Democracy plagued many stalwart Democrats during July and August.[19] Some Democrats even feared that the Bryant men would organize a formal third party, to be known as the "People's" or the "Conservative" party in an effort to unite all those opposed to prolongation and to "wipe out Democratic lines."[20] Understandably, Democrats proved reluctant to sacrifice their own party

[19] Judson Clements Ward, Jr., "Georgia Under the Bourbon Democrats, 1872–1890" (Ph.D. dissertation, University of North Carolina, 1947), 46–47. See also James R. Randall to Alexander H. Stephens, Augusta, July 23, 1870, in Alexander Stephens Papers, Library of Congress.

[20] Sidney Dell to Alexander H. Stephens, Atlanta, August 5, 1870, and Peterson Thweatt to Stephens, enclosing a clipping from an unidentified paper, quoting the LaGrange *Reporter*, Milledgeville, August 15, 1870, in Alexander Stephens Papers, Library of Congress. Bryant's "National Republican Club" seemed likely to back independent candidates throughout the state, but it had no regular statewide party organization.

organization and identity to a new, untested, and possibly suicidal coalition. Yet they knew that refusal to cooperate with the Bryant Republicans or to welcome their support for Democratic candidates could result in a Republican victory in December. To find a middle ground which would preserve their own party while preventing the defection of the old-line Whigs and the possible success of the Republicans, then, became the object of Democratic strategy during the fall campaign.

That the Democratic party was once more painfully divided in its attitude toward the dissident Republicans became evident at the party convention held in Atlanta on August 17. A compromise platform sought to avoid all divisive party questions; politics, the Augusta *Chronicle and Sentinel* observed, would be left out of the canvass.[21] The platform denounced Republican corruption and pledged the party to stand on the national Democratic platform of 1868, and it invited all to join in the campaign to overthrow Radical rule.[22] In a major concession to the old-line Whigs whose support the Democrats so desired to retain, the convention chose as its permanent chairman Alfred H. Colquitt, a former Whig and one of the wealthiest planters in the state. The details of party organization it left to district conventions, which it charged with the task of mobilizing the local committees in preparation for the campaign.

Failing to comprehend the need for an equivocal platform, many Democrats denounced the willingness of the state organization to cooperate with the independent Republicans.[23] Calling the party's policy "timid" and continuing to stigmatize the Bryant men as "Radicals," these Democrats

[21] Augusta *Chronicle and Sentinel,* August 20, 1870.
[22] Atlanta *Constitution,* August 18, 1870.
[23] See, for example, Athens *Southern Banner,* September 16, 1870. See also C. P. Culver to Alexander H. Stephens, September 13, 1870, in Alexander Stephens Papers, Library of Congress.

urged their colleagues to "make a bold aggressive onslaught on the blunders and crimes of Radicalism." The Democratic party, they declared, "must go before the people panoplied with the Constitution . . . and smite the centralists, and the extravagant usurpers, hip and thigh."[24]

The Democratic State Executive Committee and its chairman, Edward Clifford Anderson, favored working within the framework laid down by the convention. In October, Anderson urged his fellow Democrats to relinquish their lingering hopes of holding an election in November as specified in the state constitution and to bend all their efforts to the December contests.[25] For the local committees and clubs, the executive committee established two goals: harmony within the party, and the prevention of Republican fraud during the elections.[26]

The appeal of the Democratic state committee, like that of the party's convention, went out to all who were dissatisfied with Bullock's rule. "All classes of citizens," Anderson declared in a formal "Address to the Democracy of Georgia," "deplore the rule of the present regime. Their pride and their pockets alike rebel against its continuance. The colored people are ready to be delivered from their new bondage." Despite the welcome which he offered to independent voters, however, Anderson refused to bestow his blessing on independent candidates. Such candidates, he warned, must withdraw from the race; should they refuse to do so, Democrats must deny them any aid.[27] Independent Republicans, in short, should formally fuse with the Democratic party.

Appeals in the Democratic and the independent press

[24] Athens *Southern Banner,* October 21, 1870.
[25] Savannah *Morning News,* October 26, 1870.
[26] Atlanta *Constitution,* December 3, 1870.
[27] Anderson's address, quoted in the Augusta *Chronicle and Sentinel.* December 9, 1870.

throughout the campaign remained remarkably similar. Both groups focused on the "crimes" of the Radical regime. "The whole weal of the State," they agreed, "depends upon our having an honest set of officers this year particularly in the Legislature."[28] In tones alternately sarcastic and sweetly reasonable, the press repeated the old, familiar charges against Bullock—charges of misuse of public funds, of improper payments to state-supported railroads, of extravagance in the state administration. Bullock, not the Republican party as a whole, became the target of Democratic attacks; the entire case of the Democracy and of the independent Republicans as well rested on the public's opinion of a single man.[29]

Officially, the Democratic party called upon all its members to maintain peace during the elections and to abide by the provisions of the Akerman election statute, however unfair or distasteful they might be.[30] Unofficially, however, the Democrats prepared to carry the election by any means at their command. Following the precedent set by Bullock's proclamation in the fall of 1868, the General Assembly soon after it passed the election bill had declared state poll taxes unconstitutional and suspended their collection. Now, in addition to their regular activities in Ku Klux dens or "military companies," Democrats prepared under Linton Stephens' direction to arrest for fraudulent voting any Republicans who appeared at the polls without having paid their taxes.[31]

Only one thing seemed likely, in the final stages of the

[28] Atlanta *Constitution,* December 21, 1870.

[29] See, for example, *ibid.,* November 6, 15, 17, 20, and December 3, 10, 1870; Augusta *Chronicle and Sentinel,* December 20, 1870; and Athens *Southern Banner,* November 18, 1870.

[30] Anderson's "Address," Augusta *Chronicle and Sentinel,* December 9, 1870; see also the *Chronicle and Sentinel,* December 20, 1870.

[31] Atlanta *Daily Intelligencer,* December 17, 1870.

campaign, to upset Democratic hopes—the defection of their most prominent spokesman. Benjamin H. Hill, for so long the Democracy's most stalwart voice, issued an open address to the people of Georgia on December 11. The Fourteenth and Fifteenth Amendments, he announced, were now a part of the Constitution; all Georgians must accept them in good faith.[32] His address sounded suspiciously like the one issued by Joseph E. Brown in 1867, and puzzled, angered Democrats at once raised cries of treachery. Some saw Hill and Brown ready to join hands to "start a new party in Georgia . . . alike antagonistic to extreme Radicalism and Bourbon Democracy."[33] Others, more cautious, thought Hill to be "after something" which they could not as yet identify.[34] Rumors flew that Hill and Foster Blodgett had become fast friends.[35] The Milledgeville *Federal Union* assured its readers that Hill had "embarked on board the Radical ship with all his traps." "The inducements for such a venture" would "all come to light in due time."[36] All Democrats worried about the effect Hill's address would have on party morale.

In fact, Hill had not wholeheartedly joined with the Radicals. Instead, he had combined with Brown, Bullock, and others in an effort to salvage the business profits, if not the political policies, of Radical rule. His purpose, however, became clear only after the December balloting.

[32] The address was widely reprinted; it first appeared in the Augusta *Chronicle and Sentinel,* December 11, 1870. See also Pearce, *Benjamin H. Hill,* 204–209.

[33] Griffin *Star,* undated clipping, filed under December 28, 1870, in Alexander Stephens Papers, Library of Congress.

[34] James R. Randall to Alexander H. Stephens, December 15, 1870, *ibid.*

[35] Undated clipping from an unidentified paper, filed under December 28, 1870, *ibid.*

[36] Undated, unidentified clipping, *ibid.* See also Bard's *Daily True Georgian,* December 22, 1870, rejoicing in Hill's supposed conversion to Radicalism.

Ordinary statistics tell little about the balloting which took place on December 22, 23, and 24. In the Congressional elections, the only ones for which statistics are available, Republicans increased their share of the total vote by 8 percent, and the party polled over 10,000 more votes than it had in the presidential contest of 1868. The Democratic vote, by contrast, dropped by over 4,000.[37] Seemingly, the patterns of support for the Republican party differed in no way from those of 1868.[38] In North Georgia, Republicans continued to receive the backing of white farmers; in the Black Belt and seacoast counties, their votes came from Negroes and probably from those who worked in or owned the regions' few manufacturing establishments. In the wiregrass region, the party apparently retained the support of Negroes and laboring men.

But the Republicans had sustained a crushing defeat. They had held most of their former supporters to the party, but they had failed to attract the old-line Whigs, independent Democrats, and former Union men at whom their campaign appeals were directed. Democrats elected four of Georgia's seven Congressmen, seventy-one of eighty-six new members of the house of representatives, and nineteen of twenty-two senators.[39] In the Black Belt and along the coast, Chatham, Richmond, and Burke counties, strongholds of Republicanism which in 1868 had each returned three Negro members to the state house of representatives, now each returned three Democrats. Two Democrats replaced two Republicans as representatives from the Black Belt counties of Columbia, Hancock, Jefferson, Muscogee, Newton, Oglethorpe, Pulaski, Talbot, Warren, and Wilkes; Banks, Bryan,

[37] In 1868, Republicans polled 57,134 votes and Democrats 102,822 in the presidential election; in the congressional elections of 1870, Republicans received 67,643 votes, and Democrats, 98,413.

[38] See Appendix.

[39] Thompson, *Reconstruction in Georgia*, 270–71.

Campbell, Henry, Laurens, Lincoln, and Pierce each replaced their single incumbent Republican member with a
Democrat. Only five counties—all of them in the Black Belt
—returned a solid Republican delegation to the state house
of representatives.[40] The legislature which would convene
in November, 1871, then, would have an impressive Democratic majority in both the house and senate.

Predictably, the Republicans cried fraud, and contested
election cases continued to plague the state well into 1871.[41]
Democratic editors alleged that Radical election managers in
Richmond County refused to number the ballots as required
by law, "in order to shield and protect their hordes of illegal
voters."[42] In Savannah, Democrats claimed, Radicals trans-
ported "great hordes of negroes from the Ogeechee and
South Carolina" to stuff Republican votes into the ballot
boxes.[43] In Calhoun County, Republicans were supposed
to have stolen the ballot boxes when it appeared that Democratic candidates had won.[44] But the Radicals charged that
Democrats had won the election only by marching Negroes
to the polls, by resorting to intimidation and Klan rides,
and by themselves tampering with the ballot boxes.[45] Almost
none of these charges can be verified, but one well-docu-
mented episode in Sparta suggests that once more, both
sides shared some guilt. When Negroes in Sparta attempted
to vote without having paid the poll taxes declared uncon-

[40] *Ibid.*

[41] See, for example, T. J. Simmons to Bullock, February 7, 1871, in
Rufus B. Bullock Papers, Georgia Department of Archives and History.

[42] Augusta *Chronicle and Sentinel,* December 21, 1870.

[43] Anderson Diary, December 28 [?], 1870, in Anderson Papers, University of North Carolina.

[44] Dawson *Journal,* January 5, 1871.

[45] *Ku Klux Conspiracy,* VII, 1038, testimony of Henry M. Turner. See
also Stearns, *Black Man of the South,* 287–89, alleging fraud in Washington,
Jefferson, Burke, Columbia, Warren, Glasscock, Hancock, Talliaferro, Oglethorpe, Elbert, Lincoln, Wilkes, and McDuffie counties.

stitutional by the Republican General Assembly, Linton Stephens and other Democrats obtained warrants for their arrest and for the arrest of the three election managers who had knowingly encouraged "illegal" voting.[46] In turn, Stephens was himself arrested for violating the Enforcement Acts, federal statutes which provided penalties for interfering with any citizen attempting to vote. A grand jury sitting in Macon in April, 1871, refused to indict him.[47]

That the Democrats could have won an entirely fair election under the Akerman law seems doubtful; certainly the law itself was so blatantly partisan that it invited the equally partisan reaction which it provoked. The Radicals, however, knew they were beaten, and they had no hopes of overturning the election results. Few even bothered to pen the usual protests to Radical Congressmen in Washington.[48] Bullock and his colleagues could only attempt to salvage something for themselves from the wreckage.

II

Bullock's efforts to broaden the economic and social base of his party by wooing former Democrats to the Republican camp produced their most obvious results in a remarkable agreement hammered out between warring economic and political interests during the fall of 1870. As it became increasingly clear that, despite the Akerman bill, Republicans

[46] Mary Stephens [Mrs. Linton Stephens] to Alexander H. Stephens, December 21, 1870, in Alexander Stephens Papers, Manhattanville College of the Sacred Heart.

[47] Richard Malcolm Johnston and W. H. Browne, *Life of Alex. H. Stephens* (Philadelphia: J. B. Lippincott & Co., 1884), 503–504.

[48] The only protest from Georgia Republicans in the papers of such prominent national leaders as Grant, Butler, William E. Chandler, or John Sherman, came from one William Graham, a scalawag, and concerned only the election in Augusta. See Graham to Benjamin F. Butler, Augusta, January 23, 1871, in Butler Papers.

would lose control of the General Assembly in the December elections, the governor once again began his search for ways of perpetuating his influence in Georgia politics. At the same time, a restive legislature, angered by the waste and corruption in the state road under the management of Foster Blodgett and by Blodgett's failure to pay the profits of the Western & Atlantic's operations into the state treasury, determined to remove the road from state control. In the proposal by Democratic leader Dunlap Scott that the road be leased for a term of years to a private corporation, Bullock and his friends apparently found the opportunity they sought.

Under Scott's bill, the road would be leased to a private firm for a minimum fee of $25,000 a month. Each company which submitted a bid must prove to the governor's satisfaction that it had financial resources adequate to guarantee the fulfillment of its obligations. Bullock received the power to reject any or all bids. The bill passed each house of the legislature by a wide margin—the house, 90–31, and the senate, 25–7.[49] Bullock men voted for passage; so did many Moderates and Democrats. Some thought later that $50,000 allegedly expended by Bullock's henchman Hannibal Kimball at about this time had helped persuade laggards in the General Assembly, but no proof of bribery could ever be offered.[50] Bullock signed the lease bill on October 24.[51] The next day, he announced that he would receive until December 25 bids meeting or exceeding the minimum payment of $25,000.[52]

Almost at once, the reason for Bullock's extraordinary

[49] Thompson, *Reconstruction in Georgia*, 245.

[50] *Ibid.*, 246; *Report of the Majority [and Minority] of the Joint Committee Appointed . . . to Investigate . . . the Lease of the Western & Atlantic R. R.* (Atlanta: W. A. Hemphill, Public Printer, 1872), 13, hereafter cited as *Reports, Lease Investigation*.

[51] *Acts and Resolutions*, 1870, Title XVII, No. 288, pp. 423–27.

[52] Bullock's proclamation, October 25, 1870, in Executive Minutes of the State of Georgia, Georgia Department of Archives and History.

willingness to permit the lease of the road became clear.
Joseph E. Brown had resigned as chief justice and had, it
appeared, allied with Kimball and John P. King of the
Georgia Railroad to form a company which would serve the
interests of the Georgia Railroad, the Nashville & Chat-
tanooga, and doubtless also the Republican-controlled Brunswick & Albany and the Republican party.[53] When Brown's
alliance with Kimball became known, directors of the Demo-
cratic-controlled Georgia Central and its subsidiaries, the
Macon & Western and the Southwestern, tried to purchase a
half interest in the Brown company. Their attempt failed,
and the representatives of the Macon roads formed their
own competing group.[54] Unable to secure pledges of financial backing in Atlanta, the Macon company, which was
composed primarily of Democrats, looked to Washington.
Recognizing that the lease would go only to friends of the
Bullock administration, they secured the cooperation of
Senator Simon Cameron, of John Delano, who acted for his
father, the Secretary of the Interior, in the enterprise, and
Thomas A. Scott, whose Pennsylvania Railroad was attempting to expand its operations throughout the South.[55] It was
at about this time, also, that Benjamin H. Hill, the most
politically active of the Democrats in the Macon company,
issued his conciliatory "address" accepting the results of
Reconstruction and urging his fellow Georgians to do the
same.

The Brown company, meanwhile, had secured its own

[53] [*Testimony in Regard to the Lease of the Western & Atlantic Railroad*] ([Atlanta] [1872]), 121, testimony of Benjamin H. Hill. Hereafter
cited as *Testimony, Lease Investigation.*

[54] *Ibid.,* 7–11. W. M. Wadley, the powerful president of the Central and
long an opponent of Kimball and Bullock, refused to become associated
with the Macon company. *Ibid.,* 7.

[55] John F. Stover, *The Railroads of the South, 1865–1900. A Study in
Finance and Control* (Chapel Hill: The University of North Carolina
Press, 1955), 99–121, and especially the map, 106.

bipartisan accessions, for in mid-December Alexander H. Stephens asked to pledge $10,000 to the undertaking.[56] The company was delighted to add the name of so respected a Democrat, but Brown was less pleased when Stephens suggested that the road would be worth a bid of $40,000 a month. His company, Brown replied, would bid only $25,000. The Macon group would probably bid more, but, Brown hinted, the governor might not be "controlled simply by the highest bid."[57]

Bullock was, apparently, in a quandry. He never considered awarding the lease to the Seago–Blodgett company, which included Foster Blodgett and which promised to bid $35,000 a month. The company, Bullock explained lamely, could not prove adequate financial backing.[58] But the Macon company had influential Northern supporters, and Brown's company, especially with Kimball's participation, was also powerful. Both the Macon and the Brown companies, Bullock decided, must participate in the lease. He spread the word that, unless the two interests combined, he would exercise his right to refuse both bids.[59]

After an all-night bargaining session on December 24, Bullock got his wish. The Brown and Macon companies, swallowing their political differences, combined forces. Brown received the presidency of the Western & Atlantic, and the Macon company—or the Hill company, as it was known to the public—the choice of a superintendent and

[56] Stephens to Brown, December 15, 1870, in Joseph E. Brown Papers, private possession.

[57] Brown to Stephens, December 16, 1870, in Alexander Stephens Papers, Library of Congress.

[58] Brown believed that Bullock's personal sympathies lay "with Blodgett's company." Brown to Linton Stephens, July 30, 1871, in Joseph E. Brown Papers, Felix Hargrett Collection.

[59] W. C. Morrill to Simon Cameron, Atlanta, December 29, 1870, in Cameron Papers.

treasurer.[60]   Of twenty-three directorships, each side received eleven. "Director Number 23" was W. B. Dinsmore,
a close friend of Bullock and the president of the Southern
Express Company, of which Bullock had been an official before and during the Civil War.[61]

When the opponents of the lease heard that Bullock had
accepted the $25,000 bid of the Brown–Hill company in
preference to the Seago–Blodgett offer of $35,000,[62] they
charged that Dinsmore was merely acting for Bullock and
that the governor, not the express company official, was
really "Director Number 23."[63] The arrangement, in fact,
was more complex. Bullock was apparently promised the
profits due the twenty-third member of the company—but
he was to receive them only after his term as governor had
expired.[64] The immediate consideration which Bullock received for his willingness to grant the lease was, apparently,
assurance that Bullock's Senators, Farrow and Blodgett,
would be seated in Congress.[65] The governor also hoped that

[60] *Ibid.*

[61] *Testimony, Lease Investigation*, 107.

[62] For the most convenient summary, see Thompson, *Reconstruction in
Georgia*, 251.

[63] See, for example, Milledgeville *Southern Recorder*, February 14, 1871;
Linton Stephens to Alexander H. Stephens, Sparta, January 8, 1871, in
Alexander Stephens Papers, Manhattanville College of the Sacred Heart.
For refutations of these charges, see *Testimony, Lease Investigation*, testimony of A. L. Harris, 68–70, and Brown's testimony, 287. Harris admitted
that two or three weeks before the bids were accepted, Bullock told him
that the governor and his friends would control the company.

[64] Or so Bullock claimed in 1877; see the following letters, all in Joseph
E. Brown Papers, private possession: Bullock to Brown, April 20, 1877;
W. P. Walters to Brown, March 31, 1877; Brown to Bullock, April 14, 1877;
Brown to Walters, April 4, 1877; Bullock to Brown, March 29, 1877; and,
especially, Bullock to Brown, May 25, 1877. Brown, however, denied
making any agreements with Bullock; see Brown to Bullock, May 2, 1877,
copy, in Joseph E. Brown Papers, Felix Hargrett Collection.

[65] Linton Stephens to Alexander H. Stephens, Sparta. January 8, 1871,
in Alexander Stephens Papers, Manhattanville College of the Sacred Heart.
Miss Thompson hints at but does not directly suggest a connection be-

Secretary of the Interior Columbus Delano and Cameron could have the election in Georgia's Fifth Congressional District set aside and thus prolong for a few more months the Reconstruction process in the state.[66]

On December 27, after Bullock had awarded the lease but before the agreement was announced, he staged a banquet at the Kimball House hotel in Atlanta. Those present included the prominent Georgia members of the Brown and Hill companies and their Northern backers, Columbus Delano, Simon Cameron, and Thomas A. Scott. Hill led in toasting Bullock and Reconstruction, and the next morning, the press announced his conncetion with the lease award.[67] To Democrats who had wondered at Hill's sudden "conversion" during the last stages of the fall campaign, all now seemed painfully clear.

Clear, also, was the broader significance of the Kimball House banquet and the transformation of the lease measure from the realm of economics to that of politics. Through the bipartisan lease agreement as it was finally concluded, Bullock hoped he could maneuver to retain control of Georgia at least until the end of his term. Prominent Democrats as well as Republicans were now financially as well as politically in his debt.[68] In the course of negotiations for the Western & Atlantic lease, Bullock had succeeded brilliantly in forging the alliance which he and members of his faction had rejected until 1870. The lease agreement brought together the same groups to whom Georgia Republicans had

---

tween the lease agreement and Bullock's hopes for the seating of Farrow and, especially, Blodgett. Thompson, *Reconstruction in Georgia*, 251.

[66] Thompson, *Reconstruction in Georgia*, 251.

[67] Augusta *Chronicle and Sentinel*, December 29, 1870.

[68] Correspondence in the Cameron Papers, during the first few months of 1871, especially letters from W. C. Morrill, the new treasurer of the Western & Atlantic, makes it clear that the lessees were profiting handsomely from the operations of the road.

belatedly directed their campaign appeals in the fall of
1870: moderate Democrats, Republicans of all persuasions,
and old-line Whigs like Hill. The new combination came
too late to save either Bullock or the Republican party in
Georgia. It did mark, however, a step toward the kind of
economic-political alliance which would characterize the
New South of the later 1870's and 1880's.

Requiem for Radicalism

For Rufus Bullock and the remnants of Georgia's Radical faction, the year 1871 opened on a somber note. Defeated in the December elections of 1870 and fearing the charges of malfeasance in office which woud doubtless be raised when the newly elected legislature convened, the Radicals could cling only to a single hope. The Western & Atlantic lease might yet prove the salvation of the Bullock regime. The governor might be able to trade on the newly-won support of former Whigs—Democrats throughout most of Reconstruction—who had joined or supported the lease company. Perhaps, too, he could count on the renewed loyalty of Republicans like Brown who now found themselves tied by tighter bonds of financial as well as political allegiance to the Radical administration. The odds, however, seemed against the governor and his clique. Democratic reaction to Benjamin H. Hill's defection in December, 1870, had

213

made it clear that no alliance such as Bullock contemplated could be quickly or easily forged; it would require more than the conversion of a single major leader to make Georgia's Democrats forget the grievances of three years. Bullock himself sensed the near hopelessness of his situation. During most of 1871, the governor remained unusually aloof from politics.

If Bullock hoped to use the lease to bolster his own prestige, his hopes were doomed to disappointment. In fact, the transfer of the Western & Atlantic to the new lease company effectively removed the Radicals from positions of power within the Republican party. As in 1867, power had passed from the hands of the Union League to those of the Augusta Ring, so now, in 1871, it passed finally from the hands of Bullock and his colleagues to those of Moderates like Brown. The change had long seemed in the offing; hints had appeared as early as 1868, when Bryant and Caldwell had staged their coup within the State Executive Committee. As long as the Bullock men controlled the state patronage, however, the Augusta Ring's fall from power would be only temporary. In January, 1871, when control of the Western & Atlantic shifted to the Brown company and Foster Blodgett was supplanted as superintendent, the Bullock faction lost control of the major patronage of the state.[1] Blodgett's influence within the party diminished. Hannibal I. Kimball was associated with the lease, but his interests were always subordinated to those of Brown. Bullock himself—his power now precariously tied to the Brown company's favor—dared not cross the new Western & Atlantic president.

In the first months of 1871, however, Brown faced difficulties which temporarily drove him toward the Radical camp. He and his associates, he frankly avowed in May,

[1] C. A. Nutting to Simon Cameron, January 26, 1871, in Cameron Papers.

were "energetically at work . . . perfecting an organization of the Republican party in the state that . . . [would] combine more elements of strength and have more of the confidence of the people . . . than heretofore."[2] Brown probably knew that he and his supporters would have little chance of success if they formed a third party outside both the regular Republican and the regular Democratic organizations. However much they distrusted Bullock and intended to relegate him to a subordinate role within their new coalition, the Moderates recognized that their success at the ballot box would depend in good measure on votes from Radical Republicans. As long as Brown and his colleagues elected to remain within the Republican party, then they would need Radical support. They could as ill afford to alienate the Radicals and Bullock as Bullock could afford to alienate the Moderates.

The first suggestion of the Moderates' dilemma came when Foster Blodgett sought to occupy the Senate seat to which he had been illegally elected in the spring of 1870. Moderate Republicans had abstained or voted against Blodgett then, and the Brown men hated him and rejoiced in any misfortune which came his way.[3] In ordinary circumstances, they would never have sustained his claims, but the circumstances in 1871 were far from ordinary. Bullock himself exerted no direct pressure on the lease company, but he made his wishes regarding the senatorship clear.[4] And the award of the lease contract to Brown instead of to the Seago–Blodgett company quite probably depended partly on promises by Brown, Cameron, and Columbus Delano to advance Blodgett's claims in Washington. When Blod-

[2] Joseph E. Brown to Simon Cameron, May 4, 1871, *ibid.*
[3] W. C. Morrill to Simon Cameron, June 29, 1871, *ibid.*
[4] Rufus B. Bullock to Zachariah Chandler, Atlanta, February 18, 1871, in Zachariah Chandler Papers.

gett's claims came before the Senate, then, the lease company felt obliged to support the Radical partisan.[5] Blodgett, however, was never seated.

Bullock had failed to award the lease to the highest bidder, and throughout 1871 members of Brown's company worried that the new session of the General Assembly would hold the contract a violation of the agreement contemplated by those who had voted for the lease bill. The new legislature would be strongly Democratic, and Benjamin H. Hill lost no chance to remind his associates of the fact. He could have blocked the lease award in 1870; now, he could withdraw from the company and induce Democrats to vote against the contract when the test came. "Now I am in [a] position to aid you in making sure this lease," he wrote pointedly to his Republican associates. For so great a service, of course, he would expect payment. "You are in [a] position to aid me with at least sufficient funds to bridge over my present embarrassments & enable me to make good cup & then my pecuniary troubles will be over."[6] What Hill's "embarrassments" might be, his colleagues in the lease company did not stop to inquire. They could not risk losing Hill's backing or that of the Democrats whose votes he might still control.

As long as Republicans in the company continued to placate Hill, Democrats elected to the new General Assembly indeed seemed reluctant to attack the lease. Before the legislature convened in November, a bipartisan coalition formed as Democrats and Republicans united to support the Western & Atlantic contract.[7] Democratic lead-

[5] W. C. Morrill to Simon Cameron, Atlanta, February 24, 1871, in Cameron Papers.

[6] Benjamin H. Hill to Messrs. Cameron, Delano, Walters & Scott, Athens, February 27, 1871, *ibid.*

[7] J. Henly Smith to Alexander H. Stephens, Atlanta, October 18, 1871, in Alexander Stephens Papers, Library of Congress. Stephens had long

ers who hoped to secure both the abrogation of the lease agreement and the impeachment of Bullock found themselves in an awkward position. "We could not impeach Bullock without the aid of the RR ring," explained one party spokesman, "and . . . we must not drive the Democrats who voted for and are interested in the RR Charter over to the support of Bullock."[8] Certain parties seemed to be identifying the lease with the fortunes of Bullock, and any debate on the lease question would cost the Democrats votes for the governor's impeachment.[9] Disgusted party stalwarts grumbled that "corruption . . . [would] do much . . . to carry the Legislature astray." They branded the Democrats who supported Republicans on the lease question "New Departurists"[10] and complained that "Moderation tion [was] their perpetual note and grand refrain."[11]

As the meeting of the legislature drew closer, it became clear that the Democrats would, for the time being, let the lease contract stand. Bullock's impeachment was, after all, their primary objective. Probably, Democratic leaders planned as soon as the legislature convened to bypass the lease issue and mount a full scale assault on the alleged corruption of the Bullock regime.

Had members of the Brown company been willing to permit a prolonged debate on the lease contract, they might

since withdrawn from the lease company. Brown denied the existence of any combination. See his "To the Political Editor of the [Atlanta] Sun," October 11, 1871, *ibid.*, and Brown's copy, signed, in Joseph E. Brown Papers, Felix Hargrett Collection.

[8] J. Henly Smith to Alexander H. Stephens, October 17, [1871], in Alexander Stephens Papers, Library of Congress. Smith claimed to be summarizing the views of Robert Toombs.

[9] J. Henly Smith to Alexander H. Stephens, October 7, 1871, *ibid.*

[10] In the political language of the 1870's, a "New Departure Democrat" was a party member who sought to bypass the old issues of Reconstruction campaigns and focus attention on economic problems.

[11] Smith to Stephens, Atlanta, October 18, 1871, in Alexander Stephens Papers, Library of Congress.

have temporarily saved the Bullock administration. Their strategy, however, had changed since they had been forced to back Foster Blodgett in May. Perhaps the lease company had simply decided to save itself, even at the cost of sacrificing a Republican state administration. As the crucial test of their loyalty approached, in the last weeks before the General Assembly met, the lease men did nothing to support the governor. Instead, they flocked to Atlanta in great force, lobbying vigorously to prevent the lease question from coming before the legislature.[12]

However dubious the Democrats were about their ability to impeach Bullock, the governor by the autumn of 1871 sensed his approaching downfall. Mounting evidence of frauds committed during his administration had appeared during the summer, and by September rumors were thick that Blodgett—and by implication Bullock himself—would be cited for wrongdoing in the management of the Western & Atlantic.[13] Nothing had yet been proved, but Bullock was apprehensive. He knew that he could no longer control his own party—indeed, that he had lost the party reins to Brown and that Brown and the lease coalition could depose him at will.

Bullock also knew that, should the incumbent governor die, resign, or be impeached before the expiration of his term, the office under Georgia law passed to the president of the state senate. The legislature of 1868–70 had been Republican, and its senate president was an old member of the Augusta Ring, Benjamin F. Conley. The legislature scheduled to convene on November 1, 1871, however, would undoubtedly elect a Democrat in Conley's stead. Should

[12] *Ibid.*

[13] W. C. Morrill to Simon Cameron, Atlanta, September 8, 1871, in Cameron Papers.

Bullock be impeached, therefore, a Democrat would immediately become governor.

Faced with what he believed the inevitable prospect of impeachment, Bullock in October, 1871, chose to make his final play to perpetuate Radicalism if not himself in power. On October 23, he wrote out his resignation, addressing it "To whom it may concern": "Be it known that good & sufficient reasons me thereunto moving I do hereby resign the office of Governor of this State to take effect on Monday next the thirtieth day of October in the year of our Lord one thousand eight hundred & seventy one, and on that day & date deliver over to the Honl. Benjamin Conly [*sic*] President of the Senate the Executive powers of the Government until the election & qualification of a Governor . . . ."[14] Bullock quietly left the state, and only Conley knew of the resignation until the new governor took the oath of office on October 30, two days before the first meeting of the new Democratic assembly.

The situation confronting the Democratic legislators when they assembled at Atlanta was a novel one, for no one knew whether Conley should serve as governor only until the election of a new senate president or whether he should serve out the remaining year of Bullock's term. Democrats found Bullock's resignation a last, galling reminder of the former governor's political acumen. The timely resignation and the accession of Conley, they agreed, meant that Georgia had merely "swapped the devil for the witch."[15]

In hastening Bullock's departure, the Democrats in the General Assembly had secured what they most wanted.

[14] Bullock's resignation appears in the Rufus B. Bullock Papers, and in the Executive Minutes of the State of Georgia, in the Georgia Department of Archives and History.

[15] Atlanta *Constitution*, quoting the Savannah *Morning News*, November 3, 1871.

Once the Assembly met, they made no concerted effort to install the new senate president, Democrat L. N. Trammell, in Conley's stead. In fact, they seemed remarkably eager to cooperate with Republicans of Brown's persuasion. Conley, who perhaps failed to appreciate that Brown had renounced Radicalism and would sacrifice nothing to sustain a Radical regime, gloated that "Joe Brown runs the legislature." There was, so W. C. Morrill informed Simon Cameron, a "good deal of truth" in the new governor's boast.[16]

The assembly did little which failed to meet the approval of Republican Moderates. Democrats united to pass resolutions calling for investigations of Bullock's conduct as governor and of the award of the Western & Atlantic lease, but even these seemed not to disturb Brown. His associates in the lease company reported him "perfectly" satisfied with the composition of the investigating committees;[17] and, although the probes took place and the committees returned adverse reports, they recommended no legislation, and the lease contract was allowed to stand. The legislature did pass over Conley's veto on November 22 a bill calling for a special election for governor on the third Tuesday in December.[18] Republicans who had long opposed Bullock voted for the bill and then to override Conley's veto; apparently, many Moderates within the party were now willing that

[16] W. C. Morrill to Simon Cameron, Atlanta, November 20, 1871, in Cameron Papers.

[17] *Ibid.* For the resolutions passed on December 1 and December 5 by the senate and house of representatives calling for investigation of Bullock's conduct, the administration and management of the state road, the lease, and the conduct of commissioners appointed to audit claims against the Western & Atlantic, see the Georgia *Acts and Resolutions,* 1871, Resolution No. 9. Each investigating committee was to consist of two sentaors and three representatives.

[18] *Acts and Resolutions,* 1871, Title V, No. 21. Conley's veto appears in the Executive Minutes of the State of Georgia, November 21, 1871, Georgia Department of Archives and History.

Republican government of Georgia should at least temporarily end.

The campaign of 1871 was virtually nonexistent. Democrats held a convention at Atlanta on December 6, at which a fight first threatened to develop among rival candidates for the nomination. W. T. Wofford and Herbert Fielder withdrew their names, however, and the nomination went by acclamation to James M. Smith, a hitherto obscure and rather colorless Columbus lawyer recently elected the new speaker of the state house of representatives.[19] Though Republicans held a caucus in Atlanta, they failed to nominate a candidate. In a move which reflected the new structure of the party hierarchy, Republicans voted to accept the "resignation" of Blodgett as state chairman and offered endorsement for governor to James Atkins, a leader of the Moderate faction.[20] Atkins declined to make the race, and, when Republicans could agree on no one else, they urged their supporters to remain at home on election day. Smith, then, was the sole candidate for the governorship. He received a mere 39,705 votes.[21]

County-by-county returns for the special election of 1871 were never published, but it is clear that prominent Republicans feared little from a Democratic "redemption" of Georgia. Though invited to attend the Republican caucus, Joseph E. Brown refused. Democrats claimed that he voted for Smith, and later that he contributed $100 toward the costs of an inaugural ball.[22] Perhaps politicians like

[19] Anderson Diary, December 4, 1871, in Anderson Papers, University of North Carolina; Milledgeville *Federal Union,* December 13, 1871; Avery, *History of the State of Georgia,* 466–68.

[20] P. Thweatt to Alexander H. Stephens, Atlanta, January 41, 1872, in Alexander Stephens Papers, Library of Congress.

[21] *Journal of the House of Representatives of the State of Georgia, 1872,* p. 25.

[22] P. Thweatt to Alexander H. Stephens, January 14, 1872, in Alexander Stephens Papers, Library of Congress.

Brown saw in Smith's election new possibilities for con-
summating the union of Georgia industrial interests they
had long sought, a union which would be bipartisan and
more lasting than the coalition forged for the Republican
party by Bullock and the Radicals between 1867 and 1870.

Conley contested the legality of Smith's election and
insisted that he remained the lawful acting governor of
Georgia, but few heeded his protests.[23] To most Georgians,
Smith's inauguration on January 12, 1872, was a joyous occasion. It marked, exulted a Savannah paper, "the spon-
taneous outpouring of the people in rejoicing over the ad-
vent of the new era." And it "recalled in salient contrast the
sham of inauguration that occurred when Bullock took the
reins of government. Those who had the misfortune to witness that spectacle, with its immense concourse of negroes
and its small attendance of whites, can realize the contrast
between that occasion and one in which the sympathies
and convictions of the people are enlisted."[24]

The "redemption" of Georgia, a slow, tortured affair,
occurred not in a single sharp political campaign, but was
dragged out over a period of twelve months.[25] The disputes
within the party which hastened its downfall in 1871 left
Republicans in Georgia divided and disorganized in 1872.
So badly split that its members besought national leaders
to support a purge of old Radicals who had blocked the
adoption of the Moderate program, the party in effect admitted that it could never again win in Georgia unless it
could attract new votes.[26] Even the Republican national

[23] *Journal of the House of Representatives,* 1872, p. 25.

[24] Savannah *Daily Republican,* a Democratic paper, January 14, 1872.

[25] Shadgett, *Republican Party in Georgia,* is a competent history of the
party after 1871.

[26] M. M. Hale to [?], October 22, 1871, in Butler Papers; J. Clarke
Swayze to Benjamin F. Conley, March 1, 1872, in Benjamin F. Conley
Papers, Atlanta Historical Society; Hale to William E. Chandler, March 25,
1872, in Chandler Papers.

committee despaired of Georgia. Preferring to concentrate its financial resources in the presidential election of 1872 where they could do the most good, the national committee rejected Georgians' pleas for aid and left the shattered remnants of the state party to their own devices.[27]

To many former Republicans, the Liberal Republican ticket headed by Horace Greeley and reluctantly endorsed by the national Democratic party proved a convenient bridge back to the Democracy.[28] Republicans in Georgia continued in 1872 to draw their support from the yeoman whites of North Georgia and from the state's Negro population, and they elected three members to Congress. But their losses were greater than their gains, for the party's most powerful spokesmen, including such Moderates as Brown, returned in 1872 to the Democratic fold.

In fact, 1872 saw the final repudiation of Radicalism in Georgia and with it the exposure of the alleged corruption of Bullock's regime. Investigating committees appointed by the legislature in 1871 submitted their reports in 1872. By both Democrats and Republicans, Bullock stood accused of frauds in the purchase and furnishing of a state capitol building at Atlanta, in payments for the printing of state notices and documents, and in disbursements to Democratic lawyers kept on the Radical payrolls presumably to ensure their silence should they uncover evidence of frauds or corruption in the state administration. Bullock could not be held personally responsible for the mismanagement of the Western & Atlantic, but investigations of Blodgett's conduct as the road's superintendent strongly suggested the gov-

[27] Broadside, written by Henry P. Farrow, September 12, 1872, in Henry P. Farrow Collection, University of Georgia.

[28] Thomas B. Alexander has noted a similar pattern in other southern states in 1872; see his "Persistent Whiggery in the Confederate South, 1860–1877," *Journal of Southern History*, XXVII (August, 1961), especially p. 322.

ernor's complicity. The state promptly issued warrants for
Bullock's arrest, and Governor Smith dispatched messen-
gers to New York to ferret out the fugitive.[29] But the former governor could not be found. Not until 1876 did he
return to Georgia and stand trial. By then, potential witnesses against him were scattered, and a few, prominent
in the Democratic politics of the New South, feared that
testimony against Bullock would expose their own trans-
gressions of the Reconstruction era. Bullock won acquittal
on all the charges against him. He remained in Georgia for
most of the rest of his life. Though he continued a member
of the Republican party and served on the Board of Trustees of the Negro Atlanta University at a time when such
activities were unpopular, he took a prominent role in civic
affairs and was among the directors of the Atlanta Piedmont Exposition in 1887.[30]

To Georgians concerned with the industrial development
of their state, "redemption" brought little change. The promoters who had most benefitted from state aid grants and
other favors under Republican rule now found Democrats
equally receptive to their programs and plans. Negroes and
white farmers—the supporters of Radical Republicanism—
on the other hand found themselves politically deserted,
deprived of the place they had enjoyed at the center of
Reconstruction politics. Their votes still counted, and campaign orators continued to pay lip service to their demands,
but not until the 1890's would they again fill a role in
Georgia politics comparable to that they had played in the
Reconstruction years. In its broadest sense, therefore, "re-

[29] In the Rufus B. Bullock Papers, Georgia Department of Archives and
History, is correspondence dealing with attempts to arrest the former gover-
nor and with the search made for him in New York state. See, for example,
J. B. Cumming to James M. Smith, April 23, 1872.

[30] C. Vann Woodward, *Origins of the New South 1877–1913* (Baton
Rouge: Louisiana State University Press, 1951), 24.

demption" in Georgia meant the open acceptance on a bipartisan, statewide level of the "new era" which Joseph E. Brown had long since proclaimed the true result of the Civil War.[31]

In the years between 1865 and 1872, the politically disaffected in Georgia probably formed a majority of the population, but it was not a majority which could easily be welded into a viable political party. A Republican party built primarily around the votes of Negroes and yeoman whites was doomed almost as soon as it perfected its organization. Though the two groups had similar economic interests and demands, the social antipathy between them was deep-seated. Moreover, the Negroes were too few, the yeoman whites were too poor, and the leadership which both groups could furnish was inadequate to sustain the party without outside help. The failure of the yeoman white–Negro coalition to overcome the normal Democratic majority in Georgia made it plain after 1868 that Republicans could not continue to dominate the state unless they could broaden the base of their party. Radical strategists, however, chose instead to rely on Congressional aid. Finding it, they prolonged the life of the party in Georgia for a few months, but their tactics did nothing to correct the basic flaw in the Republican organization. As soon as Congress withdrew its support and the Democrats healed the divisions within their own party, the Radical faction would topple from power.

Could the Republicans have united the former Whigs of Central Georgia, the Negroes, and the white farmers and workers of North Georgia and the wiregrass region, they could probably have achieved the natural majority of voters they long sought. On paper, such a combination seemed possible, and, had it been attempted in the early days of

[31] See Chapter Two.

Reconstruction before party lines had solidified and before Republicans had come to be identified with corruption and misrule, it might have worked. There would have been difficulties, of course. Appeals to the former Whigs of Central Georgia—the "progressive men" repeatedly wooed by Brown and finally by Bullock himself in 1870—inevitably meant less emphasis on appeals to Negro voters and to the white farmers and laboring men. Inevitably, too, they meant the adoption of programs and policies repugnant to the Negro and white laboring groups. But the single attempt to form a broad-based Republican coalition in Georgia came too late to be regarded as the final test of whether a strong Republican organization could have been achieved. For by 1870 few self-respecting Democrats found it possible to cross party lines and unite with those they had for two years been branding as despots and usurpers.

The impact of the Republican party on Georgia politics cannot be measured by the shadow of a once-proud organization which lingered in the state after 1871. Three years of Republican rule had ensured that Georgia politics would never again be quite what they had been before 1865. The real contributions of Republicanism to Georgia lay less in legislation, of which there was little, than in a fundamental reshaping of the direction state politics would take after Bullock's regime had collapsed and the Radical governor had fled the state.

The conduct of the Bullock regime and Republicans in general gave a fatal blow to the two-party system which had seemed likely in 1868 to develop in Georgia. As whites who had supported the Republicans continued to creep back to the Democracy after 1871, the Democratic party became once more what it had been in the 1850's—an unwieldy and precarious coalition. Now, however, it was a coalition tied together by determination to maintain white supremacy and never again to allow the state to fall prey to Republican rule. No longer would the factional feuds which had divided the Democracy in the 1850's and 1860's be paraded before the Georgia electorate. Chastened by the lessons of Reconstruction, Democrats determined to present a united front in public. The one issue on which all could agree was race solidarity.

A white supremacist Democracy and a solidly Democratic state were not, however, the only legacies of the Republicans in Georgia. Republican encouragement of industrial promoters and merchants had brought these groups to a new position of influence in state politics. With the notable exception of Joseph E. Brown, these men under "Bullock's administration had operated on the fringes of the political hierarchy—always present, but rarely seen or heard in the official party councils. After 1871, however, they moved easily into the Democracy, and there they assumed, not again the subordinate places they had occupied in the Republican coalition, but a dominant role. Railroad promoters, bankers, and corporation executives, they also became state legislators, party committeemen, and even United States Senators. As C. Vann Woodward has suggested, there was a remarkable "continuity between Reconstruction and Redemption" throughout the South.[32] For its leaders, as well as more obviously for its programs, the New South Democracy would draw in Georgia on the policies and personnel of the Reconstruction Republican organization. But it would be a party far less open and far less responsive to the needs of the Georgia electorate than the one Republicans might have built in the state between 1867 and 1871.

[32] Woodward, *Origins of the New South*, 15.

APPENDIX

The following tables express relationships between Republican votes and various social and economic indexes as coefficients of correlation. Analysis of election returns in this manner is one method of suggesting patterns of party strength and weakness, as well as changes in these patterns over time. It does, however, have certain limitations. Coefficients of correlation cannot indicate that any individual voted Republican in any given election; nor can they prove that voters were attracted to the party only by particular appeals or slogans. They can merely suggest, for example, that, in certain regions of Georgia, counties which had the poorest land and least productive farms gave the largest Republican majorities. Only when interpreted in connection with more conventional evidence from newspaper and manuscript sources can coefficients of correlation be truly meaningful.

A correlation of +1.00 indicates a perfect, direct relationship between variables; a correlation of −1.00 indicates a perfect, inverse relationship. Correlations of ±0.5 or greater indicate significant direct or inverse relationships between variables.

For every election analyzed, I have calculated the relationship between Republican votes and Negro population; acres of land improved, per capita; cash value of farms, per capita; cash value of farm implements, per capita; value of manufactures, per capita; Joseph E. Brown's vote in the gubernatorial election of 1857, when he defeated Benjamin H. Hill; and the average of the combined Whig vote in the presidential elections of 1840, 1844, and 1848. I have made separate analyses for each of five geographic divisions: the Blue Ridge area of North Georgia, the Upper Piedmont, the Black Belt, the coastal counties, and the Wiregrass Country. For a description of these regions, see Robert Preston Brooks, *The Agrarian Revolution in Georgia 1865–1912* (Madison:University of Wisconsin, 1914).

Election returns appear in the *Tribune Almanacs* for the Reconstruction period. Some election data for Reconstruction Georgia have proved unavailable at various archives in the state, in the contemporary press, and at the Inter-University Consortium for Political Research, Ann Arbor, Michigan.

Census data appear in the *Statistics of the Population* and the *Statistics of the Wealth and Industry of the United States* compiled in the *Ninth Census of the United States* (1870).

Counties included in each of Georgia's five regions are listed in the Notes to Table A.

Table A

SOURCES OF REPUBLICAN STRENGTH IN GEORGIA

Coefficients of Correlation Between Republican Votes in the Gubernatorial Election, April, 1868, and Various Indexes

	North Georgia[1]	Upper Piedmont[2]	Black Belt[3]	Wiregrass Country[4]	Seacoast Counties[5]
% Negro	−0.520	+0.138	+0.966	+0.238	+0.329
Acres Improved	−0.331	−0.054	+0.618	−0.126	+0.106
Cash value, farms	−0.782	−0.411	+0.255	+0.195	+0.066
Cash value of farm implements	−0.793	+0.005	+0.951	+0.149	+0.198
Value of manufactures	−0.489	−0.212	+0.736	+0.347	+0.206
Brown's vote, 1857	+0.599	+0.309	+0.937	−0.367	+0.807
Average Whig vote, 1840, 1844, 1848	+0.036	+0.094	+0.043	+0.569	−0.072

[1] Catoosa, Chattooga, Dade, Dawson, Fannin, Gilmer, Gordon, Habersham, Lumpkin, Murray, Pickens, Rabun, Towns, Union, Walker, White, Whitfield.

[2] Banks, Bartow (Cass, in 1868), Campbell, Carroll, Cherokee, Clayton, Cobb, Crawford, DeKalb, Fayette, Floyd, Forsyth, Franklin, Fulton, Gwinnett, Hall, Haralson, Hart, Heard, Jackson, Madison, Milton, Paulding, Polk, Walton.

[3] Baker, Baldwin, Bibb, Brooks, Burke, Butts, Calhoun, Chattahoochee, Clarke, Clay, Columbia, Coweta, Decatur, Dooley, Dougherty, Early, Elbert, Glasscock, Greene, Hancock, Harris, Henry, Houston, Jasper, Jefferson, Jones, Lee, Lincoln, Lowndes, Macon, Marion, Merriwether, Miller, Mitchell, Monroe, Morgan, Muscogee, Newton, Oglethorpe, Pike, Putnam, Quitman, Randolph, Richmond, Schley, Screven, Spaulding, Stewart, Sumter, Talbot, Taliaferro, Taylor, Terrell, Thomas, Troup, Twiggs, Upson, Warren, Washington, Webster, Wilkes, Wilkinson.

Table B

SOURCES OF REPUBLICAN STRENGTH IN GEORGIA

Coefficients of Correlation Between Republican Votes in the
Congressional Elections of April, 1868, and Various Indexes

	North Georgia	Upper Piedmont	Black Belt	Wiregrass Country	Seacoast Counties
% Negro	−0.553	+0.065	+0.971	+0.024	+0.172
Acres Improved	−0.303	−0.309	+0.634	−0.105	−0.089
Cash value, farms	−0.743	−0.362	+0.267	−0.041	+0.050
Cash value of farm implements	−0.731	+0.091	+0.957	−0.100	−0.009
Value of manufactures	−0.469	+0.115	+0.805	+0.506	+0.361
Brown's vote, 1857	−0.580	+0.336	+0.953	+0.186	+0.754
Average Whig vote, 1840, 1844, 1848	+0.052	−0.046	+0.143	+0.179	−0.234

Table C

SOURCES OF REPUBLICAN STRENGTH IN GEORGIA

Coefficients of Correlation Between Republican Votes in the
Presidential Election of 1868 and Various Indexes

	North Georgia	Upper Piedmont	Black Belt	Wiregrass Country	Seacoast Counties
% Negro	−0.484	+0.046	+0.631	+0.291	+0.604
Acres Improved	−0.152	−0.236	+0.350	+0.019	−0.226
Cash value, farms	−0.538	−0.085	+0.054	+0.202	+0.131
Cash value of farm implements	−0.587	−0.418	+0.582	−0.110	+0.358
Value of manufactures	−0.238	+0.212	+0.551	+0.581	+0.437
Brown's vote, 1857	+0.397	−0.034	+0.649	+0.011	+0.765
Average Whig vote, 1840, 1844, 1848	+0.348	−0.235	+0.180	+0.270	+0.071

[4] Appling, Berrien, Bulloch, Charlton, Clinch, Coffee, Colquitt, Echols, Effingham, Emanuel, Irwin, Johnson, Laurens, Montgomery, Pierce, Pulaski, Tatnall, Telfair, Ware, Wayne, Wilcox, Worth.

[5] Bryan, Camden, Chatham, Glynn, Liberty, McIntosh.

Table D

SOURCES OF REPUBLICAN STRENGTH IN GEORGIA

Coefficients of Correlation Between Republican Votes in the
Congressional Elections of 1870 and Various Indexes

	North Georgia	Upper Piedmont	Black Belt	Wiregrass Country	Seacoast Counties
% Negro	−0.579	+0.399	+0.930	+0.543	+0.723
Acres Improved	−0.243	+0.069	+0.614	+0.220	−0.169
Cash value, farms	−0.527	+0.084	+0.326	+0.270	+0.411
Cash value of farm implements	−0.618	−0.404	+0.915	−0.061	+0.577
Value of manufactures	−0.352	+0.073	+0.677	+0.443	+0.722
Brown's vote, 1857	+0.335	−0.170	+0.889	+0.012	+0.866
Average Whig vote, 1840, 1844, 1848	+0.164	−0.214	−0.018	+0.142	+0.358

BIBLIOGRAPHICAL ESSAY

The literature on Reconstruction is now so vast that no bibliographical essay can claim completeness. General histories, specialized monographs on such agencies as the Freedmen's Bureau, and biographies of national political leaders often contain material on Georgia. Where they have proved especially helpful, they are cited in the text. Discussed in this essay are only primary sources and specialized works on Georgia politics.

Readers who desire a more comprehensive list of works on Reconstruction may find James G. Randall and David Donald, *The Civil War and Reconstruction* (2nd ed.; Boston: D. C. Heath and Company, 1961) helpful.

UNPUBLISHED PERSONAL PAPERS

Despite their limitations as sources for the study of political behavior, collections of personal papers have proved invaluable. For neither Georgia's Republicans nor Democrats are many extensive collections available, but the papers of Democratic politicians are more plentiful than are those of Republicans. Unfortunately, there are for the Reconstruction period no substantial collections of the papers of Robert Toombs, Benjamin H. Hill, or—most disappointing of all—Rufus B. Bullock. There is some evidence that a group of Bullock papers exists, but my efforts to locate and use them have met with no success. Existing papers of both Republicans and Democrats are widely scattered.

The Georgia State Department of Archives and History in Atlanta contains a few large and many small collections. The most important of these, official manuscript records of state agencies, are discussed separately below. Among the personal papers at the archives, the most valuable for my purposes were the small collections of Rufus B. Bullock, Joseph E. Brown, Charles Jones Jenkins, and N. L. Angier Papers. Bullock's papers contain few of the governor's own letters, but they include some patronage correspondence, letters concerning the financial affairs of the state, and originals or copies of the charges and evidence in impeachment proceedings against State Treasurer Nedom L. Angier. The most interesting item in the Brown Papers is a letter from Mr. George M. Brown to Miss Ruth Blair, Georgia state historian, October 23, 1936, announcing the family's intention to burn most of the governor's papers for the post-Civil War period. Much of the material in both the Jenkins and Angier collections was published in official state records.

The Georgia Department of Archives and History holds dozens of small collections. Though few contain significant items, most are useful to fill gaps or add illustrative material. They include papers of Amos T. Akerman, Garnett Andrews, Samuel Bard, Madison Bell, Henry Lewis Benning, Foster Blodgett, John E. Bryant, John H. Caldwell, Tunis G. Campbell, Jr., Howell Cobb, Benjamin F. Conley, David G. Cotting, Henry P. Farrow, Varney Gaskill, John Brown Gordon, Lemuel P. Grant, A. L. Harris, Iverson L. Harris, Benjamin H. Hill, Joshua Hill, Ed. Hulbert, Herschel V. Johnson, John Jones, Hannibal I. Kimball, R. L. Mc-Whorter, W. C. Morrill, Eugenius A. Nisbet, J. R. Parrott, James M. Smith, Alexander H. Stephens, Linton Stephens, Peterson Thweatt, Nelson Tift, Robert Toombs, Dawson A. Walker, and Campbell Wallace.

Also in the archives are collections titled simply County Files, Reconstruction Files, and Election Files. They contain miscellaneous materials—occasional census or election returns, reports of outrages against Negroes, and, most important, reports made by the military officers assigned to individual counties during the spring elections in 1868.

The Atlanta Historical Society holds fewer materials of importance than do the archives, and its collection of Joseph E. Brown Papers contained nothing of value for my study. Of greater use are the Benjamin F. Conley Papers. The collection is especially strong on the factional disputes within the Republican party after Bullock's resignation and the inauguration of Democratic Governor James M. Smith.

For the historian of Reconstruction, the most valuable items at Emory University in Atlanta are the Alexander H. Stephens Papers, which detail Stephens' bid for the governorship in 1865. Other papers at Emory include those of James P. Hambleton and L. N. Trammell. The papers of Joseph E. Brown and John Brown Gordon proved disappointing.

The University of Georgia Library at Athens holds several important collections. The Joseph E. Brown and Elizabeth G. Brown Papers, a collection of personal correspondence and scrapbooks of the Brown family, have long been available. More significant are the Joseph E. Brown Papers of the Felix Hargrett Collection, papers sold or given to Mr. Hargrett by members of the Brown family and others and held by him until the autumn of 1965. The papers are uneven in quality. They contain hints of Brown's attitude on Reconstruction and its aftermath, transcripts and memoranda concerning the Mitchell Heirs case, one of the scandals of the Bullock administration, and valuable materials on Brown's role in post-Reconstruction national politics. Until a collection of Brown papers remaining in private hands becomes widely available, however, the full context of correspondence in the Hargrett Collection will not easily be appreciated. Fortunately, I have been able to inspect the collection still held in private hands.

The Henry P. Farrow Collection at the University is, probably, the single most valuable collection of papers of a Georgia Republican politician. It contains disappointingly thin materials on Farrow's Union League activities before 1867 but is fuller on events after the passage of the Military Reconstruction Act. The Telamon Cuyler Collection fills some gaps for the 1865–66 period, but much of its contents are more easily available in published state records.

The Howell Cobb Papers, on deposit with the University of Georgia, are disappointing for the political history of early Reconstruction. The most valuable correspondence has already been published in the *Georgia Historical Quarterly* and in the Phillips volume cited below, and scholars have mined the collection thoroughly.

Other collections at the University of Georgia which proved only moderately helpful include the Baber–Blackshear Collection and the papers of David C. Barrow, Foster Blodgett, Rebecca A. Latimer Felton, William Smith, Nelson Tift, and Robert Toombs. The University has an extensive broadsides collection upon which I have drawn. Most broadsides are catalogued separately, but those in the Felix Hargrett, Henry P. Farrow, and Reconstruction Collections are particularly relevant and helpful.

The Duke University Library contains one of the most valuable and best catalogued collections of Georgia material in the country. The most important papers are those of Herschel Vespasian Johnson; they contain correspondence and Johnson's own letterbooks. Also of some use are smaller collections of Joseph E. Brown, the Charles Jones Jenkins Papers, and miscellaneous material in the Broadsides, Georgia Portfolio, and Georgia Miscellaneous Manuscript files. The William Worth Belknap Papers contain one letter on the prolongation question. Other collections at Duke include the papers of Richard Dennis Arnold, Samuel Houston Brodnax, Howell Cobb, Alfred Holt Colquitt, Edward Harden, Iverson L. Harris, Columbus Heard, J. A. Hill, Henry W. Hilliard, Andrew Johnson, Charles Colcock Jones, Jr., Samuel J. Lazenby, Augustus Reese, William E. Smith, William Patterson Smith, Alexander H. Stephens, Ella Gertrude Clanton Thomas, George H. Thomas, and Robert Toombs. Particularly disappointing is the large collection of Eugenius A. Nisbet Papers. Nisbet, a Democrat, was a frequent correspondent of party leaders like Alexander H. Stephens, but his papers contain only business correspondence of little interest to the political historian.

The Southern Historical Collection at the University of North Carolina, Chapel Hill, also contains important papers. Especially significant are the Edward Clifford Anderson Papers. Anderson's correspondence and diary give a remarkably full picture of politics from the standpoint of a Savannah Democrat. The Arnold–Screven Family Papers also contain correspondence on Democratic politics, particularly of the later Reconstruction years. Of less use are the Julian Allen and Kate Lamar Scrapbooks and the Garnett Andrews and Fleming Family Papers.

The Amos T. Akerman Letterbooks at the University of Virginia contain virtually nothing on Akerman's role in pre-1871 Georgia politics—nothing on the convention of 1867–68, or his opposition to Bullock during the prolongation fight, or the passage of the election bill in the fall of 1870. They do contain one nostalgic letter rationalizing after a lapse of several years Akerman's decision to join the Republican party during Reconstruction.

At the Historical Society of Pennsylvania, Philadelphia, are the George Gordon Meade Papers. Most of Meade's correspondence appears in official government publication, but this collection provides evidence of Brown's role in the trial of the Columbus prisoners in 1868.

Manhattanville College of the Sacred Heart, Purchase, New York, holds a large and valuable collection of Alexander H. Stephens Papers which includes almost daily correspondence between Stephens and his half-brother, Linton. The collection is widely available on microfilm; I have used film copies at Duke University.

The Massachusetts Historical Society holds several collections which helped to fill gaps or furnished illustrative material. Most helpful were the papers of John A. Andrew, Edward A. Atkinson, and Horatio Woodman, which contain letters commenting on conditions in Georgia in 1865 and 1866. The Otis Norcross Autograph Collection contains several letters describing Georgians' reactions to major national events.

Houghton Library of Harvard University houses the Charles Sumner Papers. Sumner received many letters from Georgia, but his correspondents were seldom men prominent in the Georgia Republican party. The few letters he did receive from state party leaders were form letters sent with minor variations to all prominent Congressional Radicals.

The most valuable papers for my purpose at the Library of Congress include those of Andrew Johnson, Edwin M. Stanton, Ulysses S. Grant, Benjamin F. Butler, Alexander H. Stephens, Edward McPherson, William E. Chandler, and Simon Cameron. Of next importance are the Hamilton Fish, James A. Garfield,

John Sherman, and William Tecumseh Sherman Papers. There is little Georgia material in the Zachariah Chandler and Benjamin Franklin Wade Papers, and the Lyman Trumbull collection is especially thin and disappointing. I have drawn some material on Democratic politics from the voluminous Blair–Gist Family Papers. Other collections upon which I have drawn include the papers of Nathaniel P. Banks, Jeremiah S. Black, Salmon P. Chase, William Pitt Fessenden, Duff Green, Horace Greeley, Joseph Holt, Hugh McCulloch, Carl Schurz, Thaddeus Stevens, Elihu B. Washburne, Gideon Welles, and Henry Wilson.

Through the kindness of friends who prefer to remain anonymous, I was permitted to use and to quote freely from the Joseph E. Brown Papers which are still in private hands and which provide a crucial supplement to the Brown Papers of the Hargrett Collection at the University of Georgia. I examined items selected by the owner of the papers—probably all the documents pertaining to the post-Civil War years. Included in the collection are Brown's drafts of letters written while a prisoner in 1865, a draft of a letter to Bullock protesting the Radical governor's plan to subject Georgia to a second military Reconstruction, and important correspondence concerning the lease of the Western & Atlantic Railroad and the affairs of the road after the lease arrangement was concluded.

PRINTED PERSONAL PAPERS

Important personal papers relating to Georgia Reconstruction have been published. Myrta Lockett Avary (ed.), *Recollections of Alexander H. Stephens* (New York: Doubleday, Page & Company, 1910), contains Stephens' prison diary for the summer of 1865. In the *Georgia Historical Quarterly*, V and VI, Robert Preston Brooks published extensively from the Howell Cobb Papers now on deposit at the University of Georgia. For my purposes, the selections published in the *Georgia Historical Quarterly*, VI (December, 1922), 355–94, were most useful. Walter Lynwood Fleming (ed.), *A Documentary History of Reconstruction* (2 vols.; [New York]: The Arthur H. Clark Company, 1906) is still the best documentary collection. It includes one important Cobb letter and several other Georgia items. For Georgia history, the most useful printed source is Ulrich B. Phillips (ed.), *The Correspondence of Robert Toombs, Alexander H. Stephens, and Howell Cobb,* Annual Report of the American Historical Association for the Year 1911, II (Washington: Government Printing Office, 1913).

MANUSCRIPT GOVERNMENT DOCUMENTS

Important Georgia state records are deposited in manuscript form at the Department of Archives and History in Atlanta. The Executive Minutes of the State of Georgia contain proclamations, copies of messages to the General Assembly, and records of all other business, however routine, of the executive office. The most important correspondence in the governor's letterbooks for the 1865–68 period was published in Georgia's *Confederate Records,* cited below, but the letterbooks contain unpublished correspondence relating primarily to financial and patronage problems confronted by the James Johnson and Charles Jones Jenkins administrations. If Rufus Bullock kept governor's letterbooks, they have eluded all searchers. For the routine business of his administration, the only sources are the Executive Minutes and the letterbooks of the secretary of the Executive Department.

The archives also contain the voluminous manuscript records of the Western & Atlantic Railroad. These records would be an important source for those interested in the patronage practices of the Reconstruction governments were they not now so badly faded as to be nearly illegible and useless.

The Federal Records Center, East Point, Georgia, holds the records of the U.S. Circuit Court for the Southern District of Georgia, and those of the U.S. District Court for both the northern and southern districts of the state. The court records include information on indictments and lists of jurors. Manuscript records of Internal Revenue officers serving in Georgia are disappointing and contain nothing on the activities of the few agents who became prominent members of the Republican party.

The National Archives of the United States, Washington, holds records of various government departments. The best guides to their use are Kenneth W. Munden and Henry Putney Beers, *Guide to Federal Archives Relating to the Civil War* (Washington: The National Archives, National Archives and Records Service, General Services Administration, 1962) and the staff members in individual archives divisions. I have found helpful the Station Records, Lists of Civil Officers, General and Special Orders, and Records of Letters Sent in the Records of the Bureau of Refugees, Freedmen and Abandoned Lands, all in Record Group 105. Among the records of the War Department, I have consulted in Record Group 98 the books of Letters Received, Letters and Telegrams Sent, the records of the Headquarters Post, Atlanta, and those of the Headquarters Post, Augusta. In Record Group 107 are the official papers of the Secretary of War, including Telegrams Sent and Telegrams Received. Most papers in Record Group 46, Senate Records, and Record Group 233, Committee Papers of the House of Representatives, have been published. The Manuscript Returns of the United States Census, Schedule I, Population, are time-consuming documents to be consulted only as a last resort for obtaining information on obscure state politicians. The information they provide on age, place of birth, occupation, and estimated wealth can, however, be of great value. I consulted the manuscript returns for the Eighth Census, 1860, and the Ninth Census, 1870.

PUBLISHED GOVERNMENT DOCUMENTS

Government publications for the Reconstruction period, both state and national, are voluminous. The most important state publications include the *Acts and Resolutions of the General Assembly of the State of Georgia* and the *Journals* of the state senate and house of representatives, published at the close of each legislative session by the state printer. Of great value is Allen D. Candler (comp.), *The Confederate Records of the State of Georgia* (6 vols.; Atlanta: By order of the Legislature, 1909–1911). Only Volumes I–IV and VI actually appeared; Volume V has never been published. For the Reconstruction period, the *Confederate Records* contain the records and correspondence of the provisional government, the journal of the convention of 1865, the records of the Jenkins administration, and the journal of the constitutional convention of 1867–68. Also useful are the *Annual Reports of the Officers of the Western and Atlantic Railroad*, and the *Annual Reports of the Treasurer of the State of Georgia*, and the *Annual Reports of the Comptroller General of the State of Georgia*, which often contained miscellaneous statistics of population, voting registration, and election returns. Investigations during and after Reconstruction resulted in an outpouring of reports and testimony. Reports on the management of the Western & Atlantic include: *Report of the Joint Committee [of the General Assembly] to Investigate the condition of the Western & Atlantic R. R. submitted to the Two Houses of the General Assembly, Thursday, February 25, 1869* (Atlanta: Samuel Bard, Public Printer, 1869); *[Majority and Minority Reports of the Committee of the General Assembly, appointed . . . to investigate the administration and management of the Western & Atlantic Railroad, and the management of its finances]* ([Atlanta]: [1872]); *The Evidence Taken by the Joint Committee of the Legislature of the State of Georgia, Appointed to Investigate the Management of the State Road, Under the Administration of R. B. Bullock and Foster Blodgett* (Atlanta: J. Henly Smith, at the *Daily Sun* Office, 1872); and *Evidence Taken by the Joint Committee of the Legislature . . . Appointed to Investigate the Indebtedness of Foster Blodgett and his Securities, as Treasurer and Superintendent of the Western & Atlantic Railroad* (Atlanta: W. A. Hemphill & Co., Public Printers, 1872). Investigations into the award of the Western & Atlantic lease contract are reported in the *Report of the Majority [and Minority] of the Joint Committee Appointed by the General Assembly to Investigate the Fairness or Unfairness of the Contract Known as the Leases of the Western & Atlantic R. R., Made December 27, 1870, by Rufus B. Bullock Late Governor, and to Investigate the Question of Fraud in said Contract, if any exists* (Atlanta: W. A. Hemphill, Public Printer, 1872). The testimony appears in *[Testimony in*

Regard to the Lease of the Western & Atlantic Railroad] ([At-
lanta]: [1872]). Investigations of charges against Bullock are reported and described in: *Report and Proceedings of the Committee to Investigate the Official Conduct of Rufus B.
Bullock,
Late Governor of Georgia* ([Atlanta]: [1872]), and *Appendix,
Additional Testimony on the Claim of the Mitchell Heirs; Proceedings of the Investigating Committee: Charges and Testimony
against N. L. Angier, State Treasurer* ([Atlanta]: 1870); and
*Proceedings of the Investigating Committee Appointed to ex-
amine Governor Bullock's management of the finances and the
charges of Angier against Bullock* ([Atlanta]: 1870). The most
complete collection of these reports is in the Georgia State
Library, Atlanta; unfortunately, many of the reports have been
bound without title pages. The *Georgia Reports* contain the decisions of the state supreme court.

Publications of the federal government contain Congressional
debates on the situation in Georgia and the testimony on Georgia
affairs taken by Congressional committees. For debates, the *Congressional Globe* for the Thirty-ninth through the Forty-first
Congresses is the basic source. The various indexes to the United
States Serial Set provided the best guide to material scattered
through the *Reports, Executive Documents,* and *Miscellaneous
Documents* of the Senate and the House of Representatives.
Among the most helpful items in the Serial Set are: *Condition of
Affairs in Georgia. Evidence before the Committee on Recon-
struction relative to the condition of affairs in Georgia,* in *House
Miscellaneous Documents,* 40th Cong., 3rd Sess., No. 52; *Letter
from Governor Bullock of Georgia, in reply to the statement by
Hon. Nelson Tift to the Reconstruction Committee of Congress,*
in *House Miscellaneous Documents,* 40th Cong., 3rd Sess., No.
52, Pt. 2; *Report of the Committee on the Judiciary,* in *Senate
Reports,* 41st Cong., 2nd Sess., No. 58; and the *Report of the
Committee on the Judiciary,* in the *Senate Reports,* 41st Cong.,
2nd Sess., No. 175. The *Annual Reports of the Secretary of War*
contain correspondence between military commanders in Georgia
and authorities in Washington. The reports covering 1867 and
1868 are especially important. General Meade's correspondence

also appears in *Report of Major General Meade's Military Operations and Administration of Civil Affairs in the Third Military District and Dep't of the South, For the Year 1868, with Accompanying Documents* (Atlanta: Assistant Adjutant General's Office, Department of the South, 1868). The *Testimony Taken by the Joint Select Committee to Inquire into the Condition of Affairs in the Late Insurrectionary States* (13 vols.; Washington: Government Printing Office, 1872), VI and VII, contains the Georgia testimony in the so-called Ku Klux Conspiracy investigation. Democrats denied any knowledge of the Klan's existence, and Republicans, especially Negro witnesses, recounted tales of Klan atrocities. The reports must be used only with extreme caution. The Appendix to this volume indicates the use I have made of the social and economic statistics available in the volumes of the United States Census for 1860 and 1870.

NEWSPAPERS

Republicans never succeeded in developing a strong party press in Georgia, and few copies of most Republican papers survive. The only Republican daily for which a complete file remains readily available is the Atlanta *New Era*. As a source of opinion among Radical leaders, it is defective for the later months of 1868 and the year 1869, for its editor, Samuel Bard, broke with Bullock during the fall campaign of 1868. A file of another important Republican paper, the *American Union*, edited by J. Clarke Swayze and published at Griffin and Macon, is available in Topeka, Kansas, but I was unable to consult it. No extensive files of other Republican papers exist; short runs of the Augusta *Loyal Georgian*, the Augusta *Daily Press*, and the Atlanta *Daily Opinion* are, however, helpful.

Of the more plentiful Democratic papers, the Atlanta *Daily Intelligencer*, the Atlanta *Constitution*, the Augusta *Constitutionalist*, the Augusta *Chronicle & Sentinel*, the Macon *Telegraph*, the Macon *Georgia Journal & Messenger*, and the Savannah *News & Herald* have proved most consistently useful. I have also consulted files of the Albany *Patriot*, Atlanta *Daily Sun*, Athens

Southern Banner, Columbus *Daily Sun,* Dawson *Journal,* Milledgeville *Federal Union,* Milledgeville *Southern Recorder,* Rome *Courier,* and Sandersville *Central Georgian.* The New York *Times,* the New York *Tribune,* and the New York *Herald* suggested Northern reaction to Georgia events.

PAMPHLETS

The most complete information about the Georgia Equal Rights Association appears in pamphlets issued by association officers. The first statewide Negro convention in Georgia is described in *Proceedings of the Freedmen's Convention of Georgia, Assembled at Augusta, January 10, 1866. Containing the Speeches of Gen'l Tillson, Capt. J. E. Bryant and others* (Augusta: Office of the *Loyal Georgian,*1866). The expansion and purposes of the association can be noted in *Proceedings of the Council of the Georgia Equal Rights Association. Assembled at Augusta, Ga. April 4, 1866.* (Augusta: Printed at the Office of the *Loyal Georgian,* 1866); *Proceedings of the Convention of the Equal Rights and Educational Association of Georgia, Assembled at Macon, October 29, 1866: Containing the Annual Address of the President, Captain J. E. Bryant.* (Augusta: Office of the *Loyal Georgian,* 1866); and *[Rules and Regulations of the] Loyal Georgian Publishing Association* ([Augusta: Office of the *Loyal Georgian,* 1866]).

Several pamphlets containing political propaganda were distributed by both parties during the postwar years. Those concerning the trial of the Columbus prisoners in 1868 include *Radical Rule: Military Outrage in Georgia. Arrest of Columbus Prisoners: With Facts Connected with their Imprisonment and Release* (Louisville: John P. Morton and Company, 1868), and *Governor Brown and the Columbus Prisoners* (n.p., n.d.), a justification of Brown's service as prosecuting attorney against the alleged Ashburn murderers. Bullock's speech at Albion, New York, October 17, 1868, appears in his *Have the Reconstruction Acts been fully Executed in Georgia?* (Washington: Chronicle Print., n.d., but probably 1868). *An Appeal to Republican Sena-*

tors by *Wealthy and Influential Republican Leaders of Georgia* (Washington: Gibson Brothers, Printers, 1870) is an argument by anti-Bullock Republicans against prolongation of the state legislature. Other pamphlets published during the prolongation debate include: *Col. J. E. Bryant of Georgia, and the Washington Chronicle* (Washington: 1870); *The Georgia Question before the Judiciary Committee of the United States Senate. Arguments of Hon. J. H. Caldwell and Hon. J. E. Bryant* (Washington: Gibson Brothers, Printers, 1870); *Letter from Rufus B. Bullock, of Georgia, to the Republican Senators and Representatives in Congress who Sustain the Reconstruction Acts* (Washington: Chronicle Print., 1870); and *A Letter to Hon. Charles Sumner, of the United States Senate, Exposing the Bullock–Blodgett Ring in their Attempt to Defeat the Bingham Amendment* (Washington: Gibson Brothers, Printers, 1870). Foster Blodgett advanced his claims to a Senate seat in *Brief of Facts and the Law, on Behalf of the Hon. Foster Blodgett, Senator Elect from Georgia* (n.p., n.d.). Rev. W. W. Pierson's *A Letter to Hon Charles Sumner, with 'Statements' of Outrages upon Freedmen in Georgia, and an Account of my Expulsion from Andersonville, Ga., by the Ku Klux Klan* (Washington: Chronicle Print., 1870) is a product of the Radical propaganda mill. *The Campaign Speech of Hon. Foster Blodgett, on the Issues Involved in the Georgia Campaign, Delivered at Augusta, November 3, 1870* (Atlanta: New Era Printing Establishment, 1870) is an attempt to make progress and the safety of Georgia's freedmen seem tied to the continuance of Radical rule in the state. It indicates, also, the attempt made by Radicals in 1870 to broaden the base of their coalition by appealing to all who sought economic progress for Georgia. Bullock's *Address of Rufus B. Bullock to the People of Georgia* (n.p.: October, 1872) is the deposed governor's bitter denunciation of his critics. Most of these pamphlets, and several others of less consequence, are included in the DeRenne Collection, formerly located at Wormsloe, Savannah, but now owned by the University of Georgia. An excellent catalogue of this collection is readily available.

TRAVEL ACCOUNTS AND GUIDEBOOKS

Travel accounts are more valuable to the social than to the political historian, for travelers rarely commented on political events. The most complete bibliography of travel accounts for the Reconstruction South is Thomas D. Clark (ed.), *Travels in the New South: A Bibliography* (2 vols.; Norman: University of Oklahoma Press, 1962), I. Among the accounts which comment on affairs in Georgia, I have found a few helpful. Sidney Andrews, in *The South Since the War: As Shown by Fourteen Weeks of Travel and Observation in Georgia and the Carolinas* (Boston: Ticknor and Fields, 1866), noted the speed with which Atlanta had rebuilt from the war and commented unfavorably on the members of the 1865 constitutional convention. John H. Kennaway, *On Sherman's Track: or, The South After the War* (London: Seeley, Jackson, and Halliday, 1867), described Georgia in 1865 but said little about politics. A strongly partisan Radical Republican account by a Northern carpetbagger who settled in Georgia after the war is Charles Stearns, *The Black Man of the South, and the Rebels* (New York: American News Co., 1872). Equally partisan, but Democratic, is Frances Butler Leigh's bitter *Ten Years on a Georgia Plantation since the War* (London: Richard Bentley & Son., 1883). Georgia guidebooks of some use include Joseph Tyrone Derry, *Georgia: A Guide to its Cities, Towns, Scenery, and Resources* (Philadelphia: J. B. Lippincott & Co., 1878). and Samuel A. Drake, *Georgia: Its History, Condition, and Resources* (New York: Charles Scribner's Sons, 1879).

GEORGIA BIOGRAPHICAL DIRECTORIES

Efforts to identify obscure state politicians are aided by material in both national and state biographical directories. The standard directories are well known. In addition to the state histories cited below, the *Bulletin of the University of Georgia, Alumni Number, October, 1906, Catalogue of the Trustees, Officers and Alumni of the University of Georgia from 1785 to 1906* (Athens: The E. D.

Stone Press, 1906) is remarkably helpful. Also useful are Jesse Oslin and A. J. Cameron (comp.), *The Executive Officers, Senators and Representatives of the General Assembly of the State of Georgia for the Years 1865 and 1866* (Milledgeville: J. W. Burke & Co., Stationers and State Printers, 1866), and A. St. Clair-Abrams, *Manual and Biographical Register of the State of Georgia, for 1871–2* ([Atlanta]: [1872?]). St. Clair-Abrams, however, pointedly omitted biographical sketches of Negro legislators from his *Register*.

STATE HISTORIES

There are three monographs on Georgia Reconstruction. The oldest—and least complete—is Edwin C. Woolley, *The Reconstruction of Georgia* (New York: Columbia University Press, 1901), an account remarkable for its fairness to Republicans but based almost entirely on material in government publications. Broader in scope, more accurate, and based upon much wider research is C. Mildred Thompson's *Reconstruction in Georgia: Economic, Social, Political, 1865–1872* (New York: Columbia University Press, 1915). Moderate and fair-minded in its discussions of the Negro and of the Republican regime, it was one of the most outstanding of the "Dunning" state studies of Reconstruction and remains the best book on its subject. Its major flaws are those of organization; most errors which the modern researcher would note crept into the text because materials easily accessible today were unavailable to Miss Thompson. For only one mistake can Miss Thompson justly be held accountable—her failure to recognize that Republicans and not Democrats had a majority in the Georgia house of representatives in 1868.

The publication of Alan Conway's *The Reconstruction of Georgia* (Minneapolis: University of Minnesota Press, 1966) marked a new venture for a Welsh scholar who has contributed much to our knowledge of the Welsh immigrant in the United States. Conway's failure to exploit materials now readily available leads him to perpetuate Miss Thompson's faulty analysis of the political composition of the 1868 legislature. Though he is more perceptive when writing about Democrats than when describing Republicans—perhaps because his major manuscript source for political events was the collection of Alexander H. Stephens Papers at Emory University—he adds little to Miss Thompson's findings about Reconstruction politics. He is, however, considerably kinder to Rufus Bullock than was Miss Thompson, believing that Bullock himself had little to do with the corruption of his regime. The major contribution of Professor Conway's monograph is to social, rather than to political, history.

Other accounts supplement the Woolley, Thompson, and Conway monographs. I. W. Avery's *The History of the State of Georgia from 1850–1881* (New York: Brown & Derby, 1881) is a mine of ill-digested information. Robert Preston Brooks, *The Agrarian Revolution in Georgia, 1865–1912* (Madison: The University of Wisconsin, 1914) is a competent special study. It contains valuable maps and statistics, as does W. E. Burghardt DuBois, "The Negro Landholder of Georgia," *Bulletin of the Department of Labor,* No. 35, July, 1901 (Washington: Government Printing Office, 1901), 647–777. Henry P. Goetchius, *Litigation in Georgia during the Reconstruction Period—1865 to 1872* (Atlanta: Franklin Print. Co., n.d.) is brief and of little value. Louis Turner Griffith and John Erwin Talmadge, *Georgia Journalism 1763–1950* (Athens: University of Georgia Press, 1951) contains limited information on newspaper policies and the politics of individual publishers and editors. James Houston Johnston, *Western and Atlantic Railroad of the State of Georgia* (Atlanta: Stein Printing Company, State Printers, 1931) contains valuable statistics for the Reconstruction period but is written almost entirely from the reports of investigating committees. The standard constitutional history of the state, Albert Berry Saye, *A Constitutional History of Georgia, 1732–1945* is disappointingly thin on Reconstruction. Olive Hall Shadgett's *The Republican Party in Georgia from Reconstruction through 1900* (Athens: University of Georgia Press, 1964) contains little on Reconstruction and is based on only limited sources for the later period. It makes full use, however, of the Henry P. Farrow Collection at the University of Georgia. Ralph Wardlaw, *Negro Suffrage in Georgia, 1867–*

1930 (Athens: The University of Georgia, 1932) does too little with a promising topic.

Filio-pietistic state histories are less helpful for their accounts of Reconstruction politics than for the information they provide on the careers of Georgia politicians. The same may be said of the general run of laudatory, uncritical county histories. The authors of these studies apparently wished to forget the "horrors" of Reconstruction, and the county studies generally contain little of use beyond basic biographical material. Of the state histories, the most helpful are: Absalom Harris Chappel, *Miscellanies of Georgia, Historical, Biographical, Descriptive, &c.* (Columbus: Gilbert Printing Co., 1874), Parts 1 and 2; Walter G. Cooper, *The Story of Georgia* (4 vols.; New York: The American Historical Society, Inc., 1938); Lucian Lamar Knight, *A Standard History of Georgia and Georgians* (6 vols.; Chicago: The Lewis Publishing Company, 1917); William J. Northen (ed.), *Men of Mark in Georgia* (6 vols.; Atlanta: A. B. Caldwell, Publisher, 1907–12); Orville A. Park, *The Bench and Bar of Macon, Georgia, 1823–1923* (Macon: 1923); and George G. Smith, *The Story of Georgia and the Georgia People, 1732 to 1860* (Macon: George G. Smith, Publisher, 1900).

BIOGRAPHIES

For biographies of national leaders of the Republican and Democratic parties during Reconstruction, the reader should consult Randall and Donald, *The Civil War and Reconstruction*. Adequate biographies of Georgia politicians are virtually nonexistent. There is no biography of Rufus B. Bullock. On Joseph E. Brown, the best study is Louise Biles Hill, *Joseph E. Brown and the Confederacy* (Chapel Hill; University of North Carolina Press, 1939), which includes a chapter on Reconstruction. See also Emory Speer, *Joseph E. Brown of Georgia* ([Atlanta: 1905]) and Herbert Fielder, *A Sketch of the Life and Times and Speeches of Joseph E. Brown* (Springfield, Mass.: Press of the Springfield Printing Company, 1883). On Howell Cobb, one must consult without much profit Zachary Taylor Johnson, *The Political Poli-*

cies of Howell Cobb (Nashville: George Peabody College for Teachers, 1929). The only full biography of John Brown Gordon is uncritical and disappointingly thin on Reconstruction: Allen P. Tankersley, *John B. Gordon: A Study in Gallantry* (Atlanta: The Whitehall Press, 1955). Haywood Jefferson Pearce, Jr., *Benjamin H. Hill: Secession and Reconstruction* (Chicago: The University of Chicago Press, 1928) puts the best construction on everything Hill did. So, more understandably, does Benjamin H. Hill, Jr.'s *Senator Benjamin H. Hill of Georgia, His Life, Speeches and Writings* (Atlanta: T. H. P. Bloodworth, 1893). Charles Jones Jenkins is eulogized in Charles Colcock Jones, Jr., *The Life and Services of Ex-Governor Charles Jones Jenkins* (Atlanta: Jas. P. Harrison & Co., Printers and Publishers, 1884). Percy Scott Flippen used the Johnson Papers now at Duke University in the preparation of his *Herschel V. Johnson of Georgia, States Rights Unionist* (Richmond: Press of the Dietz Printing Company, Publishers, 1931). There is as yet no good biography of Alexander H. Stephens, but for the postwar period, one must consult Richard Malcolm Johnston and W. H. Browne, *Life of Alex. H. Stephens* (Philadelphia: J. B. Lippincott & Co., 1884), and Rudolph Von Abele, *Alexander H. Stephens: a Biography* (New York: Alfred A. Knopf, 1946). William Y. Thompson's *Robert Toombs of Georgia* (Baton Rouge: Louisiana State University Press, 1966) helps fill a gap which had existed for too long. Older and thinner in their coverage are Plesant Stovall, *Robert Toombs, Statesman, Speaker, Soldier, Sage* (New York: Cassell Publishing Company [1892]), and Ulrich Bonnell Phillips, *The Life of Robert Toombs* (New York: The Macmillan Company, 1913). For a somewhat disappointing biography of a Reconstruction Democratic politician, based on family papers as yet inaccessible to other scholars, see Lynwood Holland, *Pierce M. B. Young, The Warwick of the South* (Athens: University of Georgia Press, 1964). There are virtually no biographies of Negro political leaders. M. M. Ponton, *Life and Times of Henry M. Turner* (Atlanta: 1917) is laudatory. More detailed, though quite hostile to Turner, is E. Merton Coulter's "'Henry M. Turner: Georgia

Negro Preacher–Politician During the Reconstruction Era,"
Georgia Historical Quarterly, XLVIII (December, 1964), 371–
410.

ARTICLES IN PERIODICALS

The files of the *Georgia Historical Quarterly* contain dozens of
articles on Georgia Reconstruction. To list here all those I have
examined would serve little purpose; my discussion includes only
those I have found most helpful. Roberta F. Cason, "The Loyal
League in Georgia," *Georgia Historical Quarterly*, XX (June,
1936), 125–53 repeats some of the old myths but is the best available account of league activities. Theodore B. Fitz-Simons, Jr.,
"The Camilla Riot," *ibid.*, XXXV (June, 1951), 116–25, is based
on careful research in newspaper files. William Best Hesseltine
and Larry Gara, "Georgia's Confederate Leaders after Appomattox," *ibid.*, XXXV (March, 1951), 1–15, offers useful information
but little analysis. Peter S. McGuire, "The Railroads of Georgia,
1860–1880," *ibid.*, XVI (September, 1932), 179–213, provides
the best and most convenient account of railroad building during
Reconstruction and the New South years. Willard Range, "Hannibal I. Kimball," *ibid.*, XXIX (June, 1945), 47–70, details the
misadventures of that railroad builder and financial wizard.
William A. Russ, Jr., "Radical Disfranchisement in Georgia, 1867–
1871," *ibid.*, XIX (September, 1935), 175–209, makes it clear
that there was disfranchisement in Reconstruction Georgia. Olive
Hall Shadgett, "James Johnson, Provisional Governor of Georgia,"
ibid., XXXVI (March, 1952), 1–21, is a convenient summary of
Johnson's nomination and his brief administration, based almost
entirely on published and newspaper evidence. John F. Stover,
"Northern Financial Interests in Southern Railroads, 1865–1900,"
ibid. XXXIX (September, 1955), 205–20, contains important
information also available in his *The Railroads of the South, 1865–
1900* (Chapel Hill: University of North Carolina Press, 1955). C.
Mildred Thompson's "The Freedmen's Bureau in Georgia in
1865–6," *Georgia Historical Quarterly*, V (March, 1921), 40–49,
is a reasoned defense of bureau policies in the state and of the

competent Georgia commander General Davis Tillson. Ralph A. Wooster, "The Georgia Secession Convention," *ibid.*, XL (March, 1956), 21–55, and his "Notes on the Georgia Legislature of 1860," *ibid.*, XLV (March, 1961), 22–26, provide full information from the manuscript returns of the United States census on nearly every member of each of these two groups.

Several articles provided hints for my own research. The connection between railroads and politics in Alabama is brilliantly traced in Horace Mann Bond's "Social and Economic Forces in Alabama Reconstruction," *Journal of Negro History*, XXIII (July, 1938), 290–348. Thomas B. Alexander, "Persistent Whiggery in Alabama and the Lower South, 1860–1867," *Alabama Review*, XII (January, 1959), 35–52, and "Persistent Whiggery in the Confederate South, 1860–1877," *Journal of Southern History*, XXVII (August, 1961), 305–29, suggest that antebellum Whigs played a major role in both Republican and Democratic Reconstruction politics. Carter Goodrich, "Public Aid to Railroads in the Reconstruction South," *Political Science Quarterly*, LXX (September, 1956), 407–79, is the most important and incisive article on its topic. It includes tables giving comparative data on state aid and railroad construction for all southern states. Also important are Patrick Riddleberger, "The Radicals' Abandonment of the Negro During Reconstruction," *Journal of Negro History*, XLV (April, 1960), 88–102, and William A. Russ, Jr., "The Negro and White Disfranchisement During Radical Reconstruction," *ibid.*, XIX (April, 1934), 171–92. Russ shows that the Negro generally opposed stringent disfranchisement measures directed against the whites. See also his "Registration and Disfranchisement under Radical Reconstruction," *Mississippi Valley Historical Review*, XXI (September, 1934), 163–80. Jack B. Scroggs, "Southern Reconstruction: A Radical View," *Journal of Southern History*, XXIV (November, 1958), 407–29, points out the value of the personal papers of Northern Congressmen as sources for the study of Southern Reconstruction. From both Judson C. Ward, Jr., "The Republican Party in Bourbon Georgia, 1872–1890," *Journal of Southern History*, IX (May, 1943), 196–209, and C. Vann Woodward,: "Bourbonism in Georgia," *North*

Carolina Historical Review, XVI (January, 1939), 23–36, I drew hints which later developed into the central thesis of my chapter on the election of 1870 and the lease of the Western & Atlantic Railroad.

UNPUBLISHED THESES AND DISSERTATIONS

Clarence A. Bacote's "The Negro in Georgia Politics, 1880–1908" (Ph.D. dissertation, University of Chicago, 1955) covers a period later than that encompassed by my own study, but it contains a comprehensive bibliography and information on several Negro politicians whose careers I had been unable to trace. Charles G. Bloom's "The Georgia Election of April, 1868. A Re-examination of the Politics of Georgia Reconstruction" (M.A. thesis, University of Chicago, 1963) is a brilliant analysis, to which I am much indebted. Bloom's conclusions are accepted by Wallace Calvin Smith, "Rufus B. Bullock and the Third Reconstruction of Georgia" (M.A. thesis, University of North Carolina, 1964). Donald Hubert Breese, "Politics in the Lower South During Presidential Reconstruction, April to November 1865" (Ph.D. dissertation, University of California, Los Angeles, 1964) I believe claims too much for the organization of politics in Georgia in 1865. Ethel Maude Christler, "Participation of Negroes in the Government of Georgia 1867–1870" (M.A. thesis, Atlanta University, 1932) is a remarkably full narrative but contains little analysis. Theodore Barker Fitz-Simons, Jr., "The Ku Klux Klan in Georgia 1868–1871" (M.A. thesis, University of Georgia, 1957) is a competent narrative and contains a good account of the Ashburn murder and trial. Henri H. Freeman, "Some Aspects of Debtor Relief in Georgia during Reconstruction" (M.A. thesis, Emory University, 1951) is based upon research in county archives. Morton Strahan Hodgson, Jr.'s "Georgia Under Governor Charles Jones Jenkins" (M.A. thesis, University of Georgia, 1934), relies entirely on published accounts. So does Jessie Pearl Rice, "Governor Rufus B. Bullock and Reconstruction in Georgia" (M.A. thesis, Emory University, 1931). Derrell C. Roberts, "Joseph E. Brown and the New South" (Ph.D. dissertation, University of Georgia, 1958) hints that Brown joined the Republican party for selfish financial reasons. I do not accept Dr. Roberts's suggestion. Mrs. Olive Hall Shadgett's "A History of the Republican Party in Georgia from Reconstruction through 1900" (Ph.D. dissertation, University of Georgia, 1962) is less complete than her book of virtually the same title. Allen Candler Smith, "The Republican Party in Georgia 1867–1871" (M.A. thesis, Duke University, 1937) goes far beyond the usual M.A. essay of its time in scope of research and skill of narration. Though it lacks sustained analysis, it is a competent account. Judson Clements Ward, Jr., "Georgia Under the Bourbon Democrats, 1872–1890" (Ph.D. dissertation, University of North Carolina, 1947) contains a stimulating chapter on Reconstruction. Edward Barham Young, "The Negro in Georgia Politics, 1867–1877" (M.S. thesis, Emory University, 1955) is less skillful than Miss Christler's thesis. Because Richard Lee Zuber tended to accept at face value everything that Rufus Bullock said, I found his "The Role of Rufus Brown Bullock in Georgia Politics" (M.A. thesis, Emory University, 1957) of only limited usefulness.

POSTSCRIPT

A major collection of the papers of John E. Bryant, co-founder of the Georgia Equal Rights Association, sometime chairman of the Republican State Executive Committee, and opponent of Governor Bullock in 1869 and 1870, was deposited with Duke University in September, 1968. The collection is rich in material on Negro history and politics and on Bryant's activities in the Republican Party during Reconstruction. It will constitute a major source for any future investigation.

INDEX

Adkins, Senator Joseph, 155
Air Line Railroad: as 1868 campaign issue, 90; bill granting state aid to, 119–20
Akerman, Amos T.: relief proposals of, 60–61; on franchise and office-holding issue, 67; seeks to have Georgia's electoral vote discounted, 148, 151; opposes Bullock's plan to restore military rule, 152, 158; becomes U.S. Attorney General, 193; favors 1870 General Assembly elections, 193; election bill of, 193–94; mentioned, 45, 104, 133, 181, 195–96
Akerman election bill, 193, 194, 196, 199, 202, 206
American Union, 20, 24
Anderson, Edward C.: urges Democrats to unite against Radicalism, 201; mentioned, 51–52, 181
Angier, Nedom L.: election of, as state treasurer, 114; charges Bullock with misuse of state funds, 184; mentioned, 71, 74, 77, 175, 181
Ashburn, George W.: murder of, 97–98; mentioned 76
Atkins, James, 221
Atlanta, Ga.: organization of Republican party in, 23; as headquarters of Third Military District, 33; Republican convention in, 41; becomes capital of Georgia, 69; 1868 General Assembly ordered to reconvene at, 167; Democratic party convention in, 200; mentioned, 36, 90, 169, 179, 211, 218
Augusta, Ga.: effects of Civil War on, 4; Republican party in, 22; Republican newspaper founded in,

24; Freedmen's convention in, 25–26; mentioned, 20, 36
Augusta Ring: dominates 1867 Constitutional Convention, 57–58; and 1867 homestead exemption debate, 63; demands removal of Governor Jenkins, 70; supports Rufus Bullock for governor, 74; controls State Executive Committee, 75; mentioned, 59, 78, 92, 103, 114, 175, 214, 218
Avery, P. J., 189

Bard, Samuel: advocates aid to Air Line Railroad, 90; elected state printer, 114; opposes Bullock's plan to restore military rule, 158; mentioned, 44, 89, 197, 199
Beaird, Simeon: establishes *Loyal Georgian,* 24, 30; founds Georgia Printing Company, 24; mentioned, 67
Belknap, William Worth, 183, 193
Bell, Madison, 114
Bethune, Marion, 143
Bingham, John A.: proposes amendment to Butler's Georgia bill, 186; mentioned, 181, 188
Black Belt: Republican party strength in, 55, 94–95; opposition of, to 1867 relief proposals, 61; and 1868 Republican party campaign, 89, 91; decline of Republican strength in, 144; reports of fraud in, during presidential election, 152; 1870 voting record of, 204–205; mentioned, 5, 57
Black Code (Georgia), 13
Black, Jeremiah S., 46
Blodgett, Foster: and Augusta Ring, 57–58; appointed temporary chair-